W9-BNW-937

CONDI

THE LIFE *of a* STEEL MAGNOLIA

MARY BETH BROWN

THOMAS NELSON
Since 1798

NASHVILLE DALLAS MEXICO CITY RIO DE JANEIRO BEIJING

Published in Nashville, Tennessee, by Thomas Nelson, Inc. Thomas Nelson is a trademark of Thomas Nelson, Inc.

Thomas Nelson, Inc. titles may be purchased in bulk for educational, business, fund-raising, or sales promotional use. For information, please e-mail SpecialMarkets@ThomasNelson.com.

Library of Congress Cataloging-in-Publication Data

Brown, Mary Beth.
Condi : the life of a steel magnolia / Mary Beth Brown.
p. cm.
Includes bibliographical references and index.
ISBN 978-1-59555-098-9
1. Rice, Condoleezza, 1954– 2. Stateswomen—United States—Biography. 3. Cabinet officers—United States—Biography. 4. Women cabinet officers—United States—Biography. 5. African Americans—Biography. 6. Bush, George W. (George Walker), 1946– —Friends and associates. 7. United States—Foreign relations—2001– 8. National Security Council (U.S.)—Biography. 9. Stanford University—Officials and employees—Biography. I. Title.
E840.8.R48B76 2007
327.730092—dc22
[B] 2007045946

Printed in the United States of America
07 08 09 10 QW 5 4 3 2 1

This book is dedicated with love and gratitude:

To my own extraordinary parents,

Eleanora and John Adams

CONTENTS

Introduction

On the evening of May 10, 2006, I was invited by my friend Ellen Clouse to attend a gala dinner sponsored by the Independent Women's Forum honoring Dr. Condoleezza Rice. Over the years I have attended many Washington, DC, galas honoring countless dignitaries. Somehow that night was different. I felt my pulse race on the lovely spring evening as we neared the Andrew W. Mellon Auditorium on Constitution Avenue by the National Mall and America's monuments.

The Andrew Mellon Auditorium is an ornate gilded hall renowned for its architecture. Designed by the famous San Francisco architect Arthur Brown Jr., it was the perfect site for the evening's event. As Dr. Rice walked through the door, I was impressed by her poise and grace. She was slightly taller than me at five foot eight, but I was struck by her small features and petite bones. Her fingers were long and slim. She extended her hand and greeted me warmly, her eyes smiling and a slight tilt to her head. With her lovely smile and graciousness, she seemed very approachable. I saw how her demeanor could possibly mislead some people and cause them to underestimate her (like President Reagan, who used it to his advantage). Could this refined and reserved figure really be the most powerful woman in the world?

As she did for so many others, Condoleezza Rice caught my attention in the days and weeks after September 11.

My publisher had recently asked me about a follow-up to *Hand of Providence*, my biography focusing on the faith and leadership of President Ronald Reagan. Could Condoleezza Rice's life be my next focus? I wasn't sure before the speeches, festivities, and pomp of that May evening, but then after hearing her speak I knew how I was going to spend the next two years.

There are two types of biographies, authorized and unauthorized. I prefer the latter because it provides the opportunity to be much more candid and honest. I have never sought permission from Dr. Rice to write this book, nor would I. I wanted to follow the facts and reach my own conclusions about her character, and I have read over two hundred thousand pages of transcripts, interviews, and original documents in preparing this story.

I hope that by reaching into her family history, we can see how her forebears and loved ones created the essential foundation for Condi's faith. It is this deeply planted belief which explains how she copes with life's difficulties, obstacles, and heartache, including the piercing pain of racism and rejection she encountered in her youth.

As Condi walked to the podium to receive her award and give her speech, her mannerisms reminded me of the times I had been with President Reagan. An obvious strength and passion were in her words as she spoke. She commanded the issues throughout her speech.

In many ways Condi has similarities to Ronald Reagan. Besides being often underestimated, they can take difficult and complex issues and explain them in language which people understand. They are both optimists and visionaries. They are able to share optimism with others as they paint a picture of what is possible, and this skill they share gives people hope. Both are strong people of faith who trust in the providence of God.

If you are ready to meet the woman who has captivated a nation, I invite you to join me on this adventure of discovery.

Mary Beth Brown
University Place, Washington

Prologue

Birmingham, Alabama, 1961

A mother never knows when an action she takes or something she says is going to leave a lasting impression on her child. Many years ago at a department store in segregated Birmingham, Alabama, a seven-year-old girl was affected by what seemed at the time of small importance.

The little girl, shopping with her mother at a local department store, happily chose a pretty dress to try on. As usual, both mother and daughter were impeccably dressed. They enjoyed their Saturday shopping trips. The girl's father was a minister, and as he was busy polishing his sermon for the next day's church service, Saturdays made for great mother-daughter time. Many of the child's earliest memories of her beloved mother are of their shopping expeditions.

Today, this seven-year-old girl learned an important lesson that would be imprinted into her character. By watching her mother confront the ugly face of racism, she learned how to be a steel magnolia, how to be assertive while retaining dignity, poise, and self-respect in the most difficult of situations.

As the two walked toward the dressing room reserved for "whites only," they were suddenly stopped by a white saleswoman stepping in their path. The saleswoman snatched the dress from the child's hands. Pointing at a storage room, the clerk told the pair, "She'll have to try it on in there."

Standing her ground, the mother remained poised, but firmly told the clerk, "My daughter will try on this dress in a dressing room, or I'm spending my money elsewhere!"

Realizing that this mother meant what she said, the saleslady backed down from the challenge. Surreptitiously, she directed them to a distant dressing room in hopes that no one would see them, so that she could still collect her commission.

"I remember the woman standing there guarding the door, worried to death she was going to lose her job," said Condoleezza Rice in a 2001 interview in the *Washington Post*.[1]

Young Condi was impressed by how her mother handled the situation. She learned by example how to remain gracious but tough, and to not back down in difficult situations. This was not the only time her mother stood up against racial prejudice and bigotry.

Condi remembers another time when she was shopping with her mother, looking at pretty hats. A saleswoman came up to them and sharply commanded Condi, "Get your hands off that!" referring to a hat she was admiring.

Without missing a beat, Mrs. Rice told the clerk, "Don't talk to my daughter that way." Then she sweetly instructed her daughter, "Condoleezza, go touch every hat in this store." Condi was only too happy to comply as she went about the store gazing at the beautiful hats.[2]

Angelena Rice was teaching her daughter to be self-confident and assertive, to act confidently in stating a position or a claim. An individual need not be rude or aggressive to be assertive. Morally conscious men and women may demand their rights without resorting to violence. This idea of non-violent resistance was at the heart of the civil rights movement. From her parents' example, Condi learned to cherish the good and despise evil. She learned to stand against whatever threats may come against the home, the church, and the community. She learned to stand for justice.

"When you do your best to right an injustice or make a stand for fairness," says author LeAnn Weiss, "a silent witness is listening with trusting little ears."[3] This is exactly what Angelena Rice modeled for her daughter.

Washington, DC, 1989

Now fast-forward to September 1989. Thirty-four-year-old Condoleezza Rice was working at the National Security Council in the West Wing of the White House. On that particular day her job was to deal with Boris Yeltsin, the arrogant, demanding Russian leader known for his bravado, as he arrived for a meeting at the White House.

The meeting had been carefully planned by President George H. W. Bush and National Security Advisor Brent Scowcroft because of the delicate situation involving Soviet general secretary Mikhail Gorbachev and Yeltsin. Both had strong personalities, but Gorbachev was the official leader and Yeltsin was the leader of the growing democratic movement in the Soviet Union. President Bush wanted to meet with Yeltsin, but he did not want to offend Gorbachev, since Gorbachev supported *Glasnost* and Bush did not want to compromise that budding progress in the USSR. They decided the best approach would be to bring Yeltsin into the White House through the west basement doors to avoid the press and meet with Scowcroft. President Bush would then "drop by"—thus making it an unofficial visit with the president.

Yeltsin arrived by car at the basement entrance where he was greeted by Condi, his escort to Scowcroft's office. But he had other things in mind. He wanted a meeting with the president and wasn't about to meet with anyone less than President Bush himself. "This isn't the door you go in to see the president," he bellowed at Condi. After she reminded him that his appointment was with Scowcroft, the burly Soviet leader shouted back, "I've never heard of General Scowcroft. He's not important enough to meet with me."[4]

Then the real showdown began. When Condi later recounted the incident she said, "Well, Boris Yeltsin is someone who is not easily programmed. . . . He is best when he, Boris Yeltsin, is in control and when everything depends on him. He's such a strong personality when he first came to the White House, for instance, he was determined to do it his way. He wanted to meet with President Bush, not in the way that we had particularly set it up. We found out something about this man. He's a very strong character."[5]

"He stood in the basement of the White House," said Condi, "and told me that he would not go until I guaranteed him that he was going to meet with President Bush. We're not accustomed to that kind of attitude in the White House, but it is part of his strength."[6]

With his arms defiantly crossed over his chest, an infuriated Yeltsin and resolute Condi had a silent standoff, which lasted about five minutes, with each one glaring at the other. Finally, Condi started to turn away and told him nonchalantly that he might as well return to his hotel. She would inform Scowcroft that he was not coming.

Then Yeltsin blinked. The duel was over. Yeltsin conceded, agreeing to meet with Scowcroft.

Taking Yeltsin by the elbow, Condi steered him to Scowcroft's office, where Bush stopped to talk to him for a few minutes according to their plans. Yeltsin was now pleased as punch and was even able to speak with some nearby reporters as he left the White House.[7]

This svelte woman was not about to be bullied by anyone, including the boisterous tough guy Boris Yeltsin. The gray-suited diplomats and West Wing aides watching this confrontation were astonished that Condi would stand up to Yeltsin and remain as poised and self-confident as she did. Needless to say, President Bush was impressed. "Condi was brilliant, but she never tried to flaunt it while in meetings with foreign leaders. . . . Her temperament was such that she had an amazing way of getting along with people, of making a strong point without being disagreeable to those who differed . . . She has a manner and presence that disarms the biggest of big shots. Why? Because they know she knows what she is talking about."[8]

Former National Security Council special assistant Coit "Chip" Blacker, a colleague of Condi at Stanford University and a longtime friend, describes her as "a steel magnolia."

"She has a wonderful kind of Southern affect in the positive sense, a kind of graciousness," he said. "But mixed with this is a very steely inner core. She always knows what she wants and is extremely disciplined, both at personal and professional levels."[9]

Children often learn by example, and what an example Condi's mother, Angelena Ray Rice, was to her only child. Toughness is one of the many attributes that Condi still admires in her mother. And Condi, too, has been known to be called "tough as nails."

One doesn't need to look far to see the similarities between mother and daughter. It is said that "the acorn doesn't fall far from the tree." Or, in this story, we could say that "the flower doesn't fall far from the tree."

Chapter One

TRANSFORMING AMERICA

Faith is what gives me comfort, and humility, and hope . . . even through the darkest hours. Like many people—here and abroad—I have turned to God and prayer more and more this past year and a half. . . . Terror and tragedy have made us more aware of our vulnerability and our own mortality. We are living through a time of testing and consequence—and praying that our wisdom and will are equal to the work before us."[1]

—CONDOLEEZZA RICE

"God is our refuge and strength, a very present help in trouble."

—PSALM 46:1 KJV

September 11, 2001

The sun rises into a beautiful day in America. The morning promises the kind of day that you wistfully dream about during the cold, bare months of winter: crystal-clear blue skies; the leaf-covered trees beginning to turn vibrant hues of red, orange, and yellow; and the warmth of the late summer sun.

5:00 a.m. Washington, DC

As the rest of the city sleeps, a woman wakes up at her usual workday time. Attractive and physically fit at age forty-six, she is ready to start her morning work-out. As she stretches and climbs out of bed, she knows nothing of the horrors this beautiful day is to bring.

5:00 a.m. Portland, Maine

Five hundred miles away, two men of Middle Eastern descent arrive at a small airport with luggage in hand. They have planned and prepared for this day for months. Mentally and physically, they arrive ready for the most important day of their lives.

They've shaved their bodies and prepared them as if for burial. But as they well know, if they succeed, no bodies will ever be found. Readied as warriors prepared for battle, they step up to the ticket counter. They appear calm and relaxed as they execute the first step in their murderous plot. They must not fail today. They must not fail Allah.

Passing by a security camera, Mohammad Atta's grim image is caught as he commences his attack against America.[2]

6:00 A.M. Washington, DC

Feeling energized from her morning work-out, the woman eats a bowl of cereal, jumps into the shower, and dresses for the day.[3] A television faces the treadmill in the den of her Watergate apartment, where she exercises for about forty-five minutes most mornings. She usually listens to music or watches the news while running. On the shelves of a bookcase are a variety of books, on topics such as Brahms, Frederick Douglass, and the Republic of Azerbaijan. The dining room has inviting, warm, red walls—good for entertainment and conversation. In the white living room stands a Steinway grand piano, a gift from her parents when she was fifteen years old.

Soon Secret Service agents will escort her to a chauffeured vehicle and off to work. Only eight months have passed since she became national security advisor, a job that is both challenging and rewarding. Today, she is looking forward to arriving at her office in the West Wing of the White House.

6:00 A.M. Portland, Maine

Back in Maine, Atta and Abdul Aziz al Omari board a flight from Portland to Boston's Logan International Airport.[4] They have prepared to meet their compatriots in Boston.

7:00 A.M. White House, Washington, DC

As she enters the White House she cannot help but reflect on the beauty of the day. Her office sits just around the corner from the president. National security advisor for the president is a dream job for her, considering all the years she has spent studying other countries' governments, politics, people, and cultures.

7:40 A.M. Boston, Massachusetts

Three other hijackers join Atta and Omari boarding American Airlines Flight 11 for a 7:45 departure to Los Angeles from Logan International Airport. This flight is to be the culmination of their festering hatred for the infidel United States. Convinced that their actions will merit the eternal favor of Allah, these men brace themselves for martyrdom.

Also boarding the plane are seventy-eight other passengers with carry-on luggage, purses, and reading materials in hand. Some travelers are returning home to California, like Berry Berenson, widow of actor Anthony Perkins. A seventy-one-year-old grandmother of ten, Thelma Cuccinello, plans to see her sister living there, and Jeffrey Coombs, husband and father of three children, is on a business trip to Los Angeles for Compaq Computer.

7:48 A.M. Newark, New Jersey

United Airlines Flight 93, with four more hijackers on the passenger list, is also boarding for its early-morning trip across the country to San Francisco. Businessman Todd Beamer, along with other passengers, finds his assigned seat and readies himself for the flight. Beamer, husband and father of two little boys, with a soon-to-be-born little girl, has no idea that today he will become a hero for his country.

7:50 A.M. DULLES AIRPORT, VIRGINIA

Five more hijackers are boarding American Airlines Flight 77 from Dulles International Airport, bound for Los Angeles. The hijackers carefully chose these airplanes with nearly identical cockpits, scheduled departures between 7:45 and 8:14 a.m., and departure cities. Because all of the planes are scheduled to fly west from the East coast, they are filled with large quantities of fuel, thus they have the potential for the greatest explosive force.

More innocent travelers board along with the terrorists including lawyer and author Barbara Olson, wife of Bush Department of Justice official Ted Olson.

8:00 A.M. BOSTON, MASSACHUSETTS

In the United Airlines terminal at Logan Airport, Flight 175 is pushing back from the gate carrying five more Islamic terrorists for its scheduled trip to Los Angeles, California.

Business men and women, families with children, and other passengers have no idea what is in store for them this morning.

At this point in time, "the 19 men were aboard four transcontinental flights," wrote the 9/11 Commission Report. "They were planning to hijack these planes and turn them into large guided missiles, loaded with up to 11,400 gallons of jet fuel. By 8:00 a.m. on the morning of Tuesday, September 11, 2001, they had defeated all the security layers that America's civil aviation security system then had in place to prevent a hijacking."

8:45 A.M. New York City, World Trade Center, North Tower

The workday is just beginning for the thousands of men and women working in this famous building. Cantor Fitzgerald Securities, Windows on the World Restaurant, and thousands of other businesses and law offices are located here.

Flight attendant Amy Sweeney, talking on a phone with the airline's office, says, "Oh my God, we are way too low!" The first plane, filled with ninety-two people, crashes into the North Tower of the World Trade Center, traveling at 378 miles an hour. All onboard, along with an unknown number of people in the tower, are killed instantly.[5]

8:45 A.M. Washington, DC

Condoleezza Rice stands at her desk in the White House waiting to go down to her senior staff meeting. As national security advisor she is one of the first to know. Her executive assistant comes in and hands her a note saying that a plane has hit the World Trade Center. Condi's first thought is, *What a strange accident!*[6] She begins watching live television coverage of the battered tower emitting black smoke where a jet has just entered it.[7]

"Mr. President," she says, calling the president in Florida, "a plane hit the World Trade Center." Like Condi, the president's first response is, *What a weird accident.*[8]

"I thought it was a pilot error," said President Bush, recalling that moment. "I thought that some foolish soul had gotten lost—and made a terrible mistake."[9]

As Condi learns more about the situation, President Bush proceeds to his previously scheduled event at a school, sits down, and begins listening to the children read to him.

First reports are that a twin-engine plane had hit the building. Not long after, though, Condi learns that it is a commercial airliner that has struck the building. She walks down to her senior staff meeting and continues to ask for reports on the situation. As she reads three different reports on what has happened, she receives a note from her executive assistant. The note simply states that a second plane has hit the World Trade Center. Her immediate thought is, *My God, this is a terrorist attack.*[10]

The national security advisor springs into action. When recounting that fateful day to Oprah Winfrey, she said, "I went into the Situation Room and began trying to gather the National Security Council principals for a meeting. But Colin Powell was in Latin America. I remember thinking, 'Is he in danger?'" She tried in vain to reach Secretary of Defense Donald Rumsfeld.[11] America was under attack, and Condi had her work cut out for her.

9:30 A.M. WASHINGTON, DC

As two more hijacked jets are soaring toward Washington, DC, those on the ground watch President Bush telling the nation on television that the country has suffered an "apparent terrorist attack."

A Secret Service agent runs into Vice President Dick Cheney's office at the White House, saying, "Sir, we have to leave immediately." He grabs him, putting a hand on his belt, another on his shoulder, propelling him out of the office. "I'm not sure how they do it," Cheney later recalled, "but they sort of levitate you down the hallway. You move very fast."

Also being evacuated from her office in the West Wing is National Security Advisor Condoleezza Rice. Later, she remembered hearing "a false report that [a] car bomb had gone off at the State Department." Before she knew it, someone came up to her and yelled, "Get to the bunker! The vice president is already there."[12] As she is leaving her office, Condi calls President Bush.

"It was brief because I was being pushed to get off the phone and get out of the West Wing. They were hurrying me off the phone with the president and he just said, 'I'm coming back,' and we said, 'Mr. President, that may not be wise,'" said Condi, referring to the advice she and the vice president gave Mr. Bush that morning.[13]

Rice, Cheney, and other senior staff are swiftly escorted by Secret Service agents to the bunker deep below the White House called the Presidential Emergency Operations Center (PEOC). Cheney and Condi are already talking about mobilizing an antiterrorism task force.[14] Together they collect and discuss information while keeping in contact with the president as the day unfolds. In short, the PEOC is fulfilling its purpose of being a command center where top officials work during times of extreme danger. Explaining later in an interview with Oprah, Condi said, "The bunker is protected by advanced security systems and stocked with emergency supplies and communication devices."[15]

Condi continued, "I remember stopping briefly to call my family, my aunt and uncle in Alabama, and saying, 'I'm fine,'" as she arrived in the bunker. "'You have to tell everybody that I'm fine.' But then settling into trying to deal with the enormity of that moment, and in the first few hours, I think the thing that was on everybody's mind was how many more planes are coming."[16] Condi began "calling other governments to make sure they knew that the United States government was up and running."[17]

While all this is going on, the Capitol and the Supreme Court are also being evacuated.[18] The Secret Service implements the emergency plan to ensure the presidential line of succession for the first time ever. The fifteen officials in line to become president if the others are killed are quickly gathered by Secret Service agents and brought to a secure location. Naturally, the vice president is the first to succeed the president, then Speaker of the House. Next are members of the president's cabinet in the order each position was created, starting with secretary of state. The agents want to move Vice President Cheney, but when he hears that the president and fourteen others are safe, he decides to stay in the bunker, even though agents fear he is in danger even there. "It's important to emphasize it's not personal," said Cheney talking about his duty as Vice President. "You don't think of it in personal terms. You've got a professional job to do."[19]

Tension levels remain high in the PEOC room as planes filled with frightened passengers fly like deadly missiles toward the nation's capital. In a CBS television interview, Transportation Secretary Norman Mineta remembers hearing the FAA counting down the hijacked planes heading toward Washington, DC. "Someone came in and said, 'Mr. Vice President, there's a plane fifty miles out,' then he came in and said, 'It's now ten miles out; we don't know where it is exactly, but it's coming in low and fast.'"

Plane Heads for Nation's Capitol and Symbols of America

Now, almost an hour after Condi and senior staff assembled in the PEOC, air traffic controllers note a plane on the radar screen heading quickly back east toward Washington. It is American Flight 77 with sixty-four passengers and crew on board. It took off late at 8:20 a.m. from Washington-Dulles Airport in Northern Virginia. Outside the city the plane abruptly turns 270 degrees and points like an arrow toward its target: the Pentagon. Flight 77 is fully loaded for a trip across the country with jet fuel, a mixture of kerosene and gasoline. The aircraft is now flying directly toward the no-fly zone over the Washington Monument, the Capitol, and the White House. An air-traffic controller desperately tries to contact the unresponsive plane, to no avail: the cockpit is silent, and the transponder has been turned off as was done with the three other hijacked airplanes. At 9:24 a.m. NORAD (North American Aerospace Defense Command) sends an alarm to Langley Air Force Base in Hampton, Virginia.[20] According to the 9/11 Report, "NORAD is a bi-national command established in 1958 between the United States and Canada. Its mission was, and is, to defend the airspace of North America and protect the continent."[21] A few minutes later two F-16 fighter jets take off to intercept American Flight 77.

Flight 77 swoops over Arlington National Cemetery in Virginia as it draws near the Pentagon, the military headquarters of the United States.

9:38 A.M. ARLINGTON, VIRGINIA

On the ground near the Pentagon, firefighter Alan Wallace is working on the Pentagon fire station ramp when he hears the screaming of engines from Flight 77. He looks up and sees the Boeing 757 flying two hundred yards away and twenty-five feet off the ground.[22] "Runnnnn!" Wallace shouts to a fellow firefighter. "[Wallace] made it about thirty feet, heard a terrible roar, felt the heat, and dove underneath a van, skinning his stomach as he slid across the blacktop, sailing across it as though he were riding a luge," wrote the *Washington Post*.[23]

"We remember where we were that day," wrote Secretary of Defense Donald Rumsfeld in the *Wall Street Journal* as he described what it was like being inside the Pentagon when the airplane flew into it traveling 530 miles an hour.[24] The jet was flying "full power, no flaps," according to an Alexandria police officer, as it hit the nation's top military building.[25] "At 9:38 a.m., the entire Pentagon shook," said Rumsfeld. "I went outside and saw the horrific face of war in the 21st century. Those present could feel the heat of the flames and smell the burning jet fuel—all that remained of American Airlines flight 77."

"Destruction surrounded us: smoldering rubble, twisted steel, victims in agony," remembered Rumsfeld.[26] He immediately began helping the injured onto stretchers for about fifteen minutes, according to the *New York Times*.[27] Knowing that much would be required of him after this assault on our nation, he then heads back to his office to get back to work.

American Airlines flight 77's crash into the Pentagon marked the first time since the War of 1812 that Washington had been attacked. Now America's military headquarters was a fiery furnace with smoke pouring out of a 150-foot gaping hole. Five stories collapsed.

Meanwhile, Condi is notified by Russian president Vladimir Putin not to worry about Bush raising the Defense Readiness Condition up a level. Normally, this move would have been matched by the Russians, but in a show of support, Putin orders his troops to stand down instead.[28]

As the last hijacked plane zooms toward Washington, an order to evacuate the entire White House is issued. People are literally running for their lives just as others had earlier that morning in New York City as they evacuated the World Trade Center towers.

A surreal feeling encompasses Washington, which now looks like a scene from a movie. Bumper-to-bumper traffic streams out of the city, but none is going in as people frantically evacuate the place where many of America's hallowed symbols stand. U.S. fighter jets begin patrolling the skies above the nation's capital as the residents and the workforce flee for safety.[29] Meanwhile, Condi keeps working in the bomb-proof bunker below the White House.

9:40 A.M. WASHINGTON, DC

Two minutes after the plane hits the Pentagon, the FAA suspends all flight operations at U.S. airports. Secretary Mineta supervises the grounding of the thousands of planes that are still up in the air above our vast nation (and that could potentially be used as lethal missiles).[30]

This is the first time in U.S. history that air traffic has been halted nationwide.[31] The seriousness of the situation is finally impacting the public.

Condi compiles information on the number of airplanes that have flown from U.S. airports that morning and their destinations. She finds at least twenty-two airplanes that are unaccounted for. Talking about it later she said, "We could imagine planes coming down all over the place. We know now that the plane that went down in Pennsylvania was probably headed either for the White House or the Capitol Building."[32]

9:57 A.M. SARASOTA, FLORIDA

Air Force One takes off like a rocket with the president on board. It speeds down the runway with dust clouds whirling. It lifts off and goes almost straight up for nearly ten minutes, trying to get high in the sky as quickly as possible to avoid being attacked by a terrorist-piloted plane.

While the president is leaving Florida, almost an hour after the World Trade Center Tower Two is hit, the tower begins to waver and then unbelievably implodes like a building that has been purposefully set with dynamite for destruction.

Condi remembers watching the 110-story tower collapse on a TV newscast: "Someone said to me, 'Look at that.' I remember that, 'Look at that,' and I looked up and I saw and I just remember a cloud of dust and smoke and the horror of that moment." She also recalls another emotion she felt at that moment, "that we've lost a lot of Americans and that eventually we would get these people. I felt the anger. Of course I felt the anger."[33]

10:08 A.M. WASHINGTON, DC

Secret Service agents armed with automatic rifles are sent to stand guard in Lafayette Park across the street from the White House.[34]

Down below, the question in the bunker is, how many more hijacked planes are coming? Condi now counts as many as eleven hijacked planes that are feared to still be flying in America's skies. With the planes tracking toward Washington, President Bush gives the order to shoot down the airliners that had been hijacked.

President Bush called it a "sobering moment to order your own combat aircraft to shoot down your own civilian aircraft." He went on to say that it was an easy decision given the fact "that we learned that a commercial aircraft was being used as a weapon . . . I knew what had to be done."

One of those planes heading toward Washington, and only fifteen minutes away, is United Flight 93. Heroic passengers take matters into their own hands when they realize what the terrorists flying their plane are planning. Some passengers are receiving calls telling them about the assault on the World Trade Center. A group of passengers in the back of the plane, after praying and saying the Lord's Prayer, vote to act. The men decide to rush the terrorists in an effort to gain control of the plane.

Shortly after 10 a.m. The skies over Pennsylvania

The heroes of United Flight 93 successfully foil the suicide hijackers and prevent their captors from crashing the plane into symbols of the American republic. "With the sounds of the passenger counter-attack continuing" (heard from the plane's tape recordings), "the aircraft plowed into an empty field in Shanksville, Pennsylvania, at 580 miles per hour, about twenty minutes' flying time from Washington, DC," writes the 9/11 Commission Report.[35]

"Clearly, the terrorists were trying to take out as many symbols of government as they could: the Pentagon, perhaps the Capitol, perhaps the White House," said Condi, when speaking in an interview on CBS News about the passengers on United Flight 93. "These people saved us not only physically but they saved us psychologically and symbolically in a very important way, too."[36]

10:32 a.m. White House, Washington, DC

Vice President Cheney phones President Bush to tell him that a caller has just warned the White House switchboard that the next target was the president's plane, Air Force One. The terrorist even knows the plane's secret code name is Angel.[37]

2:50 P.M. Offutt Air Force Base, Nebraska

Air Force One arrives at Offutt Air Force Base, delivering President Bush to a safe and secure location where he can also confer with his top officials and cabinet in Washington, DC.

The president's principal advisors, including National Security Advisor Condoleezza Rice, meet with President Bush via secure video teleconferencing equipment. Bush begins the meeting by saying, "We're at war." Vice President Dick Cheney and Condoleezza Rice remain in the bunker at the White House, while Defense Secretary Donald Rumsfeld stays at the Pentagon.

They discuss mounting evidence that the attacks had been conceived by Osama bin Laden, head of the al Qaeda terrorist organization. By now, they know that several al Qaeda members were on the passenger list on the plane that hit the Pentagon. After the meeting ends, Air Force One takes off from Offutt Air Force Base with President Bush flying back to Washington.

8:30 P.M. White House, Washington, DC

Condi works with the president and others on the contents of the speech he is giving to the nation that evening. After the speechwriters present a draft, Condi and her deputy, Steve Hadley, contribute additional policy positions they want included in the speech. Karen Hughes says in her book *Ten Minutes from Normal* that reassurance was the primary goal of the president's speech.[38]

In President Bush's speech, he said, "I've directed the full resources of our intelligence and law enforcement communities to find those responsible and bring them to justice. We will make no distinction between the terrorists who committed these acts and those who harbor them." This became known as the "Bush Doctrine," a policy position that Condi played a major role in devising.

Almost twelve hours after the first plane flew into the World Trade Center, America is irrevocably changed. The country is now facing a new kind of war. Not a war against a country with borders, but against a fanatical group of Islamic terrorists filled with hate toward America. With these changes, Condi would play a key role in the fight against terrorism. She strategized with others in the Bush administration concerning the challenging goal of making America safe from her enemies.

At the National Prayer Breakfast in 2003 Condi spoke about how she dealt with those extremely difficult and testing times following the terrorist attacks on September 11:

> Faith is what gives me comfort, and humility, and hope . . . even through the darkest hours. Like many people—here and abroad—I have turned to God and prayer more and more this past year and a half. . . . Terror and tragedy have made us more aware of our vulnerability and our own mortality. We are living through a time of testing and consequence—and praying that our wisdom and will are equal to the work before us.

Chapter Two

Entering a New World

"When I'm concerned about something, I figure out a plan of action, and then I give it to God. I just ask to be carried through it. God's never failed me yet."[1]

—Condoleezza Rice

"I will both lie down in peace, and sleep; for You alone, O Lord, make me dwell in safety."

—Psalm 4:8

In the days following the terrorist attacks, Condi said many inspiring words in order to convey to the American people the new world in which they now lived. Throughout the week Condi was called upon to speak. Her face became a familiar sight to Americans seeking reassurance.

How unlikely it is that Condi, born and raised in segregated Alabama, would play such an important role of uniting a divided nation. Looking back on her life, she has often told the story of the first time, as a child, she saw the White House.

Summer 1965, Washington, DC

The family of three strolled down Pennsylvania Avenue hand in hand until they stopped at the gates of the large, classic white building. The little girl, with a thick braid and bow in her hair, held a tour book about the building. She and her mother were both, as always, impeccably dressed. Standing outside the gate, the girl peered in at the beautiful colonial house. It was the summer of 1965, and the girl's parents had brought her to Washington, DC, to tour all the sites in this historic town.

Due to segregation laws, there wasn't a hotel between Birmingham and Washington where they could stay. Consequently, the family packed up their car with food before leaving on the twelve-hour trip, and in Washington they could sleep in a hotel.[2] They'd had a great vacation touring the nation's capital—seeing the majestic monuments, including those to Jefferson, Washington, and Lincoln, and enjoying the numerous museums. Of course, a visit to Washington would not be complete without seeing the president's home and office.

History was all around them, and now she was finally standing before the place she had been dreaming about: the White House. Standing outside the gate, peering in at the majestic colonial building, the little girl turned and said to her parents, "One day I'll be in that house."[3]

Now, flash forward four decades. The young girl who peered in the gate and dreamed about the White House is now one of the most powerful women in the world.

The Days Following September 11

Speaking with White House correspondents live on national television on September 13, National Security Advisor Condoleezza Rice called the September 11 terrorist attacks "a transforming event for all of us, for the country, and clearly for the President of the United States."

She told those gathered, "We've always known that something like this could happen on American soil. We've all had it as a nightmare, but you couldn't watch those planes go into the World Trade Towers, you couldn't go out to the Pentagon like we did yesterday and see the side of the Pentagon cratered, you couldn't go through the moments when we didn't know how many planes were still in the air, what else was next on the list, and not be transformed by it."

When questioned as to the president's first reaction upon learning of the attacks, she describes it as "a defining moment" for him. She goes on to say the president's reaction was "in many ways, almost immediate."

"The interesting thing is that we were all trying to deal with the immediacy of the situation, we were all trying to deal with the consequences of the situation, we were all trying to assess what was happening," she said, mentioning some of her own experiences that horrific day.

Condi described those first hours after the attack as "pretty remarkable—coming out of the Situation Room," Condi said, "we heard that there was a second plane into the World Trade Towers, and then as we were coming out, that something had hit the Pentagon, that something was likely headed for the White House."

She continued to describe the chaos of the day, saying, "To get down then to the secure facility and hear the code name for Air Force One, there's something headed for Air Force One—I don't think that you can underestimate, at that moment, that you're sorting lots of information and you're trying to deal with the consequences, but you recognize that something's changed forever in the way that the United States thinks about its security."

Condi concluded by resolutely saying that something President Bush "has been very focused on is that even though we are going to make sure that we do everything we can in terms of security measures, we're not going to let the terrorists win by changing our way of life."[4]

After the speech Condi went home and cried. The week was exhausting and nerve-racking. America had been challenged to its core. But that week, America was at its finest. The Western world was at its finest. Across the nation and across the world, men and women had united in an expression of common humanity, in affirmation of liberty and justice.

When Condi cried, her tears were not the tears of desperation, though there was sorrow mingled in them. She cried because when she returned to her condominium late at night and turned on the television, she saw the scene at Buckingham Palace. There in the forecourt was the queen's military band playing the American national anthem. It was the first time the British had performed the American anthem in their history.[5] Indeed, it was the first time the British had performed any national anthem but their own, a remarkable gesture of solidarity.[6]

Later, on Thursday of that horrendous week, President Bush said in a proclamation to the nation, "We mourn with those who have suffered great and disastrous loss. All our hearts have been seared by the sudden and senseless taking of innocent lives. We pray for healing and for the strength to serve and encourage one another in hope and faith." Quoting Matthew 5:4, he said, "Blessed are those who mourn, for they shall be comforted." He then went on to "call on every American family and the family of America to observe a national Day of Prayer and Remembrance, honoring the memory of the thousands of victims of these brutal attacks and comforting those who lost loved ones."[7]

Rain was falling on Friday, which matched the mood of the day as mourners entered Washington National Cathedral for the National Day of Prayer and Remembrance service.

The Gothic-style cathedral stands majestically, with the top of its tower being the highest point in the nation's capital. The cathedral is the sixth largest in the world, second largest in the United States. It is built primarily of one hundred fifty thousand tons of hand-carved Indiana limestone, along with leaded glass, mosaics, wood carving, and more than two hundred stained-glass windows, and it took more than eighty years to build. When the idea for the church was initially conceived in 1792, it was to be a "great church for national purposes."[8]

On that dreary September day, it fulfilled its purpose by helping a grieving nation. A special memorial service was held and packed to capacity with people, including the president, his family, members of Congress, diplomats, generals, Supreme Court justices, and leaders of industry—a complete list of Who's Who in Washington.

The service was carefully planned by First Lady Laura Bush and Karen Hughes, counselor to the president, in just thirty-six hours and reviewed by President Bush. Mrs. Bush felt it was important for it to be both dignified and comforting: "I wanted Psalms and everything to be read to be comforting," said Mrs. Bush, "because I think we were a country that needed, every one of us, needed comforting."[9] The Remembrance service was extremely moving and emotional.

With help from one of the church ministers, eighty-two-year-old Billy Graham slowly walked up to the lower stone pulpit when it was his turn to speak. His hair was white as snow. Shaking off the burdens of age, once Graham was in the pulpit, his voice became strong and powerful. He spoke about light in darkness and hope in the midst of despair. Concluding his speech, he said, "My prayer today is that we will feel the loving arms of God wrapped around us and will know in our hearts that He will never forsake us as we trust in Him. We also know that God is going to give wisdom, and courage, and strength to the president, and those around him. And this is going to be a day that we will remember as a day of victory. May God bless you all!" His prayer for those around the president included Condi, who was sure to need it in the times to come.

Karen Hughes, counselor to the president, said that when they were planning the service, they decided a great way to end the service was with a note of defiance; hence it ended with the sixteen members of the U.S. Navy Sea Chanters singing the "Battle Hymn of the Republic."[10] Beginning with the tapping of a snare drum, moving on to a trumpet fanfare, and then adding the cathedral's 10,600-pipe Great Organ, the great hymn opened:

> Mine eye have seen the glory of the coming of the Lord,
> He is trampling out the vintage where the grapes of wrath are stored;
> He hath loosed the fateful lightning of His terrible swift sword,
> His truth is marching on.
> Glory! Glory! Hallelujah! Glory! Glory! Hallelujah!
> Glory! Glory! Hallelujah! His truth is marching on!

Voices rang out throughout the National Cathedral with tears streaming down many faces.

> Glory! Glory! Hallelujah! Glory! Glory! Hallelujah!
> Our God is marching on!

Writing in his book, *Fighting Back*, Bill Sammon says President Bush "could think of no better hymn with which to conclude this service, which combined the healing power of prayer with the cold resolve of retribution."[11]

The "Battle Hymn of the Republic" had the desired effect. Condi told Karen Hughes, "It felt like the mood had shifted from sadness to readiness." The hymn steeled them, and the nation, for the "difficult days ahead."[12]

A year later Condi recalled the Remembrance Service to CBS News: "As we stood to sing the 'Battle Hymn of the Republic,' you could feel the entire congregation, and I could certainly feel myself stiffen, and this deep sadness was being replaced by resolve." She said, "We all felt that we still had mourning to do for our countrymen who had been lost but that we also had a new purpose in not just avenging what had happened to them but making certain that the world was eventually going to be safe from this kind of attack ever again."[13]

By the time the service was over, the sun was shining as if it mirrored the determination of those inside. Where before was defeat and sadness, now there was purpose and resolve. Condi felt renewed and ready to get back to work.

One journalist asked Condi how she slept the week of September 11. She replied, "The first night, not well at all. I probably woke up every thirty minutes or so. . . . After that, pretty well. There isn't much that keeps me from sleeping. I've always been capable of putting things aside. I will occasionally wake up and think, *Oh, did I take care of that?* But I'm not a worrier. When I'm concerned about something, I figure out a plan of action, and then I give it to God. I just ask to be carried through it. God's never failed me yet."[14]

That weekend, key advisors, including Condi, met with the president under extraordinary security at Camp David in western Maryland. They sat around a table, casually dressed, discussing America's response to terrorism and its strategy for war.

During her opening statement before the 9/11 Panel in April 2004, National Security Advisor Condoleezza Rice spoke movingly about September 11 and succinctly summed it up this way: "So the attacks came. A band of vicious terrorists tried to decapitate our government, destroy our financial system, and break the spirit of America. As an officer of government on duty that day, I will never forget the sorrow and the anger I felt. Nor will I forget the courage and resilience shown by the American people and the leadership of the president that day."

She reminded those in attendance, "We owe it to those that we lost, and to their loved ones, and to our country, to learn all that we can about that tragic day, and the events that led to it."

Halifax, Canada, September 2006

Speaking five years after the attacks at a ceremony at Halifax International Airport, Condoleezza Rice thanked the volunteers, firefighters, and police officers who helped stranded passengers on September 11, 2001. Although she mentioned it, she didn't focus on the death and destruction of the fateful day. Forever the optimist, she focused on the human response of hospitality and compassion seen in those gathered:

> Today, September 11, is a day of remembrance. It's a day to think about the lives lost, those whose lives were cut short. These were people with a history and with future plans. They have left behind loved ones who will forever feel the pain and the scars of what happened on September 11th.
>
> It's a day, of course, also to recognize that our lives did change forever, because for the United States and for people around the world, the sense of vulnerability that your skies could be taken over by terror in quite that way still exists today. . . .

> It's a day, of course . . . to know and to remember that there is indeed evil in the world and that we saw its awful face on that horrible day. But it's also a day to recognize that very often when the worst in human behavior and in human nature exhibits itself, so does the best in human nature and in human behavior. And that is what we saw here.

Condi spoke about first going to a church service that morning to commemorate the fifth anniversary of 9/11, and then having a moment of silence on the lawn of the White House with Bush, Cheney, and other cabinet members "to remember those who had fallen":

> And as I was standing there, I thought to myself that it seems just an instant ago that 9/11 happened and yet it seems a lifetime ago that 9/11 took place. . . .
>
> And so I know that when you awakened on the morning of September 11th, much as people did around the world, you would never have guessed that you would see the events of September 11th, but more importantly that you would be called to act because of the events of September 11th.
>
> And I am here to thank you on behalf of the people of America because you acted. . . . It is extraordinary to see these photographs and to see these planes landed as if they were on an aircraft carrier [talking about how all of the grounded planes lined up at their airport like a parking lot].
>
> The people of America will never forget your skill and your professionalism. They will never forget that you made a place for

them to be safe in a time of great danger. But more than anything, they will never forget the compassion and the kindness and the kind word and the love that was exhibited for them that day.

We share values, and we share ties of kinship. And occasionally, when tragedy strikes, we share compassion. And perhaps it is not a bad thing that when the dark and ugly side of human behavior is exposed that we are reminded of the good and that we are reminded that there is nothing like a friend in a time of need.[15]

The Day America Took Notice of Condi

That momentous day of which she spoke catapulted her out from behind the scenes to America's television screens as she calmly, yet firmly informed, encouraged, and reassured Americans about how our world had changed. She reassured an anxious and grieving nation that the government was doing all in its power to keep them safe and protected. Many Americans stopped and took notice of Condoleezza Rice for the first time and asked, "Who is she?" Americans wanted to know more about this confident, intelligent, and attractive woman who was able to maintain grace under fire. How did she become one of the most powerful and respected women in the world?

To find the answers to these questions, we must look back at her life and trace her steps to the White House. When looking closer, woven throughout the tapestry of her life we see strong cords of faith and hope holding it all together.

Chapter Three

A Strong Family Heritage

"I would say it's a story of faith. . . . It's a story of family, the importance of family ties that hold us together. . . . Now, my experience is an experience of faith and family and education, all brought together in one story."[1]

—Condoleezza Rice

"Tell your children about it, Let your children tell their children, and their children another generation."

—Joel 1:3

Remembering the Struggle

According to an old Chinese proverb, to forget one's ancestors is to be a brook without a source, a tree without a root. Condoleezza Rice has from her earliest days been inspired by the stories and examples of her ancestors.

Not only did her parents have a profound effect on her life, but she also has many other family members who have left a rich legacy of accomplishment. With a passion for history and education, Condi has always loved to look back and learn from the past. When reflecting on the past and her family, she often gains strength and inspiration.

Talking about the influence her family has had on her, Condi says, "I was blessed to have had seeds of faith planted in my soul about God's faithfulness from my childhood to fall back on."[2]

When Condi was provost of Stanford University, she delivered the commencement address to the University of Alabama graduating class of 1994, and her remarks were subsequently published in the *Birmingham News.* Condi spoke about her family and shared these worthwhile words of wisdom:

> I hope you have discovered heroes and heroines: people whose story has captivated you and upon whom you can look back when you need to tap deep down for strength in tough times. Among those heroes, there should be some ordinary people: people who are ordinary in the sense that you will never read about them in books or the newspapers, but extraordinary in how they meet life's challenges. My heroes include my grandparents, particularly my grandfathers.[3]

Firmly grounded by a strong family, Condoleezza Rice has come a long way in just three short generations, from her grandparents who were children of former slaves, to being the secretary of state of the United States.

Condi talking about her family heritage at the Southern Baptist Convention Annual Meeting, May 2006.

Speaking at the African American History Month Celebration in 2005 shortly after becoming secretary of state, Condi told about the common denominators that united those gathered in their experiences and "made this African American community prosper and thrive despite the tremendous, tremendous obstacles since Africans first landed here in America."[4]

She captured the truth best when she said that day in her speech:

> I would say it's a story of faith. . . . It's a story of family, the importance of family ties that hold us together. And you know, it's not just your mom and dad and grandmother and your grandfather, it's your aunts and your uncles and your cousins and your cousins' cousins and your aunt and uncles' cousins' cousins. [Laughter of

> audience] You know that when we talk about family, we mean extended family in the African American experience.
>
> And, of course, it's valuing education. . . . Now, my experience is an experience of faith and family and education, all brought together in one story.[5]

The Republican National Convention in 2000 was an opportunity for Condi to share her family's inspiring story with the millions of people gathered around their televisions and those in attendance: "In America, with education and hard work, it really does not matter where you came from; it matters only where you are going. . . . But truth cannot be sustained if it is not renewed in each generation, as it was with my grandfather."[6]

The Rice Family

Fondly calling him Granddaddy Rice, she recalled:

> He was the son of a farmer in rural Alabama, but he recognized the importance of education. Around 1918, he decided he was going to get book-learning. And so, he asked in the language of the day where a colored man could go to college. He was told about little Stillman College, a school about fifty miles away. So Granddaddy saved up his cotton for tuition, and he went off to Tuscaloosa.
>
> After the first year . . . he ran out of cotton and he needed a way to pay for college. Praise be, as He often does, God gave him an answer. My grandfather asked how those other boys were stay-

> ing in school, and he was told that they had what was called a scholarship. And they said if you wanted to be a Presbyterian minister, then you can have one, too. Acting as if he had planned this all along, Granddaddy Rice said, "That's just what I had in mind."
>
> And my family has been Presbyterian and college-educated ever since.
>
> But you know . . . that's not just my grandfather's story, that's an American story—the search for hope, the search for opportunity, the skill of good, hard work.[7]

Condi says her paternal grandfather was the "first one in my family to really care about education."[8] But his story really begins with his mother, Julia Head Rice. She was born in 1851, the daughter of a white plantation owner and one of his black house slaves living near Clinton in Greene County, Alabama.[9]

Most of the slaves in the Rice family lineage were house slaves, not field slaves. House slaves were often given more opportunities to better themselves. One woman who took advantage of those opportunities was Julia's mother, a house slave. Despite the fact that it was against the law, she taught Julia how to read and write. Her passion for education would continue to be an inspiration to her many descendants.[10]

Following the Civil War, Julia married John Wesley Rice of South Carolina, a former slave born in 1851 who could also read and write. The two settled in Ewtah, Alabama, a town near Birmingham, where John worked as a farmer in the western Black Belt. The Black Belt was a swath of land in south central Alabama known for its dark, rich soil and high population of black people.[11]

Faith and education played an important role in the family's life. They were Methodists, a Christian denomination that was known for helping newly freed slaves adjust to their new life, with an emphasis on education.[12]

One of John and Julia's nine children, John Wesley Rice Jr., was born in April 1895 and later became the "Granddaddy Rice" who had such an influence on Condi. As soon as he could pick cotton, he was out in the fields with his family. It was this cotton he saved and sold to pay for his education.

After graduating from Stillman College, one of the few schools of higher learning for blacks in Alabama at the time, Granddaddy Rice became an ordained Presbyterian minister. He began his first ministry in Baton Rouge, Louisiana. In 1922, at the age of twenty-six, he married Theresa Hardnet, a twenty-two-year-old half-Creole woman from Louisiana. They soon had a daughter named Angela Theresa. While Granddaddy Rice continued to pastor the church in Baton Rouge, Condi's father, John Wesley Rice III, was born on November 3, 1923.

The couple raised their children in Baton Rouge until a new Presbyterian mission in Birmingham became Granddaddy Rice's next congregation. Under his leadership and guidance it grew into Westminster Presbyterian Church, which still exists today.

Other family members called him "Uncle Doc" because he had a burning desire to see black youth in his church and community get a college education and better themselves. Granddaddy Rice helped young blacks to obtain scholarships at Stillman, his alma mater.

Giving an example of the priority her grandfather placed on books and learning, Condi told *Newsweek* editor Marcus Mabry a story about her grandfather during the Depression. One time he paid ninety dollars for a beautiful, complete set of seven gold-embossed, leather books written by Alexandre Dumas. Having her husband spend this much money on books during these hard times angered Theresa. Attempting to appease his wife, Granddaddy Rice explained to Theresa, "We can pay for them on time," by spreading out the payments. Even in the midst of economic hardship, John Wesley Rice Jr. still placed a high priority on education.[13]

Strong Christian beliefs, along with the values of education and hard work, were passed down to Condi's father, John, by his parents, and he conveyed them on to Condi. Her family took to heart Deuteronomy 6:5–7: "You shall love the LORD your God with all your heart, with all your soul, and with all your strength. And these words which I command you today shall be in your heart. You shall teach them diligently to your children, and shall talk of them when you sit in your house, when you walk by the way, when you lie down, and when you rise up" (NKJV).

Both John and his older sister, Angela, attended public schools, while their parents instilled a love of learning and an appreciation for education in them at home. Soon after graduating from McKinley High School in Baton Rouge, John went to Stillman Institute like his father before him. At that time, Stillman was accredited as a two-year junior college, so after his first two years, John transferred to another Presbyterian black college in Charlotte, North Carolina, Johnson C. Smith University. John received his bachelor's of arts in history in 1946.[14] By 1948, when he was twenty-four years old, John had received a master's of divinity from Smith University.[15]

Following in his father's footsteps, John first served a congregation in Baton Rouge and then succeeded his father as pastor of the Westminster Presbyterian Church in 1951.

John's sister Angela, equally driven, went on to higher education, receiving a PhD in English Victorian Literature from the University of Wisconsin.[16]

Although the Rice family was usually known for being stoic and serious, John stood out from the rest of the relatives with his optimistic, jovial personality and great laugh.

Condi's own father experienced racial discrimination in Alabama in many ways, but one event turned out to have a big impact on him, and eventually his daughter. Speaking during prime time at the 2000 Republican National Convention in Philadelphia, Condi said of this incident: "The first Republican that I knew was my father, John Rice, and he is still the Republican I admire most. My father joined our party because the Democrats in Jim Crow Alabama of 1952 would not register him to vote. The Republicans did," she announced. "I want you to know that my father has never forgotten that day, and neither have I."[17]

Although blacks had won the right to vote with the passage of the fifteenth amendment in 1869, some people in Southern states were still opposed to them voting, and they devised ways to prevent it. Condi's father was unable to register to vote as a Democrat in Birmingham.

On that day in 1952, college-educated Reverend John Rice stood before the Democratic Party polling official and told him that he wanted to register to vote. The official pointed toward a jar full of beans, informing John Rice that if he could guess the correct number of beans in the jar, he could vote.

That did it for John Rice. He was not about to stand for that kind of degrading treatment. Earlier he had heard from some of the Republican members at his church that the Republican party did not reject blacks by using such insulting practices. After finding a Republican woman at the court house who would secretly register blacks to vote after hours, John registered as a Republican.[18]

It was around this time that John met his future wife, Angelena Ray.

The Ray Family

With an equally compelling story, the Ray family heritage is similarly characterized by perseverance, appreciation for education, and a special emphasis on music and the arts.

Condi's maternal great-grandfather was a slave owner who had a son and two daughters with one of the house slaves, Angelena Davie.[19] Although it was illegal to teach slaves to read and write, Condi's great-grandmother came from a favored slave family which was educated. She, in turn, saw that her children were also educated.[20]

Thankfully, slavery was abolished in the United States with the Thirteenth Amendment in Condi's great-grandmother's lifetime, and her hopes for a better life for her children began to be realized when her two daughters (Condi's great aunts) both graduated as nurses. They were among the first graduates of the Tuskegee Institute founded by Booker T. Washington in 1881. The school began in the post-Reconstruction era and was originally called the "Tuskegee Normal School for Colored Teachers." It would become a major center for African American education. Washington's mission was to educate African Americans toward the goal of self-sufficiency.[21] Washington encouraged virtues such as good moral character, cleanliness, and proper etiquette, along with "habits of thrift, the love of work, economy, ownership of property, a bank account."[22] These were philosophies that rang true with both sides of Condi's family. "Success," Booker T. Washington said, "is to be measured not so much by the position that one has reached in life as by the obstacles which he has overcome."[23]

One man who overcame many obstacles was Condi's grandfather, Albert Robinson Ray III, born in 1893. Through hard work, determination, and self-discipline, his life became a success story.

Albert married Mattie Lula Parram, born in 1899 to a Birmingham seamstress named Emily (Emma) and an African Methodist Episcopal bishop from Ohio named Walter Parram. Condi's great-grandfather Parram saw to it that his daughter, Mattie Lula, not only went to finishing school but also was trained as a classical pianist.[24]

Besides working in mines starting at the age of thirteen, Albert also took on other jobs to support his wife and five children. "Albert Ray," says Condi, "worked three jobs as a mining contractor, a blacksmith and on Saturdays he built houses."[25] From their home, Mattie gave piano lessons to local children. Although the family was very industrious during the work week, they always found time on Sundays to attend a nearby colored Methodist Episcopalian church named Suggs Chapel.[26]

The Ray family's hard work and thrift paid off. They bought land and built their own house, one of the hallmarks of the American Dream. Much to Albert's surprise, his wife Mattie had been surreptitiously saving cash.[27] "When the Great Depression came," Condi said, talking about her maternal grandparents, "they had been so frugal that they bought their home outright with money saved in a mattress."[28]

Condi was probably thinking about her own family when she answered the question "What is the American Dream?" in an interview by Forbes.com in 2007. "The American Dream," she said, "is being dealt with and considered on your own merits. In America it doesn't matter where you came from; it matters where you're going. If you get ahead on your own determination and your own drive and your own merits, there should be no obstacles—not race, not creed nor color. And it's so important that be the case, that there be no obstacles in America."[29]

The Rays were one of the better-off black families in Birmingham and were able to afford a car. Albert and Mattie Lula reached their goal that all of their children go to college, so that they would not have to work in the mines like their father.[30] Albert often said, "I may have worked in the mines. My children will not."[31]

"My father was not educated himself, but he made sure we all got a college education," remarks Condi's aunt, Genoa Ray McPhatter. Condi is very close to her aunt and affectionately calls her Aunt G. "There were five of us, but he felt that you could not survive without an education. It was ingrained," says Aunt G, Condi's mother's younger sister.[32]

Education, faith, and self-reliance became hallmarks of the Ray family heritage. The three daughters, Angelena, Mattie, and Genoa, and brother Alto, all became teachers, and their brother Albert IV became a minister. Angelena's sister Mattie Ray Bonds said, "Daddy and Mother instilled something in us. It was just understood that we could go to college." Albert Ray wanted all of his children to be self-reliant and able to have good, professional jobs. Bonds said, "Daddy told us, 'Get the feel of your *own* money.' He didn't want you to have to take anything from somebody else."[33]

With education always a top priority in her family, and being a third-generation college graduate, Condi explains proudly but almost matter-of-factly, "So I should have turned out the way I did."[34]

Having a highly-educated family dating back several generations is a great achievement not only for a black family, but for any family in the United States. In Alabama in 1950, only 4.9 percent of whites had a bachelor's degree, and just 1.4 percent of blacks had the same degree. Merely 7.2 percent of blacks were even high school graduates.[35]

Along with the notion of self-reliance and perseverance, Albert Ray imparted to his family a strong belief in dignity and self-respect. Condi says her maternal grandfather impressed upon his grandchildren one of his guiding principles: "Always remember, you're a Ray!"[36] "That meant," said Condi, "you have control, you're proud, you have integrity; nobody can take those things away from you."[37]

Albert Ray was not about to allow his family to be victims of the racial segregation that was an everyday occurrence in the 1930s and 1940s in the South. He instructed his children not to drink from the "colored" fountains, use the "colored" restrooms, or ride on segregated buses. "Daddy told us, 'Wait till you get home to drink. Wait till you get home to go to the bathroom.' If you had to go in the back door, we just wouldn't go," says Condi's Uncle Alto Ray. The Ray children were also not allowed to take jobs cooking and cleaning for white families, a common practice of young black children of the day.

When talking about how well her grandparents' strategy worked, Condi said, "I think that black Americans of my grandparents' ilk had liberated themselves. They had broken the code. They had figured out how to make an extraordinarily comfortable and fulfilling life despite the circumstances. They did not feel that they were captive."[38]

Albert and Mattie's third child, Condi's mother Angelena (known as Ann or Ang), was born in 1924 and was known to be a beauty. "Angelena was very beautiful, very elegant," Connie Ray, Alto's wife, says of her sister-in-law.[39] Angelena and her older sister Mattie were less that two years apart in age and were very close.[40] The sisters enjoyed each other's company, spending most of their time together and dressing alike, so much that friends called them the "Ray twins." They delighted in dressing up and attending formal dances, wearing beautiful long gowns with long white gloves up to their elbows and their hair swept up in fashionable styles.

After graduating from Hooper City High School in 1941, Angelena went on to Miles College near Birmingham, where she received her teaching degree, as did Mattie. Part of Angelena's college experience was her membership in a cultural club for young women. The group attended operas and symphonies at the Birmingham Civic Center, although they had to sit in the coloreds-only section of the balcony.[41]

Condi's Immediate Family

In 1951, John Rice was in his late twenties, working at his father's church as director of religious education and supplementing his income as the football coach and director of physical education at Fairfield Industrial High School, a common practice of many working in the ministry.

The lovely and talented Angelena Ray, who taught music, science, math, and oratory, evidently caught John's eye, and the couple dated for several years before getting married on Valentine's Day 1954. Soon after their wedding, Angelena became pregnant. Of her birth nine months later, Condi says with a laugh, "It's a good thing I wasn't early."[42]

Whereas John has been described as a jovial, boisterous, large boned, tall, dark-skinned, handsome man, Angelena has been depicted as in many ways the opposite: a quiet, petite, and beautifully refined light-skinned woman with a biting wit at times.[43] Despite their opposite personalities, John and Angelena shared many values, such as the importance of family, education, hard work, and a love of God.

From this rich family legacy, Condi was born with the values of faith, hard work, education, self-respect, and self-confidence. She never allowed racism or segregation to stand in her way. When Condi returned to Birmingham in 1994 to deliver the commencement speech at the University of Alabama, she declared:

> The common thread is that these people did more with their circumstances than anyone had a right to expect. If you take time to learn from these "ordinary people" you will reject the most pernicious idea of our time—that somehow life is harder for you and for me than it was for our forefathers. And you will be inoculated against today's tendency to envy others and dwell on one's troubles. If you are ever so tempted—stop! Remind yourself that it is a dangerous thing to ask why someone else has been given more. It is humbling, and indeed healthy, to ask why you have been given so much.
>
> After all, circumstances are just that—circumstances. They are not immutable laws of nature. Men and woman who refused to be denied have changed their circumstances time and time again throughout history and almost magically—those personal triumphs have propelled their country forward.[44]

Viktor Frankl, concentration camp survivor and Nobel Prize-winning psychiatrist,[45] wisely said, "Everything can be taken away from a man but one thing: the last of the human freedoms—to choose one's attitude in any given set of circumstances, to choose one's own way."[46] This is what Condi's family did, choosing not to let trials and problems destroy them but to make them stronger and better people.

Concluding her remarks at African American History Month Celebration in 2005, Condi said:

> So black Americans, African Americans, have always depended on faith and family and education. In the most hostile times, in the most difficult times, that's what saw us through.
>
> But something else saw us through, and that was a belief in America and its values and its principles. . . .
>
> That should remind us, each and every one of us, African American, European American, whatever we are, that the important thing that the founders left to us was not a perfect America by any means, but an America that had principles that allowed impatient patriots to appeal to those principles and to tell America to be true to itself. . . .
>
> That's the story of African Americans in America who, in appealing to America to be true to itself, in challenging America to be what America needed to be, participated in the second founding of America, an America in which the great civil rights leaders and those before them gave us the foundation that we have today that allows for somebody like me to emerge as America's Secretary of State.[47]

Chapter Four

Childhood Matters

"They saw no limits for me. They wanted to give me everything. But the most important thing they gave me was unconditional love. Every night I pray and say, 'Thank you, God, for giving me the parents You gave me.' I was so fortunate to have these extraordinary people as my parents."[1]

—Condoleezza Rice

"I thank my God upon every remembrance of you, always in every prayer of mine . . ."

—Philippians 1:3–4

On Sunday morning, November 4, 1954, in Birmingham, Alabama, while Reverend John Rice was giving his sermon, his wife Angelena was at the hospital giving birth to their first and only child, Condoleezza. It wasn't supposed to be that way; the doctors told John to go ahead and give his sermon at Westminster Presbyterian Church where he was now the minister, because the child probably wouldn't be born until later. But births aren't always predictable, so when he came out of the pulpit that balmy November morning, his mother surprised him by declaring, "John, you have a little girl."[2]

That little girl would become the light of John and Angelena's life, as evidenced by her father's nickname for her: "Little Star."[3] Her mother's thoughts were along the same lines. She named her daughter a variation of the Italian musical word, *condolcezza* (pronounced Con-dul-CHET-za), which instructs a musician to play the music "with sweetness." Angelena feared that Americans would have trouble pronouncing *condolcezza* correctly, so she changed the word slightly and created the name Condoleezza. Relatives say with a name like Condoleezza, she neither has nor needs a middle name.

Most of her family and friends would end up calling her Condi, but to Angelena's dismay and displeasure, John playfully gave their daughter the nickname of "Condo."[4]

All their focus and love would be directed to their only daughter, Condoleezza, which was especially true for Angelena. Once, a neighbor of the Rices was surprised when she witnessed Angelena ironing the lace on little Condoleezza's anklets. She asked incredulously, "What in the world are you doing?"

"I love her so much," replied Angelena.

"Why don't you [have] another child?" asked the neighbor. "You've got enough love," she commented.

"I can't take this love from [Condoleezza]," answered the doting mother.[5]

Love and attention would be lavished upon Condoleezza Rice by her devoted parents. John shared his beliefs about his special daughter with a friend from church.

"Condi doesn't belong to us," he said. "She belongs to God."[6]

And this is how they approached the rearing of their only child, seeing her as a gift from God entrusted to them for His glory and purpose. The Rices believed that Condi would make an impact on the world, so they were going to prepare her for that day, encouraging her and providing instruction in whatever activity interested her.

Angelena especially saw to it that Condi would make the most of the gifts that God had given her, just as Benjamin West noted when he said: "God gave me the talent, but a very secure, wise mother gave the gift wings."[7]

Although they were not wealthy, through hard work and prioritizing, John and Angelena gave Condoleezza every opportunity possible to help her succeed in life. Others in their close-knit community had similar feelings. "They all thought America would get better," says Condi. "They had faith that by the time we were older, things were going to open up. That whole generation of parents in Birmingham was determined that they would educate and expose their kids to the finer things in life, so that when America opened up, their kids would be ready."[8]

Condi may have had humble beginnings, but she did not lack the truly important things in life, such as a loving, caring, and stable family.

In 2006, speaking at the Southern Baptist Convention, Condi told about her early life:

> I grew up in Birmingham, Alabama, and in the South we have an expression . . . for people who were raised with religion. We say they grew up in the church. Well, ladies and gentlemen, when I say I grew up in the church, I'm not speaking metaphorically, because for the first three years of my life we literally lived in the back of the church, in two little rooms, where my father preached. And it was the church that my grandfather founded, and I'm very proud of that heritage.[9]

After living at the church, the Rice family next moved to a brick, two-bedroom bungalow that the church had built on a corner in a new community called Titusville. It was an attractive black middle-class neighborhood in Birmingham, made up of tidy homes with nicely landscaped yards. The new parsonage was merely eight blocks from the church, which made it very convenient for the Rice family since they spent so much time at church. Titusville was a "pretty cloistered community," said Condi, "where the families were strongly pro-education, strongly pro-religion, mostly schoolteachers, a couple of doctors, a lawyer here or there, but we were solidly middle-class."[10] The neighbors shared many common values and beliefs; they were preparing their children for the world beyond the safe haven of Titusville.

Condi elaborated on the unwritten code of her childhood neighborhood, saying, "It wasn't as if someone said, 'You have to be twice as good,' and 'Isn't that a pity' or 'Isn't that wrong.' she said explaining as a matter of fact, "'It was just you have to be twice as good.'"[11]

Her parents, especially her mother, set up a conscious and disciplined plan so that their daughter would be prepared to take on the world. "I had parents who gave me every conceivable opportunity," she said. "They also believed in achievement."[12] One could say Condi's parents really took the words of Henry David Thoreau to heart: "I know of no more encouraging fact than the unquestionable ability of man to elevate his life by conscious endeavor."[13]

And that's just exactly what they did with their only child. "My parents were very strategic," she said in 2001 when talking about her upbringing. "I was going to be so well prepared, and I was going to do all of these things that were revered in white society so well, that I would be armored somehow from racism."[14]

Beginning at a young age, Condi had lessons in everything that a well-cultured person would have, including ballet, tap dancing, French, ice skating, piano, flute, and violin—all with a special emphasis on music and the arts. "They had a plan," she says. In fact, one of the gifts her parents gave her as an infant was a tiny toy piano. Today, that special memento is displayed on the coffee table in her condominium.[15]

"My mother was stunningly beautiful," Condi said. "She was tremendously talented . . . I remember how much exposure she gave me to the arts."[16] When Condi was six years old, her mother played a

A young Condi at home with her beautiful and beloved mother, Angelena.

recording of Verdi's opera *Aida* for her. Upon hearing the "Triumphal March" in the opera, Condi recalls that her little eyes became large "like saucers."[17] This was the beginning of a lifelong love of classical music.

Like most little girls, Condi played dolls with the other girls in her neighborhood and was also a Girl Scout. She also enjoyed jumping rope and playing hopscotch, but one of her favorite things to do was play school with her friends. Not surprisingly, she often was the teacher. But play time had to wait until Condi's lessons and piano practice were over for the day. Two of her childhood friends remember "waiting for what seemed like hours for her to finish her latest Beethoven or Mozart and come outside" to play with them.[18]

The self-discipline that Condi learned as a child would remain with her throughout her life. "It was a very controlled environment with little kids' clubs and ballet lessons and youth group and church every Sunday," said Condi.[19]

Despite having this rigorous schedule as a child, she says she never felt pressured by her parents. They instilled in her a love of learning and taught her to always do her best. Part of her schedule included reading lessons, and Condi was reading fluently by the time she was five years old. One of the clubs to which she belonged was a book club. Today, she enjoys reading biographies and mysteries. "I like mystery in stories," she told a reporter, explaining her later attraction to the mystery of Sovietology. Condi is a Sovietologist, which means she is an expert on the politics, government, and culture of the former Soviet Union and Russia.[20]

Angelena wanted her advanced daughter to attend the local black elementary school, but the principal said that she was too young because she wouldn't turn five for another couple of months. Not one to be deterred, Condi's mother took matters into her own hands by taking a year off from her job so that she could teach Condi herself at home.

Her mother took that year of homeschooling very seriously. Condi's day was well-organized, challenging, and disciplined. "They didn't play," said Juliemma Smith, a close family friend. "They had classes, then lunchtime and back to classes. Condi learned how to read books quickly with a speed-reading machine. . . . Angelena and John were just interested in Condi maturing and getting the best of everything. It paid off."[21] Condi ended up skipping both first and seventh grade.[22]

When the Rices went on vacations in the summer, they often traveled in their car, but not to the typical places most families go on vacation; the threesome went to visit colleges and universities. John and Angelena often took classes in the summer on the campuses they visited, but other times they went just to tour. "Other kids visited Yellowstone National Park," Condi later told a magazine writer, with a chuckle. "I visited college campuses. I remember us driving 100 miles out of the way to visit Ohio State in Columbus."[23]

"My parents and I were very close. I was their only child and their constant companion, a role they took very seriously," says Condi. "They invested time, faith, knowledge, love, and passion into my life."[24]

Perhaps one way to understand Condoleezza Rice is to look at her birth order. It is interesting to see how well Condoleezza Rice fits the profile of only-born children. Dr. Kevin Leman writes in *The Birth Order Book* about the only child: "He or she has never had to compete with siblings for parental attention, favor, or resources . . . it helps make the only child more confident, articulate, and seemingly on top of things."[25] Leman also describes some only children as being "special jewels," meaning that all the parents' "energy and attention (along with a certain amount of doting and spoiling)" goes into them.[26] With John being thirty-one and Angelena thirty when Condoleezza was born, they also fall into the category of being older parents, especially in the 1950s. Leman says, "Special jewels often arrive when parents are older—usually in their thirties—and they make their only child the 'center of the universe.'"[27] Parents of only children are also known for sheltering and protecting their child from reality.[28] Indeed, Condi's parents tried to protect her from the damaging effects of discrimination and the tensions of the civil rights movement, pressures which were all around them. But then again, they also helped her become self-confident and prepared for the day when she would leave her sheltered environment and face the world outside of her home, church, and neighborhood.

But it wasn't just her parents who gave Condi inspiration and lessons. Although Condi's Granddaddy Rice, of whom she speaks with admiration, died two months before she was born, many other family members directly impacted her life.

Condi's maternal grandmother, Mattie Ray, also played a tremendous role in Condoleezza's life. She helped to inspire in Condi a love for music. Coming from a long line of piano players on her mother's side of the family, Condi is a fourth-generation pianist: her great-grandmother, grandmother, and mother all were talented pianists.

After Condi was born, Angelena stayed home with her baby for the first year before returning to her teaching job. When both of Condi's parents worked outside of the home, each day they delivered Condi to her grandmother's house for childcare. Mattie Ray taught private piano lessons in her home, and in this warm and stimulating atmosphere, young Condi was immersed in music. "I would go to the piano and bang at the piano when she taught her students, trying to emulate what she was doing with her students," says Condi.[29] Her grandmother noticed Condi's enthusiasm and natural talent, so she started lessons when she was only three and a half years old.

"My mother thought I might be a little young," Condoleezza explained to a music critic, "but my grandmother wanted to try it and as a result I learned to play very, very young. I could read music before I could read."[30] "I don't remember learning to read music you know, the lines and spaces and all that," Condi told another reporter. "From my point of view I could always read music."[31]

"The first song I learned was 'What a Friend We Have in Jesus,'" says Condi. "My grandmother taught me that song because she and my grandfather were people of faith, and, like my parents, wanted me to have a firm foundation in Christ. That night, after I spent eight hours learning the song, I played it for my parents. The following weekend they went out and rented a piano for me to learn on. They believed in me."[32]

"My sister always knew that Condoleezza was a different child," says Angelena's sister, Genoa Ray McPhatter, whom Condi calls "Aunt G."[33] Condi always had a long, amazing attention span from early childhood, as evidenced by her ability to practice "What a Friend" on the piano for eight hours at a time when she was but three years old. This is one early indicator of Condi's high intelligence. "Condi's always been so focused, ever since she was really, really young," explains Aunt G.[34]

To verify their belief that Condi was gifted, the Rices took her to Southern University in Baton Rouge for IQ testing by a psychologist.

The test results revealed exactly what they suspected; Condi had an extremely high IQ.

"I knew my baby was a genius!" Angelena exclaimed to family members upon returning home.

The next song Mattie Ray taught Condi to play on the piano was the timeless Christian hymn "Amazing Grace." Not only did music play an important role in Condi's childhood, but a strong Christian faith was at the heart of it. "Whenever we would leave home she always told us to take the name of Jesus with us," says Condi's Aunt G talking about Mattie Ray, Condi's grandmother. "It was a constant reminder to keep Christ in our hearts and minds, foremost."[35]

Those seeds of faith were planted when Condi was young, and the seeds came to rest on more than a theory. They grew in the rich soil of example, at home and at church. "She was always given the opportunity to say grace at dinner time," says Aunt G, who was seventeen years old when Condi was born. "We learned that if Condi said a short grace before a meal, that meant she's hungry. But if the grace was long, she wasn't hungry."[36]

Before long, at the age of four, Condi gave her first piano recital. Dressed in a taffeta dress with a little tam o'shanter perched on her head, she awed a gathering of teachers with a rendition of "The Doll's Funeral" based on a Tchaikovsky composition. Soon she was accompanying the choir at her father's church along with her mother. Her years of experience performing before audiences gave her a wonderful self-confidence and made her comfortable before crowds.[37]

Angelena continued the piano lessons with Condi in their home while she was still young, which of course entailed hours of practice. Condi says she "went through . . . the kind of normal childhood . . .

with music very much at the center of it, always piano lessons, always and the time to practice."[38]

When she was about ten she wanted to stop piano lessons, but Angelena told her that she wasn't good enough to stop and make that decision. Shortly after this, Condi became the first black student to attend the nearby newly integrated Birmingham Southern Conservatory. Soon thereafter, she began to participate in piano competitions, which she continued well into her teens, with dreams of being a concert pianist.[39] Later, she was glad that she had listened to her mother and not stopped when she was ten.

Angelena also made sure Condi knew all of the social graces. And what is at the core of good manners? Consideration and respect for others: the Golden Rule.

"She was raised first and foremost to be a lady," says Colin Powell, whose wife, Alma, knew the Rice family in Birmingham. Mother and daughter were always well dressed, since they frequented the same high-quality clothing stores as the wealthy whites in town.[40] And a childhood friend from church said about Condi, "When we were running around, she was prim and proper, playing for the adult choir."[41] Today, she is still known for her gracious Southern charm and sense of style. Her Aunt G confirms this, "She always was the little lady."[42]

John Rice: Hero and the Wind Beneath Her Wings

Although Condi loved her mother and was close to her, she idolized her father. Randy Bean, Condi's close friend from Stanford, says that one of the things that she has in common with Condi is the close relationship that they each had with their fathers, who were both ministers. "Our fathers were our primary parent," she said. "[Condi] loved her mom, too . . . but our dads were it! We would throw ourselves in front of a train for them."[43]

Much has been written about the important role a mother plays in her child's life, but not until recently has the significance of the father-daughter relationship been fully examined. The relationship of Condi and her father, John, is a perfect case study showing the positive effects of a father and daughter bonding, and it helps to explain many of her positive attributes. According to one study, "Girls with the highest confidence and self-esteem have either strongly identified with their father or have particularly significant and supportive relationships with their father.[44] Other studies reveal girls with loving and involved fathers do better in school and tend to develop the traits of competence and ambition. Furthermore, Dr. Meg Meeker, author of *Strong Fathers, Strong Daughters*, says it makes it easier for a girl to bond with God "when a daughter has a good relationship with her dad."[45]

While Angelena's areas of expertise were music, fine arts, etiquette, and a wonderful sense of style, John's contributions to making their daughter a true Renaissance woman were in the fields of history, current events, religion, and sports. Considering that John's undergraduate degree was in history, along with his doctorate of divinity, he put his education to good use. Not only that, he also worked part time as a football coach at the same high school at which his wife was a science and music teacher. He shared his passions with his daughter, and soon they were among her own passions. One of those passions is football.

"I'm a football fanatic, there's no doubt about it," Condi enthused on an Oprah television special called "Secrets of Women Who Rule." "My father was a football coach, and he was going to turn me into a great football player and my name was going to be John," Condi said with a laugh. "I think it would have been great to be a linebacker!"[46]

Having a daughter did not stop John Rice from sharing his love of football with her. "He wanted a boy in the worst way," says Condi. "So when he had a girl, he decided he had to teach me everything about football."[47]

So, beginning at the age of four, Condi began to watch football games on television, with John explaining everything about the game to her. The pair would sit together on their living room sofa on Sunday afternoons watching the games, while her father gave running commentaries on the plays, rules, and strategies. Father and daughter had great discussions of football during these times of bonding. Although the days of watching games with her father are over, Condi is still wild about football (and about her father).

But not all was to be left to their living room "classroom" alone. It was time to put theory into practice. Starting on Thanksgiving Day 1958, the two played football together in their own "Rice Bowl" championship in the backyard. She loved football so much that, as a little girl, she declared to a friend's mother, "When I grow up I'm going to marry a professional football player!"[48] More recently, Condi recalled to a reporter, "My mother learned to like football in self-defense."[49]

Condi adored her father and these special times they shared. She still loves football and has never missed one Super Bowl since watching the first one with John when she was twelve years old. She even woke up in the middle of the night in Jerusalem to watch the Super Bowl kickoff in 2005.[50] Being commissioner of the NFL is one of her dream jobs. The timing just wasn't right for her when the commissioner job recently came available.[51]

When she spoke at a dinner in 2006 at which she was being honored, a surprise video message was sent to her and played for all to see from NFL commissioner Paul Tagliabue, congratulating her on receiving the "Woman of Valor Award" from the Independent Women's Forum (a political women's group). She appeared to get a big kick out of receiving that special recognition.

Along with many others involved in foreign policy and military strategy, Condi has noticed the similarities between football and war. It's no wonder that many call football "war without death." Long before she ever attended a class on military strategy, Condi was learning, analyzing, and discussing similar topics in football: strategy, air and ground attacks, and controlling territory.[52]

Former Denver Bronco and all-pro kick returner, Rick Upchurch, who dated Condi in the 1970s, says she had great admiration for Cleveland Browns hall of famer Jim Brown. "She loved the way he played the game because he was aggressive and he went after what he wanted. And that's the way she was," says Upchurch; "she went after things she wanted. She knew how to strategize and get control."[53]

"You need to be steadfast," was one of the lessons her father taught her, according to Haven Moses, another friend of Condi's, and Broncos all-pro wide receiver. "The ones who never waver are going to be the ones who are going to effect change."[54]

But John did not just spend time with Condi discussing football; he made sure that his precious daughter Condi knew that she was loved and cherished as a gift from God. Whether he was in the pulpit or in the living room, John constantly reminded Condi of truths from God's Word. He loved the Bible—he loved to study it, to talk about it, to live by it. It was an infectious love. Condi delighted to hear her father telling the great stories of the Bible. John often returned to the story of Israel's exodus from Egypt into the Promised Land. Condi learned that she was part of the same story, unfolding in her own family heritage through the struggles of her ancestors to achieve freedom.[55] As Condi got older, she and her father spent time, among their other conversations about football and current events, talking about spiritual matters.

"My father was an enormous influence in my spiritual life," Condi told a Sunday school class in 2002.

> He was a theologian, a doctor of divinity. He was someone who let you argue about things. He didn't say, "Just accept it." And when I had questions, which we all do, he encouraged that. He went to great lengths to explain about the man we've come to know as Doubting Thomas; he thought that was a little story from Christ about the fact it was okay to question. And that Christ knew that Thomas needed to feel His wounds; feel the wounds in His side and feel the wounds in His hands. That it was what Thomas needed—he needed that physical contact. And then of course Christ said when you can accept this on faith, it will be even better.

"I [liked] that because my father didn't brush aside my questions about faith," Condi said. "He allowed me as someone who lives in my mind to also live in my faith."[56]

Clearly, research backs up the view that parents play a major role and are the most important influence over their children's lives regarding religious and spiritual issues. Children look to their parents for answers and as models of faith, just as Condi explained when she said: "Part of the foundation of my upbringing was a mutual respect between my parents and me, evident in the freedom to ask and engage in questions all the time. Since my father was a Presbyterian minister and my mother a woman of faith, questions always came up centered around the Bible, specifically, historical Jesus. So I grew up asking questions and getting sound answers."[57]

Childhood Matters

"Childhood matters," Condi observed in 2001. And she is correct. For it was in this stable, loving, and challenging environment that Condoleezza Rice grew up with a solid moral and educational foundation, surrounded by her parents, extended family, and the secure, close-knit community of her church and neighborhood.

Her parents did an outstanding job raising her to her potential as they encouraged her in using her God-given talents. Their expectations were high, but not overwhelming. They treated her with respect as a unique individual. Little did John and Angelena know how well their investments and sacrifices would pay off for their daughter, for she is now one of the most powerful women in the world.

Like many parents, the Rices attempted to give their child every advantage in the hope that she would become a functioning, mature, successful adult, and a positive influence on the future of our society. They gave her their best. But most importantly, they gave her love: "They saw no limits for me," says Condi. "They wanted to give me everything. But the most important thing they gave me was unconditional love. Every night I pray and say, 'Thank you, God, for giving me the parents You gave me.' I was so fortunate to have these extraordinary people as my parents," she says gratefully.[58]

Chapter Five

Becoming a Steel Magnolia

"I was 7 or so years old, and we traveled here to Fisk University. . . . There would have been no thought of dinner in a restaurant, or lodging in a hotel. No, the American South was still quite separate and quite unequal."[1]

—Condoleezza Rice

"Justice is turned back, and righteousness stands afar off; for truth is fallen in the street, and equity cannot enter."

—Isaiah 59:14

"To do righteousness and justice is more acceptable to the LORD than sacrifice."

—Proverbs 21:3

Not everything was rosy and idyllic in Condi's childhood.

Imagine how difficult it must be to tell your child that she can't go to the local amusement park because of the color of her skin. "My parents had to try to explain why we wouldn't go to the circus, why we had to drive all the way to Washington, DC, before we could stay in a hotel. And they had to explain why I could not have a hamburger in a restaurant but I could be president anyway."[2]

The Supreme Court's Decision

The Rices believed that one day the walls of segregation would fall, and they wanted their daughter ready for that day. Although the Supreme Court had outlawed segregation in schools in *Brown v. Board of Education* in 1954 (six months before Condi was born), it was going to take a while for its impact to trickle down to everyday life for black Americans.

Despite the Supreme Court's *Brown* ruling, little interracial contact occurred in Southern schools for quite some time. From the time Condi began school in 1960 until she moved to Denver in 1968, there was not one white student in her classes, and she had just one white teacher during that span of time.

"I remember, too, my first trip to Nashville," Condi told students during the commencement ceremony at Vanderbilt University in Tennessee in 2004, the fiftieth anniversary of *Brown v. Board of Education*. "I was 7 or so years old, and we traveled here to Fisk University to hear the Fisk Jubilee Singers. There would have been no thought of dinner in a restaurant or lodging in a hotel. No, the American South was still quite separate and quite unequal."[3]

Jim Crow Laws

The inequalities to which Condi referred were called Jim Crow laws (named after a black character in minstrel shows). From the 1880s until the 1960s, Jim Crow laws enforced segregation in a majority of American states, but the South was the worst place for these laws.

Legal punishments could be imposed on people for consorting with members of another race. Frequently, the laws forbade intermarriage and forced public institutions and business owners to keep blacks and whites separated. Signs reading "Whites Only" or "Colored" were posted, restricting non-whites from access to restaurants, restrooms, water fountains, and waiting rooms. There were also separate hospitals, schools, and other public areas.[4]

Growing up in Segregated Birmingham

Continuing to share her personal experience with bigotry and racism with those gathered at Vanderbilt, Condi said: "I grew up in Birmingham, Alabama, before the civil rights movement—a place that was once described, with no exaggeration, as the most thoroughly segregated city in the country. I know what it means to hold dreams and aspirations when half your neighbors think you are incapable of, or uninterested in, anything better."[5]

Condi divides her time growing up in Birmingham into two separate periods. "The years from the time that I was conscious, which is probably around 1957, 1958 . . . until 1962 or '63, it was like living in two separate societies. But I was fortunate." In late 1962, violence and bombings in her section of town caused the split or division in Condi's childhood in Birmingham.

In 2002, while speaking at a Sunday school class at National Presbyterian Church in Washington, DC, Condi described an important aspect of her childhood: "I was a preacher's kid," she said, "so Sundays were church, no doubt about that. The church was the center of our lives. In segregated black Birmingham of the late 1950s and early 1960s, the church was not just a place of worship. It was the place where families gathered; it was the social center of the community, too."[6]

"She was raised in a protected environment to be a person of great self-confidence in Birmingham, where there was no reason to have self-confidence because you were a tenth-class citizen and you were black," said former secretary of state General Colin Powell.[7]

John Rice: Unsung Hero

Condi's father played an important role in the lives of many young people in their community and church. He made a tremendous difference in his corner of the world—an unsung hero, for certain. "I'm his only child by birth, but my dad has influenced hundreds and hundreds of other children over the years," Condi said in 1998. "I run into them all over the country."[8] Many of those young people have since become university presidents, doctors, lawyers, professors, and engineers, and they give credit to Reverend Rice for inspiring them to achieve through education, self-confidence, and fortitude.

John Rice was a big, tall man with a positive, warm personality and a great, heart-felt laugh. He had a way of attracting people to himself: the youth from the church, the students at the school where he was a guidance counselor and football coach, the participants at the fellowship center he founded. Kids came to the center after school and on weekends for fun or for the enrichment classes he arranged, such as chess, field trips to art museums, tutoring in math, and organized sports teams. Not only that, but John also led a Boy Scout troop at his church, which even produced two Eagle Scouts.

"He treated those kids in so many ways like they were his own children," Condi remembers.[9] The kids affectionately called him "Rev." Condi often came along for the fun at the center and to be with her beloved father. As a source of inspiration, encouragement, and practical tips, he helped numerous students get into college and found them part-time and summer jobs to pay for it. John believed that by encouraging these kids in their education, he was doing his part to knock down the walls of segregation.

With the church just blocks from the Rice home, it was fairly easy to remain sheltered within their neighborhood and schools, but there was no way to avoid what was going on around the Rices in those early days of the civil rights movement.

Although Condi's father wanted her to be aware of some of the historic events occurring around them, he didn't want her to be a part of them. He didn't think it was right to put children in dangerous situations. John believed that there were better ways to fight racism. A friend of John's, Pastor Fred Shuttlesworth, was one of the most radical of the Birmingham civil rights leaders. He had different ideas than John about how to best deal with the problem. "John said that the Lord had not called him for [radical measures like protest marches]," said Shuttlesworth.[10] John believed the best way to overcome segregation was through education. Condi called her father an "education evangelist."[11] "I want you to fight with your mind," John told the kids in his youth fellowship group.[12] Condi would also become a firm believer in the importance of education, considering that she went on to get a doctorate in Soviet Studies and became a university professor.

A Turn for the Worse

Then, things began to get vicious.

Thus began the second time period of her life in Birmingham. Condi's life in Birmingham was split in two by one word: violence. By late 1962 and 1963, it became more and more difficult to evade the world beyond Titusville, especially when it started to come to them. Unfortunately, there were times and situations that simply could not be avoided. Describing this terrifying time period in the civil rights movement, Condi said, "Bombs went off in the neighborhood all the time, and some of those heroes, people my parents knew really well . . . their houses were being attacked all the time. And there were Night Riders in the community."[13]

Night Riders were marauding groups of armed white men who drove through black neighborhoods at night bent on frightening and injuring the residents by shooting, bombing, and setting fires.

When a bomb was lobbed into a neighbor's yard, John asked the police to investigate this obvious crime. They refused, most likely because of the most prominent white supremacist in Birmingham, a man named Eugene "Bull" Connor. He was the city's powerful, racist Commissioner of Public Safety. Besides controlling the police and fire departments, he did everything possible to keep segregation alive and stop those who were "challenging our way of life."[14]

This was a frightening time for black citizens in Birmingham, and little Condi was no exception. "Those terrible events burned into my consciousness," she said later. "I missed many days at my segregated school because of the frequent bomb threats. Some solace to me was the piano, and what a world of joy it brought me."[15]

Condi's Strong Beliefs About Gun Rights

What happened next helps to explain another of Condi's stances.

"I have a sort of pure Second Amendment view of the right to bear arms," said Condi in 2001. She speaks from personal experience.[16]

In order to protect his family from the Night Riders, Condi's father joined other men patrolling and guarding their neighborhood armed with shotguns. This vivid memory of her father is the basis for Condi's strong beliefs about gun rights. She realizes how important it is for individuals to be able to defend themselves and their families. Besides, as Condi recently said about her father,

> He was supportive of the civil rights movement, like everybody, [but] my father was a very strong man, and the idea of a nonviolent response where people are beating up on you was not his cup of tea. He told my mother at one point, if somebody does that to me, then

> I'm going to end up in jail, and Condoleezza won't have a father . . . His style was much more "go take your shotgun and defend the community."[17]

If those guns had been registered, Condi reasons, Bull Connor could have confiscated them under some legal pretense, thus leaving the black community defenseless.[18] Of course, a personal experience with a law makes it come to life, and it strengthens a person's convictions regarding it.

Not only was the threat coming from within the country, our enemy just ninety miles off the coast of Florida, Fidel Castro, was rattling his saber in the form of nuclear warheads. The Cuban Missile Crisis of October 1962 frightened seven-year-old Condi even more than the events at home. She saw and heard the developing story on television and in the newspapers. "We all lived within range," she said. "The Southeast was it—you'd see these red arrows coming at Birmingham. And I remember thinking that was something that maybe my father couldn't handle."[19]

Children's March Turns Violent

Peaceful demonstrations, rallies, marches, and "sit-ins" occurred around town in an effort to bring about equality and civil rights. In May 1963, thousands of black children took the day off from school in order to participate in peaceful marches in downtown Birmingham.

Unfortunately, things got ugly.

Firemen sprayed the protestors with powerful fire hoses, under orders from Bull Connor, sending innocent children hurtling down the street. Policemen were commanded to break up the crowd with force.

Instead of using their dogs just to threaten the protesters, the police turned them on the unarmed, nonviolent children and adults, thus denying them their First Amendment privilege of peaceful assembly and protest. The forceful streams of water injured some people, cutting one little girl above her eyes so that blood streamed down her face and causing a woman to suffer a bloody nose from the powerful blasts. German shepherd police dogs bit a couple of people, and two dogs nearly ripped off a man's trouser legs, leaving his pants stained in blood.

While John and Angelena believed in the civil rights movement, they thought there was a better way than protesting. "My father was not a march-in-the-street preacher," said Condi.[20] John "detested" the Children's March, and he absolutely did not want Condi in it. "He saw no reason to put children at risk. He would never put his own child at risk," she said.[21] Even so, John wanted his daughter to be aware of history in the making, so he brought eight-year-old Condi downtown, and the twosome watched the demonstrations from a safe distance in their car.

The dogs and fire hose incident made national news, and soon millions of Americans were aware of the situation in Birmingham. Consequently, the civil rights movement continued to grow and gain momentum. Shortly after the event, President Kennedy instructed his administration to begin drafting the Civil Rights Act.

Before long, the situation went from bad to worse.

Murder in a Church

Racial tensions mounted in Birmingham. The pressure within the city was rising and was ready to burst like an overinflated balloon. But instead of harmless balloons exploding, bombs were going off in Birmingham, the work of hate-filled white people who aimed to kill, maim, and destroy. Remembering those times, Condi said, "I know what it's like to live with segregation in an atmosphere of hostility, and contempt, and cold stares, and the ever-present threat of violence, a threat that sometimes erupted into the real thing."[22]

In 1963, more than forty bombs exploded in Birmingham, giving the city the nickname of "Bombingham." Instead of getting better, the civil rights situation was quickly getting worse, escalating now with murder.

Inside a church on Sunday, September 15, 1963, the lives of four innocent young black girls were violently and brutally ended by Ku Klux Klansmen who planted a dynamite bomb under a stairwell. As much as Condi's parents tried to shield their daughter from what was happening around her, the violence, brutal scenes, and unrest were inescapable. One of the girls horrifically killed that Sunday morning in the racially motivated bombing was eleven-year-old Denise McNair, Condi's neighborhood friend.

"It all happened so unexpectedly that it took a moment to sink in," said the pastor of the church, the Rev. John Cross, speaking about the bombing to a reporter at the *Birmingham Post-Herald*.[23] The previously peaceful atmosphere in the church quickly broke into chaos. Reverend Cross went on to say, "It was terrible . . . The four children who died must have been killed instantly. They were in the direct path of the explosion."[24]

The girls, all wearing white dresses, were inside a dressing room in the church basement preparing to participate in a special service for the church's "Youth Day." Two of the girls were putting on their choir robes to sing in the youth choir and the other two young ladies were preparing to serve as ushers that Sunday morning. Then ten sticks of dynamite exploded at 10:22 a.m.[25]

The explosion could be heard blocks away. Eight-year-old Condoleezza Rice heard the bomb, and she felt the vibration of the floor at Westminster Presbyterian Church. To this day, the event is burned into her memory. Condi describes the blast as "a sound that will forever reverberate in my ears."[26]

When Difference Becomes a License to Kill

Condi spoke about this life-impacting experience at Stanford University's 2002 commencement. Less than a year after the September 11 terrorist attacks, she pointed out the similarities between the church bombing in Birmingham in 1963 and the assault on New York, Washington, and United Flight 93:

> In the months past, we have been reminded in dramatic and terrifying ways of what happens when difference becomes a license to kill. Terrorism is meant to dehumanize and divide. Growing up in Birmingham, Alabama, I saw the "home-grown terrorism" of that era. The 1963 bombing of the 16th Street Baptist Church was meant to suck hope out of the future by showing that hope could be killed—child by child. My neighborhood friend, Denise McNair,

was killed in that bombing, and though I didn't see it, I heard it a few blocks away. And it is a sound that I can still hear today.

Those memories of the Birmingham bombings have flooded back to me since September 11. And, as I watched the conviction of the last conspirator in the church bombing last month, I realize now that it is an experience that I have overcome but will never forget. And so it will be for all of us, you and me, who experienced September 11.

The story is repeated—time and again—in the Middle East, in Latin America, in Africa—and it came home to America. Innocents are killed to send a message of hatred and to propel old fears into the next generation.[27]

In an interview with the BBC, Condi pointed out the parallels between the war in Iraq and the civil rights movement of the 1960s. "Just because you're a democracy doesn't mean that you're perfect. Everybody has a long journey," she said. "The United States has had a particularly long journey, given our heritage of slavery, but indeed we have made enormous progress. . . . And that is an important lesson to countries that are just beginning their struggle for multiethnic democracy."[28]

In October 2005, Secretary Rice brought her English counterpart, British Foreign Secretary Jack Straw, with her to visit her hometown of Birmingham. While speaking at a ceremony called "Tragedy to Triumph" at a park in Birmingham, Condi recalled the events of forty-two years earlier and spoke about her friend Denise:

We played together, we sang together in little musicals. We were children together and we played with dolls together. And that pic-

> ture of Denise with her doll will always be near and dear to my heart; and the other girls had similar experiences, of course. . . . And when I think of them, I think first and foremost of them like that, as little girls who were just growing up and one day they were just at Sunday school. And as God would have it, they were at Sunday school when America experienced homegrown terrorism of the worst sort, when somebody decided that on a Sunday morning, in a house of God, he was going to have a bomb planted so that human beings who were just there to worship God would be hurt.[29]

"It was meant to shatter our spirit," Condi pointed out to those gathered. She also reminded them that only a few weeks before the bombing, Martin Luther King Jr. had delivered his famous "I Have a Dream" speech; the act of terror at the church was meant to show black Americans that their dream would be denied.

When thinking of the four girls, Condi looked for the good that came out of that terrible crime: "I think of their triumph as a fact that that dream was, in fact, not denied."

"Now, sometimes when I think of them," she pondered, "I wonder what they would be doing today, because they were, of course, very near my own age. . . . There's no telling what they would have done."

In closing she said, "I know they rest with God, grateful that they are remembered for what they meant and what they did for each and every one of us."[30]

To the klansmen, the bombing of the church did not have the desired outcome. It backfired. Instead of hindering the civil rights movement, the blast powerfully propelled it forward. Soon after that, laws were changed. This tipping point gave a boost to the growing movement, which in time brought about the end of racial segregation.

Until Condi was nine years old, the only non-segregated restaurant that she had ever eaten at was on her trip to Washington, DC. Things were about to change.

On July 2, 1964, President Johnson signed the Civil Rights Act into law. Now segregation was outlawed in restaurants, schools, lodging, federally assisted programs, and racial and sexual discrimination were outlawed in employment.[31] A few days after watching the historic occasion on television, the Rice family celebrated the event by going to dinner at a fine, previously segregated restaurant. As Condi tells it, the white diners looked up from their dinner plates in shock as the Rices walked past them toward their table, then "they all went back to eating. And that was it."[32]

Condi believes that the legal changes are only part of the civil rights story. Equally important were the people who had prepared and educated themselves to take advantage of the laws when they finally did arrive. "The legal changes made a tremendous difference," she said, "but not in the absence of people who were already prepared to take advantage of them, and therefore took full advantage of them. You can't write them out of the story."[33]

It's Good to Get out of Washington

Prior to Condi's visit to Birmingham with British Foreign Secretary Jack Straw, she told the *New York Times* the reason she had invited him to visit Birmingham. "I feel pretty strongly that it's good to get out of Washington. There are other places I'd like to go around the country to do speeches about our foreign policy. And I've had the idea that it would be good to take some of my foreign minister colleagues with me from time to time."[34]

Later in the trip she explained her reasoning further: "Foreign ministers, when they come to the United States, they see Washington and maybe they see New York for the United Nations General Assembly. Maybe they see a little bit of the West Coast." Condi noted that it is unfortunate that "it's rare that they get to the South or to the middle of the country or, for that matter, to the Northwest." Condi hoped to "get the foreign ministers out to different parts of the country. It's awfully important to understand how complex America is."[35]

Women of the Civil Rights Movement

Two of Condi's favorite leaders from the civil rights movement are women. One woman Condi greatly admires is the late Rosa Parks. The beginning of the civil rights movement has been declared by many historians as December 1, 1955, the day Parks refused to give up her seat on a bus to a white passenger. In 1956, the U.S. Supreme Court struck down the law under which Parks had been fined following her arrest, thus outlawing racial segregation on public transportation. When Parks died in 2005, Condi honored her by sitting in the front row of the church at her funeral.

Another outstanding woman of the civil rights movement is Dorothy Height. Condi spoke in *Ebony* magazine about influential black leaders in her life:

> I remember the stories about all of them . . . the well-known people, like Rosa Parks and Martin Luther King, were, of course, a part of my life. But probably to me, my personal heroine is Dr. Dorothy Height. . . . People who had that foresight to see, as the struggle unfolded, that education was the key to having a whole generation of people who were ready to take advantage once the United States came to terms with segregation were my heroes.[36]

Dr. Height is one of the nation's top human rights and equality leaders. Height says it was her mother who taught her to help others and to deal with prejudice and hatred. She was the only woman in the "Big Six," a prominent group of civil rights leaders that included Dr. Martin Luther King Jr. The members made plans for the civil rights movement. The principle of self-reliance is behind many of the programs that Height started, with a special emphasis on black women and children. These values also ring true for Condi.

The U.S. Conference of Mayors proclaimed February 28, 2001, as "Dr. Dorothy Irene Height Day," commending her work to promote black family life and "to reinforce the historic strengths and traditional values of the African-American Family."[37] She has received numerous awards, including one in 1989, when President Reagan bestowed the Citizens Medal Award on her "for her tireless efforts on behalf of the less fortunate."[38] She received an even greater honor in 2004 on her ninety-second birthday—President Bush awarded her the Congressional Gold Medal in recognition of her many contributions to the nation.[39]

Height gives excellent advice not only to youth but to all ages when she says, "People need to see each other as people, not as races."[40]

At a naturalization ceremony in 2007, Condi addressed new American citizens with these inspiring words:

> America stands as a shining example that difference does not have to be a license to kill. Difference can be a source of strength. . . . It matters not that you are Ethiopian-American or Russian-American or Mexican-American or Korean-American, you are just American. And you know, too, that it did not matter from where you came, it matters where you're going. That is what it is to be essentially American.[41]

In 1994, Condi encouraged graduates of the University of Alabama to get along with one another:

> When the founding fathers said "we the people" they did not mean me. But we have made great strides to give meaning to that phrase. If you are a member of the majority, please act in ways that move the promise forward. If you are in the minority, remember that we, too, are responsible for this fragile bargain. . . . Never avert your gaze from prejudice, but try, whenever possible—if you think that someone might have slighted you—count to ten and give the other guy the benefit of the doubt.[42]

One can imagine that some of the same words of wisdom Condi shared with those young people were expressed to her when she was young. When discussing how her parents masterfully handled her childhood in regards to civil rights issues, she said, "I am so grateful to my parents for helping me through that period. They explained to me carefully what was going on, and they did so without any bitterness. It was in the very air we breathed that education was the way out. . . . Among all my friends, the kids I grew up with, there was . . . no doubt in our minds that we would grow up and go to colleges—integrated colleges—just like other Americans."[43]

The events of Condi's childhood would shape her views on terrorism, justice, democracy, and freedom from tyrants—issues she would have to face again as an adult, in her jobs as a professor of political science, as a National Security Council staffer, national security advisor, and secretary of state.

And through it all, she has stood for justice, because she knows the source of justice. When talking about where real worth comes from, Condi said in 2006, "Human dignity is not a government's grant to its citizens nor mankind's gift to one another; it is God's endowment to all humanity."[44]

Just as parents immunize their children to protect them from the pain and suffering of various diseases, Condi's parents sought to inoculate her from the harmful and destructive effects of discrimination and bigotry. They also gave her a boost of self-confidence and a wonderful education so that she would be prepared and strengthened to become anything that she wanted.

The sky truly was the limit for this steel magnolia.

Condi says it this way, "My parents had me absolutely convinced that, well, you may not be able to have a hamburger at Woolworth's but you can be president of the United States."

Chapter Six

Not Your Average Teenager

"I'm the one who speaks French. . . . I'm the one who plays Bach. I'm better at your culture than you are. This can be taught!"[1]

—Condoleezza Rice

"Be strong and of good courage, do not fear nor be afraid of them; for the Lord *your God, He is the One who goes with you. He will not leave you nor forsake you."*

—Deuteronomy 31:6

As Condi entered the second decade of her life, she faced many changes—not just emotionally, physically, and spiritually, but in new surroundings as well.

Although the church members were sad to see them go, the Rices moved to Tuscaloosa in 1966 after John stepped down from the pulpit of Westminster Presbyterian Church. He was returning to his alma mater to serve as the dean of students. The all-black school had grown since he attended, and Stillman was now a four-year college. Instead of working with high school students, John would work with college students for the rest of his career. As the trio headed off in their old Dodge for John's new job at Stillman College, Condi entertained herself in the backseat by creating games reading license plates.[2]

A small white clapboard house situated on the Stillman campus served as the Rices' home in Tuscaloosa. One nearby neighbor said that despite sleeping in Tuscaloosa, the Rices *lived* in Birmingham, due to the fact they visited there so frequently.[3]

The family made the sixty-mile trip to Birmingham three times a week for the next couple of years while John worked at the college. He stayed involved with members of his former church, but mostly, they made the trip to see the Ray family. One of the trips north was for Condi's weekly ninety-minute piano lesson at the Birmingham Southern Conservatory of Music.[4] In order to make ends meet and pay for Condi's lessons, John waited tables while living in Tuscaloosa in addition to his other job.[5] Considering Angelena, John, and Condi were so close to the Ray family, it was great to be able to visit them on a regular basis.

Many years after an incident that occurred when she was twelve years old, Condi would recount in speeches how this experience made a lasting impression and planted "a seed of faith" in her.

It all started when she returned with her parents to visit her Grandmother Ray in Birmingham. During the middle of the night, Angelena's youngest brother, Alto, became seriously ill. Condi vividly recalls the commotion and scene of "complete chaos" as her parents and aunt "rushed frantically to get him to the hospital."

During all of the confusion, Condi searched throughout the house, looking for her grandmother. Where could she be when Alto was so sick and all of this was going on? When she found her, Condi clearly saw a demonstration of her grandmother's faith in action: Grandmother Ray didn't merely "talk the talk," she "walked the walk" of her Christian faith in her life.

Grandmother Ray sat peacefully and calmly on the bed, her arms folded. Condi asked incredulously, "Grandmother, aren't you worried about Alto?"

Grandmother Ray simply replied, "God's will be done."

"That was it: four simple but profound words," Condi says as she relays the story. "Those words struck a chord in my heart that has

Condi signs official papers after receiving the oath of office as Secretary of State, January 2005. Along with the Bushes and Justice Ginsburg are Condi's Aunt G, Uncle Alto, and his wife Connie.

resonated ever since." Condi asks, "How many of us say that without meaning it? We repeat it again and again in the Lord's Prayer, but we don't walk in it, becoming chaotic when difficult circumstances arise."[6]

Condi took this lesson from her grandmother and applied it to her own life in difficult circumstances. Fortunately, Uncle Alto survived the illness and years later was able to stand at his niece's side as she was sworn in as secretary of state.

Continuing Education

Reverend Rice's years of graduate courses were beginning to pay off. Almost every summer since 1960, Angelena and John studied at the University of Denver pursuing their master's degrees. They traveled so far from their home for graduate school because the nearby University of Alabama was segregated and restricted them from attending. When it seemed like he would never attain his goal at the rate he was going, John took a year off from his job at Stillman to attend classes full-time. He received his master's degree in education in 1969. Angelena continued to take classes off and on until she reached the same goal in 1982, a master's of education.

These trips out West became the instigation of another of Condi's favorite extracurricular activities, ice skating. Since Angelena and John were both working on their degrees, ice skating classes provided supervision and fun for Condi and allowed her to do a worthwhile activity. She worked her way up to practicing skating three hours a day, every day, by the time she was thirteen years old. Whereas piano playing and classes were sedentary, ice skating was a sport that built on her years of ballet and included many similarities such as grace, strength, performance, and music.

In the summer of 1969, when America's Neil Armstrong walked on the moon and flower power and tie-dyed clothes were at their peak, the Rices left Tuscaloosa. Soon after John Rice earned his master's degree, along came a job offer: assistant director of admissions for the University of Denver. John accepted the invitation and moved the family to Denver, Colorado. John was more adventurous than the reserved Angelena, but she was willing to relocate for his new opportunity in the West.

Condi enrolled at Saint Mary's Academy, a small, highly academic Catholic school closely connected to the University of Denver. Even though the school was Catholic, it accepted students of different faiths. With many of the university administrators sending their daughters to the school, St. Mary's was an attractive place for Condi and her parents.[7] Condi entered the all-girls school as a thirteen-year-old sophomore in high school, and for the first time, she wore a uniform. Always fashion conscious, she may have found wearing a uniform every day a little disappointing, but she adapted well. At St. Mary's, she was one of only three black girls. Condi's new school was very different from her all-black school in Birmingham, but she didn't think much of the difference. Condi's mind was on ice skating. Living in Denver meant that she could skate daily, not just in the summertime.[8]

St. Mary's provided an orderly and challenging curriculum, requiring students to take Latin, three years of high school science, and two foreign languages, which made it much more academic than the Denver public schools.

During her time at St. Mary's, Condi stood out to her teachers as being different from the average teenager. "Any of us who have raised children know that certain qualities are either there or not there," said her math teacher, Therese Saracino. "In the first place she was very, very poised. And she was beautiful even then, and charming, and her manners were impeccable, which is unusual for a sixteen- or seventeen-year-old." Saracino said in all of the time she knew Condi she couldn't think of any instance that she wasn't "a perfect lady."

Condi's religion teacher, Sister Pautler, remembers her being "very self-possessed and mature." She went on to say, "A lot of adolescent girls go through a tortured time, whether from lack of self-confidence or not being able to understand their maturation process or their family. But she didn't have any of that baggage; no self-doubt or confusion about growing up or about her family dynamics."[9]

Having self-confidence helped Condi to avoid feelings of inferiority and helplessness that are common among teenagers. She was an accomplished pianist, skilled ice skater, good tennis player, and excellent student. These qualities helped to boost her self-assurance.

Condi set her alarm each morning for 4:30 to go to the ice rink for practice, then to school, and when there wasn't tennis practice after school, she practiced piano after hours at St. Mary's. As Condi stayed later into the evening to work on the piano, her father decided that it was time to buy a piano. Believing that a good piano would be an investment in Condi's future career, John Rice obtained a loan for $13,000 and purchased a Steinway Grand. Condi was stunned, and it became another incentive to achieve greatness as a pianist.[10] At the time, John was only making $16,000 a year, so buying the top-of-the-line piano for Condi was a great sacrifice for him. Among other accolades, Condi won a piano competition with Mozart's "Piano Concerto 20 in D minor."[11] Her prize for winning the competition was to perform the piece of music with the Denver Symphony Orchestra.

Condi worked her way through St. Mary's quickly, completing the graduation requirements by the time she was fifteen. She then turned her mind toward college.

When she first entered St. Mary's Academy, though she was a straight-A student, her college entrance test scores came back with some disappointment. Condi went to meet with the St. Mary's guidance counselor. The counselor explained the hard truth from looking at the scores from the PSAT and nothing else: Condi wasn't college material.

Condi, of course, was shocked by this. She went home to share the bad news with John and Angelena. They rejected the notion and encouraged their daughter to persevere in her college pursuits.[12] The Rices knew Condi had years of solid data (her grades, other test scores, and several foreign languages) to fall back on. Plus, they knew their child better than the counselor who had just met her.

She later remarked that a person with less-supportive parents than hers may not have fared as well as she did regarding the counselor's advice to her. Condi's parents were wise to advise her to keep pursuing her dreams of college and ignore the counselor's comments.

Fortunately, Condi didn't listen to the school counselor's opinion because both she and her parents knew better. She definitely was "college material."

John and Angelena wanted Condi to graduate early and begin college classes, but Condi insisted on graduating with her class. "It was the first time I ever really fought my parents on anything," Condi told *Vogue*. "I just had a sense that socially you're supposed to finish high school."[13]

Condi made a compromise with her parents for senior year, but it meant a hectic schedule. Every morning, after ice skating, Condi headed over to the University of Denver, where she was enrolled part-time in two morning classes, then she went to St. Mary's for high school classes. By the second part of the school year, Condi had grown bored with high school, and she decided to pursue college full-time. She was fifteen years old.[14]

Condi wanted to go to one of the world's premiere music conservatories, the prestigious Juilliard School of Music in New York City, but her father thought that she could be more successful in some other endeavor. "My father was fundamentally against it," she recalled. "He said, 'You might change your mind,' and I remember thinking, I'm not going to change my mind."[15]

After living in Denver a couple of years, the entire family had settled into their new life in Colorado. Condi kept busy with her school, piano, ice skating, and church. Besides caring for her family, Angelena taught the seventh grade at one of the public schools in Denver. In addition to his work with the admissions department, John worked part-time as an associate minister at the church they now attended, Mountview Boulevard. He also taught a new class on "Black Experience in America," at the university. Condi spent time with her father on campus, attending lectures, meeting guest speakers who came to his class: Howard Robinson of the Congressional Black Caucus, civil rights activist Rev. Channing Phillips, Hollywood producer Gordon Parks, and voting rights advocate Fannie Lou Hamer.

Condi's meeting with Hamer was memorable. "I will never forget meeting . . . Fannie Lou Hamer when I was a teenager," she said in her commencement address at Stanford in 2002. "She was not sophisticated in the way we think of it, yet so compelling that I remember the power of her message even today."

The Mississippi woman had become involved in a public awareness campaign after she learned at the age of forty-four that she could legally vote. Fannie Lou Hamer refused to be intimidated by those who said that blacks couldn't vote. As Condi later reflected, "Anytime you feel powerless to affect *your* world, remember all you have learned about the history of *our* world. That history teaches that it takes just a single, determined individual to bring profound change. . . . Ms. Hamer reminds us that heroes are not born—they are made; and they often come from unlikely places."[16]

The University of Denver may have seemed an unlikely place to become a great musician, but Condi was growing attached to the place. She had never been away from her family for long, and the idea of going off to Juilliard eventually faded.

Probably one reason Condi wanted to be near her parents was that in 1969 Angelena Rice was diagnosed with breast cancer. The rest of the Ray family traveled from Alabama to be with Angelena for her first surgery. After the devastating results from her surgery came back, John got onto his knees and prayed out loud. "Lord, how am I going to raise a fifteen-year-old girl—alone?" he asked. Condi wondered how she would be able to live without her mother. "My father and I prayed that she might live to see me grow up." Thankfully her mother lived until Condi was thirty.

Angelena fought for the next decade and a half, but breast cancer haunted the family all of that time. Condi was worried about the possibility of her mother dying "in the abstract every waking day," she remembered.[17] But it also caused the threesome to cherish their time together all the more. Condi also recalls what a wonderful role model her mother was in dealing with life's trials. "She was tough as nails, and she not just survived it, I mean she completely overcame it." Angelena appeared to be cancer free for some time after treatment and tried to make Condi's life as normal as possible.

In the fall, Condi began full-time classes at the Lamont School of Music at the university with the goal of achieving a degree in piano performance so that she could become a concert pianist. Besides her already busy schedule of ice skating and piano, Condi worked on the school newspaper, took honors classes, and became a debutante at the University of Denver. The debutante program was a group of young African American ladies "who excelled in academics and were also involved in community types of volunteerism."[18]

Early on, Condi made herself known as an assertive and intelligent young lady. In one class with 250 students, Condi was one of two or three blacks. One day, the professor lectured about William Shockley, the physicist and inventor who later in his life taught that black people were intellectually inferior to whites. When it was clear that the professor was supportive of Shockley's views, Condi was stunned. She stood up in class and made it clear to the professor and 250 classmates that they would make a big mistake to underestimate her. She raised her hand and said, "You really should not be presenting this as fact because there's plenty of evidence to the contrary." The professor disagreed.

Condi then said, "Let me explain to you: I'm the one who speaks French. I'm the one who plays Bach. I'm better at your culture than you are. This can be taught! It doesn't have anything to do with whether you are or are not black."[19] The professor was left speechless.

Condi gained an important perspective that day of her freshman year. "It was leaving that class that it occurred to me that I think that had been my mother and father's strategy," she said. "You had to be better at their culture than they were. Recognize that you're always going to be judged more harshly. They made certain I was never going to be found wanting."[20]

While Condi went into college with unusual confidence, she was humbled by the college experience. At the end of her sophomore year, she participated in the Aspen Music Festival summer program, where she met pianists younger and more skilled than she. Eleven-year-olds could "play from sight what had taken me all year to learn, and I thought, *I'm maybe going to end up playing piano bar or playing at Nordstrom, but I'm not going to end up playing Carnegie Hall.*"[21]

Condi began to realize that her dream of being a great concert pianist was unrealistic. She says, "One day, confronted with the incontrovertible fact that I was good but not great—that I lacked prodigious talent and didn't like to practice (a particularly unfortunate combination)—I realized that I was going to end up teaching thirteen-year-olds to murder Beethoven."[22]

"I went to my parents, who had spent a fortune and all of their time turning me into a pianist, and said, 'Mom and Dad, I'm changing my major,'" Condi told Oprah Winfrey.[23]

For the first time in her life, Condi was faced with uncertainty. She didn't know what career to pursue, or what major to pursue, much less what classes to take.

Condi often says, "I don't do life crises." She explained why in an interview: "What's the point? You don't have that much of a life—life's not that long to spend a lot of time being obsessed with things that have gone wrong. . . . I had to find a major—I knew what I had to do."[24]

Condi continues to enjoy playing the piano and occassionally performs. Here she is with Yo-Yo Ma taking a bow after performing a duet of a Brahms sonata at an awards ceremony, April 2002.

Condi learned an important life lesson in her teen years from her piano dreams and passionate but short-lived ice skating career: "You can have failures and keep going." One of Condi's defining traits is her attitude toward problems in life. Both Condi and her father have been called optimists, and experts say optimism has its roots in childhood and can be learned. Optimism "enables you to approach situations with assurance, persistence, and an expectation of success," writes Lucy MacDonald, author of a book on optimism. "Being optimistic means that you have a natural aptitude for happiness, that you can manage your perspective and that you take an active role in creating the life you want." This is exactly what Condi has done with her life.

Later in life when she was a professor, Condi advised students not to stick too closely to preconceived ideas of their majors when they first begin college, but to be open to exploring new areas like she did after her piano career fell apart.

As Condi began her junior year, she waited for a fresh spark to ignite her passion. She enrolled in various elective courses, including a course in international politics with the great Sovietologist Josef Korbel. Korbel had led a distinguished career as a Czech diplomat before fleeing to Yugoslavia with his wife and baby daughter to avoid capture by the Nazis. Many of Korbel's Jewish relatives were killed in the Holocaust, while he continued to serve the exiled Czech government from London. Eventually, Korbel made his way to Denver, where he was as popular with his students as he was with scholars and diplomats around the world.

One particular lecture changed Condi's life. Korbel's topic one day was the rise of Josef Stalin. She was captivated. It was "love at first sight," she said. "That period in Soviet history after the death of Lenin until Josef Stalin established his power is just something that reads like a novel."[25]

Condi went back to her parents, who were still recovering from the shock that she wasn't going to be a professional pianist, to announce that she would major in political science. As Condi's Aunt G recalled, "Her daddy looked at her and said, 'Condoleezza! Black people don't make money in political science.'" Condi fired back, "Music, either."[26]

Condi reflected later on the path God had set before her. "I don't regret giving up the music career because I know that I was probably—with my penchant for not practicing as much as I should have and for also not having really prodigious talent—that I was probably not headed where I wanted to be in music. But the great thing about music is that you can pick it up at different phases."[27] Condi continued to play the piano, more now for the enjoyment than the profession.

She also grew in her love for singing, joining the eighty-member choir at Montview Boulevard Presbyterian Church. The choir sang classical works, including the only oratorio ever written by Beethoven, "Christ on the Mount of Olives," which became one of Condi's favorites. It held a special place in Condi's memory during one of her first diplomatic trips to the Middle East. "One of the great moments was when I was in Israel for the first time in August of 2000 standing on the Mount of Olives and as often happens in memory, this great oratorio just comes flooding back and puts it all together for me."[28]

Condi's college education came together by 1972, when she graduated from the University of Denver. When she graduated, she was closer to the age of most freshmen than to her classmates. Nevertheless, she won the Political Science Honors Award, membership in the senior women's honorary organization, Mortar Board, and membership in the Phi Beta Kappa honor society. She was selected as the Outstanding Senior Woman that spring, and her parents could not have been prouder. During her years in college, Condi had accepted God's plan for her life, whatever it would be, and she left bursting with confidence. Through searching with an open mind, Condi found her passion and a calling in life.

Chapter Seven

Education Is the Way to Success

"Education is transformational. It literally changes lives. That is why people work so hard to become educated and why education has always been the key to the American Dream, the force that erases arbitrary divisions of race and class and culture and unlocks every person's God-given potential."[1]

—Condoleezza Rice

"For it is God who works in you both to will and to do for His good pleasure."

—Philippians 2:13

The whole idea of Russia fascinated Condi.

"For reasons I don't understand," she confesses, "my passion became Russia and things Russian."

When she tried to learn German, French, and Spanish earlier in life, she was bored. But the Russian language was exciting, in part because of its complexity. "You can communicate a much wider range of nuance and emotion than in English," she said.[2] When Condi read *Darkness at Noon* by the Hungarian novelist Arthur Koestler, her fascination with the Soviet Union grew even more. Koestler exposed the horrors of Josef Stalin and the darkness of the Soviet regime, and something about that darkness intrigued Condi. "I think it's the mystery of the system," she said. "I've always been attracted to things that were hard to divine, where you had to be part detective, and it was something of a puzzle. I like mystery in stories, and when you're studying the Soviet Union, you're operating a lot in the dark."[3]

Condi loved Soviet Studies, and besides that, there were exciting career opportunities. Somebody asked her about the job prospects. "Well," she replied, "the job market's a lot better in Russian history than it is in concert piano."[4]

Soviet Studies were a popular option in the middle- and late-twentieth century for young people interested in academic and foreign policy careers. There was a great demand for experts on the Soviet Union. "The government gathered all those it could collect to inform and guide our wartime relations and our planning for the postwar period," according to Mark L. von Hagen of the Harriman Institute. "Most graduates of these institutes found jobs waiting for them, with government almost a guaranteed employer."[5]

The U.S. Civil Rights Commission met at the University of

Denver late in 1973, and Condi was invited to provide the piano entertainment at a reception. Sitting beside University of Denver chancellor Maurice Mitchell, Colorado governor John Vanderhoof was delighted by her performance. A few months later, Chancellor Mitchell got a call from Father Theodore Hesburgh, former chairman of the Civil Rights Commission, who had been at the reception. Father Hesburgh was the long-time president of the University of Notre Dame in South Bend, Indiana; just two years earlier, he had opened Notre Dame to female students. Hesburgh told Mitchell how impressed he was with Condi, who had recently visited the Notre Dame campus with an interest in graduate studies. This chance meeting proved to be a major turning point in her life.

From Condi's childhood on, John and Angelena had been investigating numerous colleges and universities for their daughter to attend when the time was right. All those summer vacations and side trips visiting schools gave them a wealth of knowledge about post-secondary education. They'd done their homework on Notre Dame too.

The Roman Catholic university's philosophy and mission was also an important factor in the Rices' encouragement of their daughter's going to the highly rated school. Notre Dame promotes the belief that "In and through the visible world in which we live, we come to know and experience the invisible God." Their vision for their students also sees "God not only present in but working through persons, events and material things."[6]

Besides having a Christian philosophy, Notre Dame had one of the leading Soviet Studies departments in the nation. It was founded by the Hungarian diplomat Stephen D. Kertesz after he fled his country during the Communist takeover in 1947. Distinguished faculty in the department included the political philosopher and writer Gerhart Niemeyer and the political scientist George Brinkley, who wrote prolifically in books and periodicals on the political and military dynamics of the Soviet Union.[7]

Condi enrolled at Notre Dame in the fall of 1974; for the first time she moved away from her parents. She was nineteen years old as she began graduate school—an age when many are only beginning undergraduate studies.

Condi had an advantage going into the program because of her prior study with Korbel and independent readings. She knew World War II history, she had read the great Russian novelists, and perhaps most important, she had a basic grasp of the Russian language. According to Brinkley, Condi's main advisor at Notre Dame, "She came better prepared than most students."[8]

Brinkley quickly saw Condi's special aptitudes, and it wasn't difficult to identify the origins of those qualities. "She was one of those self-driven students," he remarked. "Since she was a small child she has had a sense of self-worth that comes out of a certain kind of experience. Her father motivated her with the idea that regardless of what life held during her childhood, there were very important things like education that enabled her to do what she wanted and to be a success in whatever she wanted to go into."

Professor Brinkley at Notre Dame knew that Condi was no ordinary student; she needed a personalized academic challenge. "I could see she was someone who was so highly motivated," he said, "who had also read a tremendous amount, that she would benefit from a lot of opportunities to work on her own. And she wanted to do that."[9] Brinkley worked with Condi to tailor a pathway for her specific interests, capabilities, and to release her "God-given potential." That pathway included independent studies, directed readings, and classes.

Notre Dame was a key intellectual outpost for the realist school of foreign policy. Founded in 1939 by Professor Waldemar Gurian, the Notre Dame-based *Review of Politics* was one of the original intellectual forums on foreign policy realism.[10] Condi was heavily influenced by realist writers, especially Hans Morgenthau, a political theorist who wrote the landmark book, *Politics Among Nations: The Struggle for Power and Peace* in 1948.

Realism is the idea that human beings seek power, both as individuals and as nations. They fight to gain or maintain power, and in such a world, each nation is responsible for defending its own interests against those who would encroach. Realism rejects the vain idealism of the progressives, liberals, and other ideologues who think they can make a heaven on earth full of peace and justice. Realists commit themselves to making the best of an imperfect world where various interests struggle for power.

Morgenthau based his realism on the Judeo-Christian moral tradition largely inherited from St. Augustine who taught that Christians are not exempt from the business of this life, including politics and war.[11]

Condi had held these same beliefs since she was a little girl, even if she didn't know who Augustine and Morgenthau were until later. Condi learned early in life that defending one's self and one's community is not an option; it is a serious necessity for anyone who wishes to maintain her dignity in life. Dignity is a gift from God that has to be defended.

In 2006, when speaking at the Southern Baptist Convention, Condi spoke with those thoughts in mind: "Human dignity is not a government's grant to its citizens, nor mankind's gift to one another; it is God's endowment to all humanity."[12]

Morgenthau believed that the twentieth century was characterized by a new kind of power struggle in international relations. Power was still centered in individual countries, as in the nineteenth century, but as the number of leading nations diminished, the desire for supremacy among the leading countries increased. The entire world had become an arena of national interest. Morgenthau saw a race for power commencing as Winston Churchill saw the Iron Curtain descending over Eastern Europe. Churchill coined the phrase "Iron Curtain" and used it in a speech in 1946. His speech changed the way free and democratic nations in the West viewed the enslaved Communist countries in the East. The "Iron Curtain" became known as the division of Europe into Communist and democratic countries.

Add to the new power balance the realities of modern technology and the nuclear bomb, and the stakes rise. According to Morgenthau, "We live in a period of 'cold war.'" As we approached the mid-twentieth century, he said the international situation was being reduced to the big superpowers of the East and West trying to increase their military potential to the utmost to protect themselves. The new kind of war was essentially a war of ideas and values, Morgenthau believed.

This was the world for which Condi was preparing herself in graduate school. Among the current events, the major powers were bargaining over strategic arms limitations, culminating in the SALT treaties. Condi quickly discovered the importance of the Soviet military, so she centered her studies on that topic. In the process, she not only adopted the realist view of foreign policy, she also maintained the importance of moral values in her view of America's national interest. "Power matters," she said. "But there can be no absence of moral content in American foreign policy and, furthermore, the American people wouldn't accept such an absence."[13]

Condi found plenty of time for social life at Notre Dame in addition to her studies. She frequently went dancing with her friend Jane Robinett, then a doctoral candidate, now a professor of Latin American literature at Notre Dame. Friday afternoons, the two close friends often went shopping together downtown and rode in Condi's car named Boris—certainly an appropriate name for a Soviet specialist. Condi and Jane had much in common: music, protective parents, and especially a liking for football and football players. They even went to Miami to cheer on the Notre Dame Fighting Irish at the 1973 Orange Bowl.

For several months of her first year of graduate studies, Condi dated football player Wayne Bullock, who would later play for the San Francisco 49ers. (Condi met Bullock on her first day at Notre Dame, and he helped her carry her belongings to her room. She made cookies for him in gratitude.) Though the relationship didn't work out, Condi hoped that it would. When she was about to express her hope to Wayne one day as they were walking together, her platform shoe came apart and she sprained her ankle. Wayne carried Condi back to her dorm.[14]

After only a year and a half at Notre Dame, in December 1975, Condi graduated from a two-year program receiving a master's degree in international relations and economics. She was barely twenty-one, having just had her birthday in November. With plans to work as an executive assistant to a vice president at the Honeywell Corporation, she returned home to Denver. Just before she was to begin work, the company was restructured to eliminate Condi's position. She was unemployed before her job even began.[15]

Condi thought then of going to law school and applied to several major schools around the country. While waiting to hear back, she resumed singing in the church choir, teaching piano lessons, watching Denver Broncos football, and getting to know the players themselves.

Several of the Broncos' newly drafted players regularly came to the Rice home, where John Rice "became like our papa," says Rick Upchurch, a kick returner. Condi's parents would say to them, "Come on over here, and we'll cook for you." When remembering those good times, Upchurch said, "John told us to carry ourselves as professionals, what we needed to do to be successful. He'd say, 'You're pros. The cameras will be on you. Don't get caught up in bad things and ruin your career. Get that education.'"[16]

Upchurch, the 1975 NFL Rookie of the Year, even got up the nerve to ask John Rice's daughter on a date, and the pair began seeing each other. In 1976, Upchurch set the NFL record for punt-return touchdowns. More important, he asked Condi for her hand in marriage, to which she agreed, until "she realized that he wasn't the right guy and it wasn't the right time," according to Condi's close friend, Lori White.[17] Upchurch went on to complete a successful career with the Broncos, and today he and his wife have four children and organize a youth football ministry called Rare Breed.[18]

In accordance with her law school hopes, Condi was accepted at Denver, the University of Colorado, the University of Michigan, and Notre Dame, but a providential meeting with her old professor Josef Korbel made her rethink going to law school. Korbel saw in Condi a special aptitude for teaching, and he wanted her to carry on the tradition he had imparted to her. "You are very talented," he told her; "you have to become a professor."[19] Even though Condi had not really considered the possibility before, it didn't take much to change her mind. "He was nothing but supportive and insistent, even pushy, about me going into this field," she said.[20] So Condi enrolled in the Graduate School of International Studies at the University of Denver where Korbel was a faculty member.

Like George Brinkley at Notre Dame, Josef Korbel saw in Condi a kind of character that could be cultivated into greatness. He became her mentor. Despite his reservations about women in the field of international studies, Korbel treated Condi with special attention. According to Karen Feste, another professor at GSIS, who would distinguish herself as an expert on Middle Eastern issues, "Korbel liked Condi because she was smart, she was quick, she was energetic, *and she knew Russian.* Those are factors that mattered to him."[21] Condi was far ahead of her peers in her knowledge of the Russian language. As if that were not enough, she took up lessons in Czech in addition to her continued studies of Russian.

Unlike many of the more narrow programs in the prestigious East Coast universities, the program at the University of Denver examined the complex array of cultural, political, economic, and social elements of the Soviet Union.

Another of the faculty members was the renowned national security expert Catherine Kelleher. A few years later when Condi herself was a teacher, she said that Professor Kelleher "captured my imagination because she was so articulate and clear. It's what I try to do in my own teaching—communicate your own sense of excitement, that you're reading the material because you like it." Kelleher helped to direct Condi's research toward areas where she could flower as a scholar.[22]

But it was Korbel who had the greatest influence on Condi. "He was a wonderful storyteller and very attentive to his students," she said about him. "It was that attentiveness, plus his ability to weave larger conceptual issues around very interesting stories, that made him such a powerful teacher."[23] He taught her the importance in complex foreign policy of speaking in a language that common people can understand. This is one of Condi's outstanding abilities and one reason that President George W. Bush chose her to be a foreign policy advisor during his first campaign and later national security advisor and secretary of state.[24] Condi spent many hours at Korbel's home, listening to stories of power, war, and politics in his thick Czech accent.[25] She was like an adopted daughter.

Korbel also had a real daughter who would go on to achieve distinction as the first woman secretary of state: Madeleine Albright. Albright was two years old when her parents fled Czechoslovakia with her, and like her successor in the State Department, she was inspired by Korbel to pursue a career in the study of foreign policy. Condi later remarked, "He was as proud of [Madeleine], and as aggressive about her prospects, as he was about me."[26] Several years later, Albright called Condi to ask her to join the Michael Dukakis presidential campaign. For a moment, there was silence on the phone line. "Madeleine," Condi said, "I don't know how to tell you this. I'm a Republican."[27]

Despite John Rice's Republicanism that resulted from his Democrat-imposed racial disenfranchisement at the polls in the early 1950s, Condi did not become a Republican right away.

The fall of Condi's first year at the Graduate School of International Studies was the first presidential election in which she could vote. She voted for Jimmy Carter. Three years later, she regretted that vote and switched her party affiliation. Condi became a Republican because Jimmy Carter appeared to be so naive about the Communist Soviet Union. Following the Soviet invasion of Afghanistan in 1979, less than a year before the next presidential election, Carter noted his sudden disappointment with the Soviet Union, boycotted the Moscow Summer Olympics of the following year, placed embargoes on Soviet grain and technology, put off final talks with the Soviets over a second SALT treaty, and restricted Soviet vessels from fishing in American waters.

Condi was surprised at Carter's reaction. "I remember thinking, *What did you think we were dealing with? This is a horrible government—of course they invaded some foreign country!* I thought it was time to have a tougher policy toward this repressive regime."[28] Condi later criticized the Clinton administration for "swatting at flies." Carter had swatted at flies, and Condi was ready for a tough president named Ronald Reagan.

"I was a registered Democrat and might never have changed parties were it not for what I thought was our mishandling of the Cold War," she said. "I thought the Soviets were aggressive and playing us like a violin. I thought Carter didn't understand the true nature of the Soviet Union, which was pretty dark."[29] Condi respected the Democratic Party; she appreciated the Democrats' role in the civil rights movement of the 1960s, and when she met Lyndon Johnson's daughter, Lynda Johnson Robb, at an event in Jamaica, she told her, "I'm part of your father's legacy."[30] Condi says, "But by 1980 I just thought the U.S. was not pursuing an effective foreign policy, and I was attracted to Reagan's strength. Then my political views developed in favor of smaller government."[31] She switched her registration and cast a vote for Ronald Reagan in 1980.

In the mostly liberal and Democratic world of academia, Condi understood the proper way to carry herself. "She was very self-contained, holding her cards very close to the vest, never revealing anything about her political positions or her personal life," said her professor Arthur Gilbert. "It wasn't until later that I found out she was involved with the Republicans."[32]

What was clear to Gilbert and his colleagues was that Condi would go far. "I think we all knew that she was going to do something quite superior to the average student."[33] She transcended the stereotypes, demanded excellence from herself, and made good impressions with everyone she met. "She always had such a sense of presentation. She was very well-prepared, well-dressed and made-up, not a hair out of place," said Gilbert.[34] Condi was independent and she worked hard. "She was willing to seek out help when she needed it and just do the work," said Karen Fester. "That was Condi's approach."[35]

At first, Condi wanted to specialize in Soviet civilian-military politics, but as she went deeper and learned more about the Soviet military, she discovered that she had to know everything she could about the military itself before she could comprehend its place in civilian politics. "I quickly realized," she told the *Washington Post,* "that it was hard to understand those things without understanding the 'hard' side—doctrine, strategy, and force posture—and I got to like military-technical details—ranges and characteristics of missiles, the tactics as well as the strategy of warfare, the types and uses of different kinds of aircraft, the significance of throw-weights."[36]

Condi has a good understanding of military technical details. As Secretary of State, she is shown here talking to military commanders in Cyprus.

During two summers of her doctoral work (1977 and 1978), Condi was an intern, first for the State Department, then for the RAND Corporation, a think tank researching military issues.

Condi had written a thesis paper before she graduated from Notre Dame. Working with Professor Brinkley, she created a proposal to expand the paper into a doctoral dissertation. They even discussed the dissertation over the phone after Condi was settled back in Denver.[37] The dissertation was entitled *The Politics of Client Command: The Case of Czechoslovakia 1948–1975.* Though Czechoslovakia had its own military forces, Soviet rule made those forces an extension of the

Soviet Union. The Soviet Union, she wrote, must be viewed "as an ever-present wedge between the domestic Communist Party and its own armed forces."[38]

"The [Soviet] General Staff was my life for five years," she recalled.[39] She went to Moscow and Poland for seven weeks as she prepared the dissertation, though the documentation she hoped to find beyond the Iron Curtain was not available.[40] She therefore had to rely mostly on secondary sources. Having an investigatory type of mind, sometimes she did her own detective work. "I would go to Moscow and count the windows in the Ministry of Defense General Staff building to figure out how many people worked there because the data was never published."[41] Her guess: about five thousand workers.

More than a decade later, when Condi was working in the White House, she met General Sergei Akhromeyev, who served as Chief of the Soviet General Staff in the mid-1980s. She asked General Akhromeyev how many people worked for the Soviet General Staff. The answer: "About 5,000."[42]

In 1984, Condi expanded and published her doctoral dissertation as *Uncertain Alliance: The Soviet Union and the Czechoslovak Army, 1948–1983* (Princeton University Press). It was generally hailed among Sovietologists as a groundbreaking work. *Uncertain Alliance* was "by far the best work yet written on military politics in contemporary Eastern Europe," according to Timothy Colton, professor of Russian studies at Harvard University.[43] Walter Ullmann of Syracuse University commended Condi's analysis and research depth. "Her ability to ferret out important material from seemingly insignificant articles in highly specialized periodical literature reveals the breadth of her knowledge and her familiarity with things Czechoslovak in general."[44]

There were critics too. Josef Kalvoda of Saint Joseph College gave the book a negative review. What's worse, Kalvoda assumed that Condoleezza Rice was a man; after all, women were extremely rare in the field of Sovietology. "He passes judgments and expresses opinions without adequate knowledge of facts," wrote Kalvoda.[45] Condi wrote back a brief and assertive reply, defending her scholarly standards, her painstaking efforts to identify primary sources, and reiterating her central thesis, which Kalvoda's review "does not address."[46]

Powerful men, highly placed men, and men of presumption would later come to regret having underestimated Condoleezza Rice. Perhaps Dr. Kalvoda was surprised when "he" became the most powerful woman in the world.

Chapter Eight

Professor Rice

"I love being an academic. You know, I love teaching. . . . I love having a chance to make an impact on young people's lives."[1]

—Condoleezza Rice

"God has given each of us the ability to do certain things well."

—Romans 12:6 TLB

As Chip Blacker opened the mail in his Stanford University office in 1980, he ran across a handwritten letter that caught his eye from an exceptionally young doctoral candidate at the University of Denver. She had her own letterhead—light blue stationary with gold letters at the masthead, "CONDOLEEZZA RICE." When Condi had written a similar letter to Harvard, she never heard back. (In time, Harvard realized its mistake and tried to woo Condi to the university to teach.)

But Chip Blacker was indeed interested.

"It was pretty clear she was on some type of a fast track because she was significantly younger than she should have been . . . There was a quality bar that she cleared long before anyone thought through . . . 'she's female, and she's black,'" he said.[2]

What's more, Condi's reputation had preceded her application for a pre-doctoral fellowship at the Stanford Center for International Security and Arms Control. She had met Stanford professor Alexander George at a political science conference during her trip to Moscow in 1979. He mentioned her to Chip Blacker. Condi had impressed her professors at Denver; Alan Gilbert and Josef Korbel before his death in 1977 had made recommendations. When Condi went in for an interview at Stanford, she was almost a shoo-in. Condi spent the 1980–81 academic year at Stanford, completing her dissertation.

Once again, Condi moved away from her parents. But this time it was for good, unlike when she returned to her parents' home, master's degree in hand, from her year and a half at Notre Dame. Although she lived twelve hundred miles from her parents during her first stint teaching at Stanford, she remained close to them and saw them fairly often. They visited Condi at Thanksgiving and Easter, and she routinely saw them in Denver.

Condi soon fell in love with California, Stanford's beautiful campus with its red-tiled Mission-style roofs and buildings, and the stimulating academic environment. Plus, she made some close friendships there. Condi liked Stanford so much that at the end of her fellowship year, she put in an application for an assistant professor position.

Her interview included a session before the full department of political science, lecturing on her research and her dissertation and fielding questions. She stunned the department, and she was hired. At the age of twenty-six, Condi's appointment to one of the most prestigious universities in the world was, as former Stanford president Donald Kennedy explained, "unusual enough to be extraordinary." Indeed, "Very few people go from a doctorate at the University of Denver to a first-class research university." But it wasn't the first time Condi had defied the odds. "It was a product of [Condi's] set of extraordinary talents," said Kennedy.[3]

Now, just like her parents, Condi went into teaching and education. Course titles she taught included "Soviet Bloc and the Third World," "The Transformation of Europe," "The Role of the Military in Politics," "U.S. and Soviet National Security Policies," and "The Politics of Alliances." Condi loved teaching and was in her element. She would say about teaching at Stanford, "No other environment can match the energy of a place like this, where leaders in their fields create ideas and transmit them to the best young minds in the world."[4]

Condi was a natural at teaching and truly enjoyed it. "Football is like war," she would say to begin her classes at the start of the quarter. "It's about taking territory." From that point on in the course, students who would not ordinarily be interested in war or diplomacy were hooked. "Anyone who has had the good fortune to have a meeting with Professor Rice immediately after one of her lectures can sense the excitement she brings to the classroom," one colleague said. "Just by the way she talks about the lecture she has just given; it is obvious that she is still completely engaged in her subject and in her students to a truly extraordinary degree."[5]

Condi was liked and respected by her students. "She was only a few years older than the rest of us, but she was always so mature," one of her former students, Troy Eid, told the *Denver Post.* "She was my favorite professor in college, without question."[6] Condi was a favorite because, as one student who took a seminar with Condi reflected, she "treated us all like we were her favorite students." Moreover, the student said, "By the end of the seminar, several of the students were wistfully thinking about how much we wanted to be like her. This was not idle hero-worship. She seemed to be the embodiment of everything we admired about academia. She was knowledgeable without being close-minded, prestigious without being pompous, and her lectures were complex without being dry."[7]

Condi led her students through research projects that culminated in role-playing exercises, complete with costumes, to give them a sense of the relationships and personality aspects of diplomacy. During a week-long Cold War lab, Eid played a Soviet Minister of Defense. It was a grueling week. While on duty in Professor Rice's office one day, Eid nodded off to sleep. He awoke to Condi gently shaking him and offering him coffee. "It is still the most intense week I've ever had," said Eid, who went on to law school and today serves as U.S. attorney for the District of Colorado.[8] He still has the photo of himself, dressed in Soviet Army officer's garb, standing next to his favorite professor.[9]

Little did Condi know at the time, but her experiences as a professor would also help her cope with the crisis of September 11. "I think my time in academia prepared me more strongly than even I realized," she says. "I can't tell you how many times I taught decision simulations, in which I gave my students a crisis to deal with and then sat down with them afterward to go through the lessons. I learned things like, 'The first reports are always wrong,' which I remember saying several times on September 11."[10] Just after his appointment as associate dean in the School of Humanities and Science, Professor of History David Kennedy met Condi at a faculty reception and found her captivating. "A lot of assistant professors are geeky and a little bit unworldly, but she wasn't," he recalled. "To meet a twenty-six-year-old assistant professor who had that much poise and self-possession was pretty unusual. . . . She had a very self-confident manner without being overbearing or arrogant."[11]

For Condi, relationships were the most important part of her job. Ideas could only be effective if they were set in the context of people, and Condi determined to get to know people. When the dean of the Stanford Law School, Paul Brest, announced that the owner of the San Francisco 49ers was going to headline a Stanford Law School event, Condi invited Brest and his wife to a Stanford football game. "I'm not going to let you embarrass the university because I know you don't know anything about football," she told Brest, "so I'm going to take you to a Stanford football game." Condi took the seat between Dr. and Mrs. Brest and proceeded with her course in Football 101. Again, she began with her standard teaching analogy: "Football is like war; it's about taking territory."[12]

And Condi was gaining territory at Stanford. She was very busy in her new job, always organizing seminars or attending academic conferences or serving on faculty committees, while still finding time for teaching and for an active social life.

Her childhood friend Deborah Carson was also living in Palo Alto, so they picked up their friendship where they had left off. They enjoyed talking about their dates, dining together, and shopping. (Condi particularly has a weakness for shoes and has been known to purchase multiple pairs at a time.) Sometimes Condi and her friends had fun going on road trips.

Realizing the importance of exercise, Condi always made time in her schedule for her daily rigorous exercise routine, including sometimes working with a personal trainer from Stanford's athletic department for strength training.

Friends set up Condi, now in her late twenties, with blind dates from time to time, but she preferred to find her own dates. Although she dated men from a variety of professions, Condi was still drawn to football players. One of her more serious boyfriends at Stanford was handsome football superstar Gene Washington. After graduating from Stanford, he went on to play football professionally with the San Francisco 49ers as a wide receiver from 1969 to 1977. Besides having a love of football in common, Condi and Gene both came from Birmingham. Even though the relationship didn't last, the two have remained friends, and Gene, now director of football operations for the NFL, occasionally attends social events with Condi, including some official dinners at the White House.

When Professor David Kennedy met with the Stanford deans, someone often asked about Condi's work load, concerned that she was stretching herself too thin to invest adequately in research and writing.

When Kennedy relayed the concern to Condi, she asserted herself, "Look, I'm single, I don't have a family. I don't envision having a family in the near future. My career is my life. I can manage it, thank you very much."

Kennedy learned to respect Condi's time management, and one day he defended her after a dean alleged that she was taking too long to publish her dissertation. "Whatever the pace or mix of things she's doing," Kennedy replied, "this woman has success just stamped all over her. You can't be with her and not know this. And maybe it won't be a conventional success, but the fact is she has got her life under control."[13]

Still, with all that was going on in Condi's life, it was easy to get distracted from the daily exercises and disciplines of faith. With her hectic travel schedule and heavy commitments on campus and off, Condi's church attendance was sporadic. Away from the tight bonds of family and community that had kept her tied to a local church growing up, Condi found herself without a home congregation in which to regularly worship.[14]

Then a providential encounter brought Condi back to church. As she would tell a Sunday school class years later, "One Sunday I was in the Lucky's Supermarket not very far from my house—I will never forget—among the spices, and an African American man walked up to me and said he was buying some things for his church picnic. And he said, 'Do you play the piano by any chance?'" The man had noticed her long fingers.

"I said, 'Yes.' They said they were looking for someone to play the piano at church. It was a little African American church right in the center of Palo Alto, a Baptist Church. So I started playing for that church. That got me regularly back into churchgoing."[15]

There was one problem with Condi's new position in the church. She wasn't confident playing gospel music like she was playing classical music. Gospel music required a certain skill at adapting to the preacher and the congregation, and Condi wasn't sure if she had that skill. She called her mother, a veteran accompanist who had "a marvelously improvisational ear."[16]

"Mother," she said, "they just start. How am I supposed to do this?"

"Honey," replied Angelena Rice, "play in C, and they'll come back to you." Condi took her mother's advice, and it worked. She continued playing on Sundays for about six months.

Watching how God works in her life still amazes Condi. "I thought to myself, *My goodness, God has a long reach*," she says. "I mean, in the Lucky's Supermarket on a Sunday morning amongst the spices. As a result of going there and playing and getting involved again with the church community, I began to see how much of my faith . . . I'd taken for granted."[17]

Then Condi decided to get back into the Presbyterian Church. "I'm a devoted Presbyterian," she said. "I really like the governance structure of the church. I care about the Presbyterian Church."[18] Condi began attending services at Menlo Park Presbyterian Church in Palo Alto, and it was there that one particular sermon changed Condi's life. The sermon came from the fifteenth chapter of Luke, the parable of the prodigal son. But instead of focusing on the prodigal, the minister talked about the prodigal's older brother. "It set the elder son up not as somebody who had done all the right things but as somebody who had become so self-satisfied; a parable about self-satisfaction, and content and complacency in faith [and] that people who didn't somehow expect themselves to need to be born again can be complacent. I started to think of myself as that elder son who had never doubted the existence of God but wasn't really walking in faith in an active way anymore."[19]

This sermon really struck a chord with Condi, and she realized that it was time to establish new priorities in her life. Condi recommitted herself to the Lord, not just for Sundays, but for every day. "I started to become more active with the church, to go to Bible study and to have a more active prayer life. It was a very important turning point in my life."[20]

A long-lasting friendship was struck between Condi and Stanford colleague Chip Blacker. Chip tried to get Condi involved in the 1984 presidential campaign of Gary Hart. She advised Hart on foreign policy for a brief time, and ended up impressing him with her insight. He noted "her intellect and charm—charm in the profound sense, not the silly sense. And I'd add a third dimension: inner strength."[21]

Among mostly liberal scholars, Condi was able to establish credibility and respect. Professor Rice became known among Stanford faculty as "Condi the Hawk" for her conservative foreign policy views.[22] Despite intellectual disagreement, Condi's colleagues came to regard her highly. "She got along well with everybody," said political science professor John Ferejohn, "and even when she was just an assistant professor she exhibited a lot of what you see now—a very effective leader, decisive, clear-headed. Even when you disagree with her about something, she has good reasons. She's effective when she's opposing you—she often wins."[23] Condi's colleagues liked her; she defied all the stereotypes of conservatism, and she did her job extraordinarily well. "She's very respected as a scholar," said Condi's old teacher at

Denver, Catherine Kelleher. "She has enormous poise and this ability to move very quickly into a new area and to make it her own."[24]

In 1984, as a result of an arms control class she was teaching, Condi received a prestigious Stanford teaching award at commencement. The commencement speaker was Richard W. Lyman, president of the Rockefeller Foundation. Lyman bemoaned the threat of nuclear war and the "relentless small-mindedness" of the latest arms control talks. "Humanity deserves better than that," he declared.

"As if in response," wrote *Washington Post* columnist David Broder, whose daughter was graduating that day, "the teaching award for the year went to Condoleezza Rice, a black woman political scientist who helped organize an undergraduate seminar on arms-control issues."[25] Once again, Condi was a ray of light in a dark world. As Provost Albert Hastorf presented the award, he commended Condi "for bringing enthusiasm and insight to her lectures and sparking the sense of curiosity and fascination in her students that she herself feels." Condi had given "incalculable support, encouragement, and inspiration to her undergraduate advisees."[26]

There were skeptics, but not after they met Condi. "I think what struck people at the time was a combination of all the personal stuff—charm and very gracious personality . . . a kind of intellectual agility mixed with velvet-glove forcefulness," Chip Blacker remarked. "She's a steel magnolia."[27]

So popular was Condi that on four occasions Stanford's graduating seniors selected her as their Class Day speaker, an annual recognition of a professor who is invited to speak to the class just before commencement. When she spoke to the graduates in 1985, she explained the meaning of the American Dream, not as a pretext for national arrogance, but as the culmination of ideals for all people. Still there were inequities that the rising generation would have to deal with if the American Dream was to be a reality for all. "I hope that we've taught you . . . there are other cultures to be accommodated and understood and that America herself could do with a bit less arrogance," she said, adding her hope "that you will remember that our institutions are very, very fragile . . . that even today, it makes a great deal of difference whether you were born in Menlo Park [upper class] or East Palo Alto [lower class], and [the] American Dream is going to have to be delivered to us all if we are going to be a country worth the paper on which our Declaration of Independence and our Bill of Rights are written."[28]

Condi spent 1985 to 1986 as a national fellow at the Hoover Institution. The institute is a leading think tank situated within the Stanford campus. It is a "public policy research center devoted to advanced study of politics, economics, and political economy—both domestic and foreign—as well as international affairs."[29]

She published her second book, *The Gorbachev Era,* with Alexander Dallin in 1986. She compiled and edited the collection of essays, including one of her own, by foreign policy experts discussing Gorbachev and his views. The book came to be used as a study guide at college campuses.

In 1986, California Republicans tried to get Condi into politics. She turned down the offer, explaining that she was a "strong executive-prerogatives person" who wouldn't get along well in the U.S. Congress.[30] Two years later, Condi helped her Stanford colleague, law professor Tom Campbell, in his successful race for Congress.[31]

Following her year as a national fellow at the Hoover Institute,

Condi went to work in Washington, DC, because she had been awarded a Council on Foreign Relations fellowship as a special assistant to the joint chiefs of staff. Working in the Pentagon during President Reagan's military buildup and talks with the Soviets gave Condi a ground-level perspective of the things she had studied and taught for the past decade. As an expert on the Soviet Union, Condi was able to explain to the military leaders how the Soviet leaders thought and therefore shed light on what they might do in certain situations. This worked both ways, because while studying nuclear planning, Condi was able to understand the American military better. She later observed that the military was "ill understood by the academic community and the civilian community at large," but she said she "found them welcoming, happy to have the contact with academics."[32]

Through this experience she said, "I gained so much respect for military officers and what they do. I really got an experience that few civilians have."[33] By 1987, after her year in Washington, Condi returned to Stanford and became an associate professor.

For the December 1987 Washington summit meeting between Reagan and Gorbachev, ABC News hired Condi as a commentator. The summit became a high-profile global media event, as the White House granted six thousand press passes, five hundred of which went to ABC News alone.[34] After Condi was on ABC's "Nightline" to discuss Gorbachev's arms reductions, she received two marriage proposals in the mail.[35]

From 1987–88, Condi served on the Committee on International Security Studies for the American Academy of Arts and Sciences, a national honor society of distinguished scholars dedicated to public service through collaborative research.[36] That year, along with several renowned scholars, she signed onto a report entitled "Crisis Stability and Nuclear War." The report called on policy makers and thinkers to consider the element of crisis in precipitating nuclear war. Though much had been said of nuclear weapons, too little was said of the potential crises that might prompt the use of those weapons, and of what could be done to deal with the crises. "If the risk of nuclear war is to be reduced," said the report, "more attention must be paid to the ability of governments to stay in command of events in crisis."[37]

When she spoke again at Class Day in 1988, she spoke of overcoming prejudice and bigotry. Addressing minority students directly, she said,

> I feel certain that we have taught you to call prejudice and bigotry by name and to challenge it in our institutional structures. . . . But have we equipped you to deal with bigotry in your daily lives? Do you understand that prejudice is not an impenetrable force field that cannot be overcome? The will to succeed may be your most potent weapon against the prejudice that is still deeply ingrained in [the] fabric of our country and our world.
>
> Prejudice and bigotry are brought down . . . by the sheer force of determination of individuals to succeed and the refusal of a human being to let prejudice define the parameters of the possible.
>
> If your first reaction to failure is to blame—if your first thought when you or another minority succeeds is that race or gender or physical disability must have been the patron—if when someone disagrees with you or stands in your way, you immediately suspect that that person is a bigot . . . bigotry and prejudice are winning because their mere existence has begun to define your successes,

> your failures, and your relationship to others. You have become a part of the pernicious dismissal of individual will. You are sanctioning the belittlement of the efforts of generations of nameless minorities—women who scrubbed floors to send children to college, men who were spat upon but kept their dignity—people who suffered and sacrificed so that step by step, victory by victory, the walls of prejudice would be brought down, and one and then two and then many minorities could pass through and achieve.[38]

In the 1980s Marshall I. Goldman of the Russian Research Center at Harvard invited Condi to speak at his center. What he saw amazed him. He sat in disbelief as she held forth on the Soviet military. "I said, 'Wow, where did she learn all that?' This was very technical stuff; it was stuff I didn't know," he told the *Washington Post* in 1989. "I was very taken with her competence, because she was a female. That's maybe a sexist statement. Military stuff is arcane to begin with—I don't know of any other woman who's a specialist on that."[39]

In other words, Condi was not only rare, she was singularly unique. And she left a lasting impression, not just on Goldman, but on scores of others along her path in life.

Those who knew her, even just a little, could tell that she was destined for greatness. After meeting Condi, the political scientist Francis Fukuyama mentioned to a friend, "You know, we're all going to be working for Condi some day."[40]

And twice in the late 1980s, Condi made appearances before Congress to testify about Soviet issues. In September 1987 she went before the Joint Economic Committee's subcommittee on National

Security Economics to discuss the potentials of economic growth in the Soviet Union. There were two possible impacts that such growth could have on the United States and the world, she explained. Either the Soviets would invest in political and economic influence, broadening their positive interaction with the world and the United States, or the Soviets would invest in military influence, which would bode badly for the world.[41]

Then in April 1988, Condi testified before the House Foreign Affairs subcommittee about the effects of *perestroika* on the Soviet military. Instead of dumping resources into particular types of weapons, she said that the Soviets would likely focus investment in more modest objects, such as research and development and existing plant improvements. In some areas, such as the development of certain missile technologies, the Soviets would not likely slow down.[42]

Condi made her second trip to Moscow in the spring of 1988 to address Soviet officials about nuclear strategy—in Russian. She was a woman, which was unusual for the Soviet hierarchy. And she was black, which was even more unusual in Russia. The *Moscow News* took up this curiosity from the West, noting that "men [were] wondering" why she had taken the time to study nuclear weapons when she "should be busy cooking and driving her admirers mad . . . instead she aptly juggles numbers of missiles."[43]

As Condi later explained to a reporter, "They just have no context for somebody like me."[44]

But then, America didn't have much context for Condi either. She was a trailblazer wherever she went. One day in 1988, as she recalled, "I was giving a briefing for the Air Force planners . . . in the Pentagon—one- and two-star generals from all over the country, and

I suddenly looked out at them and thought, 'You know, this is really strange, I am the only woman in this room.'"

Condi laughed as she told the story. "Then I thought, 'Well, that's life!'"[45]

Condi has made her way in a predominantly male environment of dealing with superpowers, arms control, and nuclear weapons. In 1989, when working for the elder President Bush, the topic of sexism came up with a reporter. She said, "It's usually an unintentional comment about women and whether there's enough fiber in them to believe in the use of force. Haven't they heard of Margaret Thatcher, Indira Gandhi, or Cleopatra for that matter?"[46]

Passionate About Education

Even today, through all of Condi's varied experiences and positions over the years, she remains passionate about teaching. In an interview with *Essence Magazine* she said: "I love being an academic. You know, I love teaching . . . I love having a chance to make an impact on young people's lives."

Condi continues to be a popular speaker at school graduations. Around the time of the *Essence* interview, Condi spoke about the importance of education when she gave the Boston College 2006 commencement address: "Education is transformational. It literally changes lives. That is why people work so hard to become educated and why education has always been the key to the American Dream, the force that erases arbitrary divisions of race and class and culture and unlocks every person's God-given potential."

Expanding on the topic of education, she told those gathered that education is a privilege, but along with that, "privilege confers obligation." Condi went on to suggest what she thinks are "five important responsibilities of educated people."

Condi gives the commencement address at Boston College, May 2006.

1. Find Your Passion

The first responsibility is one that you have to yourself, the responsibility to find and follow your passion. I don't mean just any old thing that interests you, not just something that you could or might do, but that one unique calling that you can't do without. As an educated person, you have the opportunity to spend your life doing what you love, and you should never forget that many do not enjoy such a rare privilege. As you work to find your passion, you should know that sometimes, your passion just finds you. That's what happened when I wandered into a course on international politics taught by a Czech refugee who specialized in Soviet studies. . . . I was hooked. . . . It just shows you that your passion may be hard to spot, to keep an open mind and keep searching.

2. Use Your Reason

The second responsibility of an educated person is the commitment to reason. . . . You haven't been taught what to think, but rather, how to think, how to ask questions, how to reject assumptions, how to seek knowledge; in short, how to exercise reason . . . but no one should assume that a life of reason is easy; to the contrary. It takes a great deal of courage and honesty. For the only way that you will grow intellectually is by examining your opinions, attacking your prejudices constantly and completely with the force of your reason.

3. Cultivate Humility

A commitment to reason leads to your third responsibility as an educated person, which is the rejection of false pride. It is natural, especially among the educated, to want to credit your success to your own intelligence and hard work and judgment . . . but it is also true that merit alone did not see you to this day. There are many people in this country and in this world who have those same qualities and are just as deserving of success as you. But for whatever reason, maybe a broken home, maybe poverty, maybe just bad luck, these people did not enjoy all of the opportunities that you have had. . . . Don't ever forget that. Never assume that your own sense of entitlement has gotten you what you have or that it will get you what you want. You have been summoned to the 'Jesuit ideals of compassion and charity for those less fortunate.' You have an opportunity and obligation, 'to graduate with wisdom and humility.'

4. Be Optimistic

The fourth responsibility of the educated person is to be optimistic. Too often, cynicism can be the fellow traveler of learning, and I understand why. History is full of much cruelty and suffering and darkness, and it can be hard sometimes to believe that a brighter future is indeed dawning. But for all our past failings, for all of our current problems, more people now enjoy lives of hope and opportunity than ever before in all of human history. This progress has been the concerted effort not of cynics but of visionaries and optimists . . . who never ever accepted that they were powerless to change that world for the better.

Here in America our own ideals of freedom and equality have been born through generations by optimists, by people of reason, to be sure, but just as importantly, by people of faith, people who reject the all too common assumption that if you can't see something happening and measure it, then it can't possibly be real. . . . But you're headed into a world where optimists are too often told to keep their ideals to themselves. . . . Remain optimistic no matter what, but that's not all. You have an obligation to act on those ideals and this, I believe, is

. . . really the most important responsibility of all, to work to advance human progress.

5. Serve Others

I believe that all human beings share certain fundamental aspirations. They want protections for their lives and their liberties. They want to think freely and to worship as they wish. . . . They want to be ruled by the consent of the governed, not by the coercion of the state. . . . It is your responsibility as educated people . . . to help close the gaps of justice and opportunity that still divide our nation and our world . . . .

Progress never unfolds passively or inevitably. No, the promise of human progress is always carried forward by men and women who serve a cause greater than themselves. . . . Know that even optimists among us sometimes feel tested today, but in moments like these draw solace from education and also from historical perspectives . . . and when you read of [America's Founding Fathers'] lives and their times, you are struck by the overwhelming sense that there is no earthly reason that the United States of America should ever have come into being. But not only did we come into being, we endured . . . . So remember, even when the horizon seems shrouded in darkness, the hope of a brighter beginning is always in sight.

Condi reminded the graduates to, "Remember your responsibilities to find your passion, to use your reason, to cultivate humility, to remain optimistic, and always to serve others."

With her passion for education and love of teaching, in 1993, when she was only thirty-eight years old, she became a full professor. Her academic career was rising at a steady pace up the proverbial ladder of success. Besides her promotion to full professor, Condi was given another prestigious award for distinguished teaching. But this time, of her two parents, only her father John sat in the audience watching his pride and joy receive her honors.

Along with the good times and her career spiraling upward, Condi faced one of the most difficult, painful, and heart-wrenching times in her life in 1985 when she was thirty years old. Sadly, her beloved mother Angelena lost her battle with cancer. The breast cancer had most likely metastasized, causing a brain tumor, which was diagnosed toward the beginning of July. Condi had plane reservations to fly home to see her on August 19, but her phone rang shortly after midnight on August 18, telling Condi her mother was gone. She'd lost her role model, confidante, and one of her biggest sources of encouragement. Condi says she has always regretted that she was not with her mother when she died. "I wish I'd gotten on a plane a day earlier, but that's the way it is. And I'm grateful that I'd been home three weeks before that."[47]

After a few hours of sleep, Condi's friend Chip took her to the airport and she flew home to Denver to help her father with the funeral arrangements as well as comfort him. Following the funeral service, close friends and family members gathered at the Rices' home. Condi led them in a prayer of thanksgiving for her mother's life. Mourners were taken by surprise when Condi suggested they sing some of Angelena's favorite hymns while Condi played the piano. She led those gathered in such songs as "What a Friend We

Have in Jesus" and one Angelena often played during her illness, "The Lord Knows How Much You Can Bear."

Later, back in California, Condi spoke to the congregation at her church. She talked about the closeness she shared with her mother and how she coped with her death:

> When I found out that my mother first had cancer when I was fifteen, I found myself asking an endless amount of questions that, for the first time in my life, no one had pat answers for. . . . I was blessed that she was able to see me finish college and teach at Stanford. . . . What a blessing those fifteen years were.
>
> But during those years, I had feared her death in the abstract every waking day. People who have cancer, and families who live in the shadow of terminal illness, clearly understand my fear. I could not fathom how I would survive her death. I tried to imagine life without her. What was I going to do? What would replace our nightly telephone call? How could I ever survive Christmas or a birthday without my mother there? She was only sixty-one years old, and no intellect could soothe the hurt that was there.
>
> I knew that I would not be able to move beyond her death because of my intellect, and certainly not by the power of reason. Instead, I would have to trust God's Word, press in closer to Him, and rest in the peace that surpasses feeling and what I needed to do in dealing with my grief. I was blessed to have had seeds of faith planted in my soul about God's faithfulness from my childhood to fall back on.[48]

Now came the time in life for Condi that many adult children must face, the switching of roles with their parents. Condi needed to help care for her father besides dealing with her own loss. Angelena's death was especially difficult for John, after more than thirty years of marriage, and he slipped into a depression.

Some time after his wife's death, John moved to the apartment that Condi had rented for him in Palo Alto so that he could be closer to her and she to him. With Condi's help, John began working with the school of education at Stanford and helping at the mostly poor East Palo Alto schools. Eventually John started to get involved again with life, mentoring and encouraging minority youth and making new friends.

One day while visiting a school superintendent, John was introduced to Clara Bailey, the principal of a performing arts school in the area, who was almost two decades his junior. The two talked for a few minutes and ended up exchanging phone numbers. Clara was attracted to the warmth of John's personality, and they started to see each other in October 1988. Within six months, they married in Las Vegas, and not long after had a Christian ceremony in Clara's Palo Alto house. Condi was the maid of honor.[49] Seeing how much Clara and John loved each other contributed to Condi establishing a close relationship with her stepmother.

Happy and relieved that her father was doing so much better now that he had Clara in his life, Condi found it much easier to take advantage of new opportunities as they came her way.

Chapter Nine

DEALING WITH THE SOVIET UNION

"You are given talents and instinct and direction through faith, and then you try to use them for the common good if you possibly can."[1]

—CONDOLEEZZA RICE

"Therefore, as we have opportunity, let us do good to all."

—GALATIANS 6:10

"I will instruct you and teach you in the way you should go."

—PSALM 32:8

Mentors can appear when you least expect it. General Brent Scowcroft went to Stanford University in 1986 to speak to a faculty seminar about arms control. Then chairman of President Reagan's Commission on Strategic Forces, the former national security advisor to President Ford went to a dinner after the seminar, where he was seated with some of the most distinguished foreign policy experts in the nation. That didn't make for an enlivening evening, however. In fact, conversation was rather "dreary," as he recalls.[2] Although the night began poorly, this was about to change.

Enter Dr. Condoleezza Rice, professor of political science. She had gone to the seminar, and then at dinner she became acquainted with General Scowcroft. She dared to challenge him on something he had said, and in the process she charmed him. "Here was this young slip of a girl who would speak up unabashedly," Scowcroft remembered. "I determined to get to know her."[3] Not only was Condi brilliant, but Scowcroft learned in the course of their conversation that she was an intellectual ally, an expert on Russia, and a foreign policy realist. "She saw where we could cooperate and where not."[4]

Scowcroft was so amazed by Condi that he visited a class she was teaching on foreign policy—not as a guest speaker, but as a guest student. Her topic that day was the MX missile. She had absolutely mastered the topic.[5]

Brent Scowcroft knew greatness when he saw it. He invited her to foreign policy seminars and conferences around the country where she could meet up with key diplomatic contacts.[6] She didn't seek these new opportunities. They fell her way because she was excellent where she already was. "She doesn't seem to try to push herself forward in any particular way," former Secretary of State George Schultz once told *Time* magazine. "But she has such a level of capability . . . that she winds up getting asked to do all sorts of things."[7]

A couple years after the dinner conversation, President-elect Bush named Scowcroft as his national security advisor. Immediately, Scowcroft tried to lure thirty-four-year-old Condi away from Stanford to serve on his staff. "One of my first phone calls was to Condi Rice," Scowcroft said.[8] But he wasn't the only one who wanted to hire her. When Condi came to Washington in January to consider her options, she was pursued by defense secretary nominee John Tower and Secretary of State James Baker.[9]

Condi chose to work for Scowcroft. "It wasn't an easy decision," she admitted, "because I really loved what I was doing as a teacher and I was very happy in California, but I wanted to work for him at what I think is a very critical time."[10] Scowcroft was delighted. "I had chosen Condi," he said, "because she had extensive knowledge of Soviet history and politics, great objective balance in evaluating what was going on, and a penetrating mind with an affinity for strategy and conceptualization. She [was] . . . conversant and up to date with military affairs." What's more, "she was charming and affable, but could be tough as nails when the situation required."[11]

Condi placed a deposit on an apartment in Washington, flew back to Stanford to pack her bags and prepare for the moving company, and returned to the White House to move into her new office. When she arrived, she was already swamped by her new schedule, but she quickly learned to handle the West Wing work load. "She took to it like a duck to water," said Condi's Stanford colleague Chip Blacker.[12]

Condi remembers well the first time she was in the Oval Office for a meeting with the president and the impact the room itself had on her. "It was amazing!" she says. "I was completely overwhelmed. Anybody who tells you that they're not overwhelmed the first time they walk into the Oval Office is lying to you, because you walk in there and there's all that history."[13]

During her first day on the job, a large, mysterious box arrived at the White House from the Soviet Union. The Secret Service bomb squad took on the task of opening the package, which turned out to be a tremendous and gloriously decorated cake. As director of Soviet and East European Affairs for the National Security Council, Condi Rice was called to identify the source of the cake. She loves mysteries, so this task was right up her alley. Her investigation pointed to a group of bakers from a village in the Soviet Union. It was a gift to the president for his inauguration. President Bush wanted to arrange a photograph with the cake to be sent to the Russian bakers with a thank-you note, but by the time a photo op could be arranged, unfortunately, some rats in the Secret Service warehouse had devoured most of the cake.

And so began Condi's career as a diplomat. The *Washington Post* reported, "Her rise is an American success story with classic elements of pluck, luck and hard work, and also marked by the special perils—or, in some cases, subtle advantages—of being a beautiful woman in the predominantly male world of superpower politics, nuclear weapons and arms control."[14] Condi's credentials were starkly different than anybody else's around her; she didn't arrive at the White House through any standard career pathway, nor was she the inheritor of a place in some inner circle. "She did not come to Washington with a team," said Michael McFaul, a political scientist at Stanford. "She was not one of the boys, or one of the girls, or one of the academics, or one of the military guys, or one of the Brookings crowd or one of the Rhodes scholars."[15]

At first, White House staffers and inside-the-beltway big-shots didn't think much of her; they thought they could take advantage of her apparently soft demeanor. "They only tried that once," said Scowcroft.[16] When an official from the Department of Treasury challenged Rice's authority by trying to undermine her, she let him know his place. "With a smile on her face she sliced and diced him," said Defense Secretary Robert Gates, who served as director of the CIA during the first Bush administration. "He was a walking dead man after that."[17]

Condi didn't last long in her post as director of Soviet and East European Affairs. Just a few months after President Bush took office, Condi was promoted to be special assistant to the president for national security affairs, while continuing to serve on the National Security Council staff as senior director for Soviet Affairs. This meant that she was to collect, organize, and relay information from the assistant secretaries and undersecretaries in the Defense and State Departments. She advised Scowcroft in his daily responsibilities by helping him to arrange his diplomatic schedule and prepare for meetings. And she wrote briefing papers about specific foreign policy issues for the president before he went to meet with foreign heads of state.

History in the Making

Little did she know at the time, but she had a front row seat in watching history being made in her area of expertise.

She worked fourteen-hour days, coming into the office at 7:30 a.m. and leaving around 8:30 or 9:00 p.m.[18] She did homework too. In addition to reading embassy reports and American press reports about the Soviet situation, Condi told *USA Today,* "I also try to take home with me every night some Soviet press. There's actually public debate going on in the Soviet press."[19] The *Los Angeles Times* caught Condi holding a copy of the official Soviet state newspaper *Pravda* and syndicated the photo across the country.[20] "It was an exciting time," Condi reflected years later. "You could go to bed one night and wake up with some country having changed its social system overnight, with a new democracy to deal with."[21]

For her first major task, Condi led a team in writing a profile of Soviet General Secretary Mikhail Gorbachev, focusing both on his record and his ideas for the future, as well as setting forth a program for working with Gorbachev. Having already written and published extensively about the Soviet leader, Condi was well-suited for the assignment. As a result of her work, the Bush administration adopted four components in its policy toward Gorbachev, according to Scowcroft. First, America had to fortify its own reputation with strong and clear foreign policies. Second, America had to emphasize its commitment to its allies and to arms control. Third, America had to use aid money and other means to promote self-government in Eastern Europe. And finally, America had to work alongside the Soviet Union to advance regional stability.[22]

Condi was in the middle of all that was transpiring with the Soviet Union. "I remember coming back from a trip to Moscow and getting a message from Brent Scowcroft," she says. "He wanted to know if I could come to the White House. He said, 'We're going to meet Gorbachev on Friday in Finland to talk about the Gulf War.' And I said to myself, *Another meeting?* Then I thought, *Listen to you! When you started this job, you would have given your right arm to meet with Gorbachev and now it's 'another meeting'?*"

When Poland overthrew Communist rule in the spring of 1989, the Bush administration had an opportunity to gain a lasting ally by aiding it on the road to independence and security. Within the National Security Council, members debated whether to send an economic aid package to the new Polish government or whether such an investment would be wasted. In the end, the NSC decided to go ahead with the aid package. Condi reviewed the U.S. federal budget to identify revenue that could be reappropriated to Poland.[23] Then Condi assisted President Bush and his speechwriter Mark Davis in preparing a speech that Bush was to deliver at the Polish National Assembly, as part of a tour Bush would make of Eastern Europe in the summer of 1989. Though the president was not a great orator, his speech in Warsaw was one of his finest. Condi was there to hear it. "Democracy has captured the spirit of our time," he declared. "Like all forms of government, though it may be defended, democracy can never be imposed. We believe in democracy—for without doubt, though democracy may be a dream deferred for many, it remains, in my view, the destiny of man."[24]

Condi believed firmly in the blessings of democratic society. More than merely an abstraction, democracy to Condi meant the hopes and dreams of individuals. Faith was crucial to the human experience, she knew; it was the universal expression of man's pursuit of higher things. "You are given talents and instinct and direction through faith, and then you try to use them for the common good if you possibly can."[25] And Condi knew something that most of the establishment men in the diplomatic ring did not; as a woman who had worked every step of the way to get to where she was, who had overcome the doubts of people who said that she wasn't qualified, who had demonstrated that no barrier was too high for those who believe, Condi knew that in the end, the struggle at the bargaining tables and the lecterns and high-level meetings was about souls of individual human beings, made in the image of God. Ultimately, she said, "issues of war and peace and human values—what we think of as political issues—they're bigger than politics. They're about human beings. . . . Politics is the playing out of human aspirations through governmental structures."[26]

Condi believed that human freedom was the best way to bring out human dignity. Philip Zelikow, who served with Condi on the National Security Council, noted her disposition to trust others to follow their own goals, to encourage them and help them, not to force them or to make them beholden to one's own plans. "She believes in empowering people," he said. "In international affairs, that means real commitment to liberty and freedom. She sees the message of her life as a message of how to realize a person's potential. No one should ever become the prisoner of other people's expectations."[27]

This disposition to freedom in its fullest sense came to bear in the Bush administration's policy toward Germany. According to Zelikow, "[Condi's] instincts all along, from the very beginning, were: We need to allow the German people to pursue their own destiny, and we need to have the Soviets accept that."[28] As part of a five-member team on the National Security Council staff that developed the Bush administration policy on German reunification, Condi was a decisive voice in favor of pushing for a quick reunification. She believed that West Germany's five-year plan would give up strategic advantages to the Soviets to intervene in the process. After Condi reasoned with Scowcroft and the reunification policy team about the disadvantages of the German plan, they decided to take a risk on the people of East Germany, who didn't want to wait any longer for liberalization. The United States would push for a quick resolution.[29]

With the decline of the Soviet Union, border restrictions eased, leading to mass demonstrations, and the East German government began to fall. On November 9, 1989, the government broadcast a message to the citizens, allowing them to freely cross the border.

The Berlin Wall crumbled and fell.

As hundreds of East Germans crossed the Iron Curtain, which had been keeping them prisoner for thirty years in the Communist country, crowds of West Germans joined in the celebration.

East Germans had broken through in a dramatic display of the human spirit. Condi was in the office of NSC director for European Affairs Bob Blackwill when Blackwill got an urgent phone call directing him to prepare a report on the Berlin situation. Blackwill didn't know what was going on.[30] Blackwill and Condi turned on CNN; they couldn't believe what they were seeing. Condi later recalled that day for *Newsweek:* "I went home that night and watched the spectacle on television, joyful but shocked that this thirty-year symbol of Europe's division had fallen with hardly a whimper."[31]

The wall separating the Communist East from the free West was broken and was completely destroyed over the next few weeks. Many people around the world wanted souvenirs of the wall, but one who justifiably received a chunk was President Ronald Reagan, who several years earlier had stood at the wall demanding, "Mr. Gorbachev, tear down this wall!"

Soviet communism was in retreat, but much work remained to be done. In fact, as Condi wrote on the tenth anniversary of the Berlin Wall's collapse, "We suddenly faced a policy problem of enormous gravity and complexity. . . . We had to find a way to make the end of Soviet power in Europe and the continued existence of NATO seem to be in everyone's interest, including Moscow's. And we needed a Soviet Union coherent enough to agree to Germany's eventual unification. It was not long before we realized that Gorbachev was the Soviet leader most likely to make that decision."[32]

Condi was part of a delegation that accompanied President Bush to the Malta Summit to meet with General Secretary Gorbachev and present the American proposal on German reunification. If Condi was rare among American diplomats, she was a completely new phenomenon in the Soviet Union. Marshall Goldman, an expert on Russia from Harvard University, likened Condi to a female boxer. "You don't find many female boxers," he said.[33]

At the negotiating table, Condi was seated beside Secretary of State James Baker, who was seated beside President Bush.[34] When the Soviet diplomats first saw Condi, they were not impressed. "I think the Russians would sometimes feel, 'What's a girl like you doing here amidst bombs and bullets?'" she recalled. "It was initially hard for the Russians to accept me."[35]

Even Gorbachev may have had his doubts about Condi when Bush introduced his special assistant to the standard bearer of the Communist world. "This is Condoleezza Rice," said Bush. "She tells me everything I know about the Soviet Union." Gorbachev seemed surprised by Condi's youthfulness. "I hope you know a lot," he said.[36]

Also in late 1989, Condi met the Russian opposition leader, Boris Yeltsin, which resulted in their famous standoff in the White House basement.

In May, Mikhail and Raisa Gorbachev visited the United States. Since Condi spoke Russian, she spent some quality time with the couple. Condi escorted the Gorbachevs as they left the White House on a helicopter flight to Andrews Air Force Base. "He was really quite easy to talk to," she observed.[37] Just a few years earlier, President Reagan had gone up in the helicopter with Gorbachev to point out to him the sights of freedom on the ground below. Perhaps Condi was an equally powerful witness to freedom for the Soviet leader. Reflecting on her historic flight, Condi told *Ebony* magazine, "Every now and then you just get incredible moments like that."[38] She also accompanied the Gorbachevs on their subsequent visits to Minneapolis and San Francisco.[39]

When Mikhail and Raisa Gorbachev were about to board their plane out of San Francisco back to Moscow, Condi stood in the reception line on the tarmac. Security was necessarily tight. While Condi was waiting her turn to bid farewell to the Gorbachevs, a Secret Service field agent suddenly confronted her and ordered her to get off the tarmac and remain behind security barricades.

"I'm a member of the official White House party," she objected, flashing her White House identification badge.

The agent didn't care. Grabbing her shoulders, he pushed Condi violently and shouted at her, "I told you to get back there!"

Condi asked the agent for his name. "I'm a United States Secret Service agent, and I said to get back there. Who are you?"

"I'm Condoleezza Rice," she replied, "the president's Soviet policy advisor."

By this time, White House officials and other Secret Service agents had rushed to Condi's side to get the agent away from her. Quickly, she returned to the line, regained her composure, and exchanged farewells with the Gorbachevs.[40]

The incident generated a lot of attention for Condi. The press was desperate to know whether the incident was racially motivated. White House Press Secretary Marlin Fitzwater said that the president was "very upset about it. It's most unfortunate. It should not have happened, and the Secret Service will take appropriate measures."[41] In her first public comments about the episode, more than a year later, Condi told *Ebony* magazine that she was surprised by the media attention, since she thought that it was a "relatively minor incident" that had nothing to do with race. To her, the agent had simply been rude, and she would let Secret Service authorities take the matter from there.[42] Her words to the media are similar to words of advice she gave to young people in Birmingham telling them "to count to ten and not assume a slight is racially motivated."

When Gorbachev returned to Moscow, political instability raised major questions about his future and the future of the Soviet Union. Members of the National Security Council worried about the effects of a hypothetical coup against Gorbachev. The CIA predicted that Gorbachev only had a 50 percent chance of getting through the next three to four years if he persisted in his reform efforts. In September, the National Security Council secretly decided to begin contingency studies in the event that Gorbachev was to be overthrown and the Soviet Union was to suddenly collapse. Late one night in September 1989, deputy National Security Advisor Robert Gates called Condi into his office. "Things are looking bad," he said. He asked her to "get some people together on an off-the-record basis" for a series of contingency planning talks. Fearing that knowledge of such talks would actually precipitate the violent collapse of the Soviet Union, the talks were so top-secret that some of the seven or eight participants didn't even list it on their office calendars. The secret meetings were held periodically for more than a year.[43]

In a National Security Council memo Condi wrote dated January 12, 1990, one can detect how tense the situation must have been. "I believe (and this is a hunch and I guess if we did this that I would spend a lot of time in church praying that I was right) that the Soviets would not even threaten the Germans. Within six months, if events continue as they are going, no one would believe them anyway."[44]

In March 1990, the East German unification party won a majority in the first free election since the election of Adolf Hitler.[45] Over the next six months, Condi flew back and forth from Germany eight times to work with diplomats from around the world in reaching a settlement. On September 12, 1990, in the lobby of the Oktyabrskaya Hotel in Moscow, Gorbachev sat down with West German foreign minister Hans-Dietrich Genscher and representatives of the other nations involved in negotiations to sign off on the reunification of Germany. Gorbachev smiled and shook hands with Genscher before toasting the end of the "German question." Condi was there to see it, as part of the American delegation.

What the experts had predicted would take years to resolve after the fall of the Berlin Wall took less than a year. "This is a testimony to statecraft," Condi wrote in her 1995 book *Germany Unified and Europe Transformed: A Study in Statecraft,* coauthored with Zelikow.[46] As they wrote in the Introduction, "The German question was resolved so smoothly and amiably that it is easy to impute a kind of inevitability to the outcome. But nothing in political history is preordained."[47]

By 1991, after having begun negotiations with President Reagan to end the Cold War in the 1980s, the Soviet Union collapsed and broke into fifteen separate countries. The world was astonished, seeing the powerful Communist country dissolve. Most people had hardly considered the likelihood of that ever happening in their lifetime. Condi, too, was closely watching the historic events take place.

"I felt such joy for the Russian people," she says. "I also felt amazement at how it happened. Everything I'd been taught as a political scientist had said 'the state will try to survive.' And this was a state with 5 million men under arms and thirty thousand nuclear weapons."

When times are tough or it seems like progress is at a standstill, Condi looks back for encouragement to those historic days when the once-mighty former Soviet Union crumbled to pieces. She advises others to do the same. "If you ever feel bogged down in your routine, or caught in a cul-de-sac, or caught at a dead end, just think back to Christmas night 1991. On that night, the hammer and sickle, the flag of the mighty Soviet empire came down from above the Kremlin for the last time. You will be reminded that no condition, no matter how permanent it seems, is immune to change."[48]

On September 12, 1990, in another part of the world, nasty portents of a new chapter in the history of human political will could be discerned—but also signs of hope. Few paid attention to the ceremony at Oktyabrskaya Hotel. In the Persian Gulf, the United States and a team of allies had come in to liberate the little nation of Kuwait from the Iraqi madman Saddam Hussein.

Back in California, Republican U.S. Senator Pete Wilson was elected governor, prompting him to vacate his seat in the Senate and seek a replacement. Many leading Republicans in and out of the state, including Vice President Dan Quayle, hoped that Wilson would appoint Condi to fill the vacancy.[49] As one official close to Wilson told the *Washington Post,* Condi's nomination would make "a bold statement."[50] If appointed, she would be the first black female senator and the only current black senator. Condi didn't get the appointment, but California was nevertheless on her mind.

After two years in the West Wing, Condi was ready to go back to teaching. Her work in policy had sharpened her for the academic world, as her academic experience had sharpened her for policy. She had been blessed to serve at a crucial moment in the history of her highly specialized profession, Sovietology. As she told a reporter in 1993, "I've been to Europe thirty times or so now, and I've never paid my own way."[51] And she had sat with diplomats and heads of state in a moment of history when the map of the world was being redrawn. "Personally, I could not believe my fortune," she wrote for *Newsweek* ten years after the Berlin Wall fell. "I was witnessing the kind of diplomacy that only comes at the end of great wars, when foreign ministers and presidents, not assistants and bureaucrats, sit across tables designing the geopolitical future."[52]

In a short time, Condi had earned the respect and admiration not only of the assistants and bureaucrats, but of the foreign ministers and presidents—the kings and kingmakers at home and abroad. Beltway Democratic power couple Vernon and Ann Jordan hosted a farewell party for Condi, and the friendships at the party crossed all kinds of boundaries. "We had more Republicans in our home that night than we had in a very long time," Vernon Jordan told *Washingtonian* magazine.[53] Condi left a legacy. As the Bush administration's NSC director of European Affairs Robert Hutchings commented, "She was first among equals of those of us who were directors."[54]

Eventually, Condi even impressed the Russians. Russian newspaper *Pravda* would later observe how well she spoke Russian: "Other American Sovietologists knew only two words in Russian—*spasibo* and *pozhalustal* [thank you and please]. Condoleezza Rice, however, would start her working day reading a fresh issue of the Pravda newspaper."[55]

Condi had built a good foundation for future high-level work in the nation's capitol. *U.S. News and World Report* speculated that Condi's "technical expertise and moderate-conservative views make her a good bet for important posts at State or Defense in either a GOP administration or conceivably a Democratic one."[56]

One close observer said of Condi after her two years in the White House, "Condi was brilliant, but she never tried to flaunt it while in meetings with foreign leaders. . . . Her temperament was such that she had an amazing way of getting along with people, of making a strong point without being disagreeable to those who differed. . . . She has a manner and presence that disarms the biggest of bigshots. Why? Because they know she knows what she is talking about."[57]

Those are the words of President George H. W. Bush, who happened to have exceptionally close ties with a future president, namely his oldest offspring. In due time the elder President Bush would arrange an introduction between Condi and his son.

Chapter Ten

Tackling a Monstrous Deficit

"Life's too short. Get over it. Move on to the next thing."[1]

—Condoleezza Rice

"Forgetting what is behind and straining toward what is ahead."

—Philippians 3:13b, NIV

It was time to go home. Even though she had enjoyed her years in Washington, DC, and learned a variety of valuable lessons, Condi was looking forward to getting back to Northern California and Stanford University. Her father, John, was living there now, and she didn't want to live away from him for too long.

"I like balance in my life," Condi said, trying to explain to a reporter why she left Washington, DC. "I wanted a life. These [political] jobs are all-consuming. I have what is a blessedly normal life here. I like going to the cleaners and the coffee shop on Saturday morning."[2]

When Condi returned to Stanford in April 1991, her colleagues held a lunch to welcome her back. She spoke about the lessons she had learned in the White House. It was very different from the world of academia, she said. "You don't have time to build up any intellectual capital. You go to Washington with whatever knowledge you have, and then you burn it down," she said, echoing an old saying of Henry Kissinger's. "The problem is that sometimes people stay beyond the time that they have any intellectual capital left."[3]

Having visited the world's apexes of power and experienced the reality of international relations, Condi adapted her teaching methods and style to what she believed her students should know. As she told the *Stanford Report,* a president may be faced with the choice of whether to go to Moscow or London to celebrate a World War II anniversary; his choice will send a strong message to the world. Condi used television news clips to communicate the power of symbolism. In the real world of foreign policy, she explained, a decision must be made by 11 a.m. eastern time to fit into the global press cycles; such a world is often characterized by a feeling of "urgency, panic and even fear."[4]

Merely telling about historical events or assigning textbook readings was not enough. "It is increasingly difficult to generate in students a sense of the complexity involved in foreign policy with the methods available in the literature of political science and history," she said.[5] The "orderly, post hoc recreations that we teach" could not account for the personalities of statesmen and diplomats, so a new approach was required. To cut through the complexity, Condi assigned more primary source documents to her students—ranging from the Federalist Papers to the Stalin-Trotsky debates, and she added new role-playing scenarios to her syllabi. Condi often based her courses on current events, awakening students to the context of those events through research, writing, and personal experience in the course of the role-playing exercises.[6]

Condi wasn't just an academic, though. She decided that she wanted some business experience, so she set out to expand her knowledge and understanding in this new area. In May 1991, Chevron's board of directors elected Condi to serve on the oil company board.[7] She served on the management-compensation and public policy committees of the Chevron board. In honor of Condi's service, Chevron christened a 136,000 dead-weight double-hull tanker the *Condoleezza Rice* during a ceremony in the summer of 1993 at the Port of Rio de Janeiro, Brazil.[8] The supertanker would be the largest to go through the Suez Canal.[9] (Condi keeps a small replica of the *Condoleezza Rice* displayed in her home.) Hoping to expand its container-leasing operation into Eastern Europe, the international investment company Transamerica Corporation also talked Condi into serving on its board. Transamerica paid Condi a $24,000 annual retainer as well as a meeting fee and expenses; Chevron paid $25,000 plus meeting and expense costs.

Despite her busy schedule, she still remained a member of the prestigious Council on Foreign Relations.[10] Condi also agreed to serve on several non-profit boards, such as that of the defense think tank RAND Corporation, the Hewlett Foundation, the San Francisco Symphony, and her alma mater, the University of Notre Dame. On top of all this, President George H. W. Bush nominated Condi to a six-year term on the advisory board of the National Council on the Humanities.[11]

Despite having many responsibilities at Stanford and on the many boards and councils, Condi sought balance in her life with her regular exercise, involvement in music, and church. Top on her list of prerequisites for choosing a place to live is the necessity that it have a good location for her treasured piano. While living in Palo Alto, Condi played with a chamber-music group twice a week, and every once in a while, she performed in concerts on campus.[12] She has said that her music "centers" her and while she is playing the piano she becomes so focused on the music that it temporarily gets her mind off of other issues or problems. Her exercise is also a wonderful stress reducer and energizer. "Exercise is a high priority for me," she says, "I do some of my best thinking on the treadmill." Mark Wateska, Condi's trainer at Stanford, said that besides her workouts keeping her sharp physically, they also kept her sharp mentally.

In October 1991, Governor Pete Wilson appointed Condi, along with four retired judges and a prominent attorney, to the Independent Panel on Redistricting, to restructure the state's legislative and congressional boundaries. Through the panel's efforts, California was redistricted to conform more closely to the boundaries of cities and counties, while making certain districts more competitive between parties and diminishing the value of incumbency.[13]

ABC News retained Condi as a commentator on Soviet issues, making her a familiar face with Peter Jennings and Ted Koppel on the nightly news.[14] Condi took part in numerous panels, wrote opinion articles for major newspapers and magazines, and delivered lectures across the globe about such topics as the Cold War, race, and sometimes even the two combined. As a keynote speaker at the National Association of Black Journalists, Condi argued that the end of the Cold War presented a new opportunity for African Americans to achieve economic and social successes. "African Americans have got to be the beacon for those who are elsewhere. I would guarantee you," she said, "this is the best place to be a minority."[15]

And Condi committed herself to community service in the Palo Alto area. After delivering the commencement address for the eighth-grade graduation in the Ravenswood City School District in 1991, Condi noticed that the commencement was rather grand for a middle school graduation. She approached the superintendent, who was a friend, and asked why. The reply was shocking to Condi: "That's because 70 percent of these kids will never graduate from high school."[16] Condi helped her father and some friends to found a nonprofit after-school and summer program "to provide educational enrichment for kids in East Palo Alto," which was literally on the other side of the tracks from Palo Alto. They called it the Center for a New Generation.

Condi explained, "The idea is that if you give kids in underprivileged circumstances hands-on support in math, science, language arts, and music, then they'll have every reason to achieve. I was given that as a child, and I try very hard to pass that on."[17] The center has some similarities to places her father established for the youth in Birmingham, Alabama. With Condi's background in music, she also wanted to remedy Ravenswood's deficiency in music education. "I insisted that we had to have a band." Condi worked to raise money for the band's uniforms, and by 1992 the Center for a New Generation was in action.[18] "I believe in getting things up and running," she explained. "If we could unify Germany in less than a year, we can do just as well for East Palo Alto."[19]

As a young black woman and a rising star in the eyes of many political analysts and powerbrokers, Condi was invited to speak during prime time at the 1992 Republican National Convention. Reluctant to accept at first, Condi finally realized, "I was in a position to address and defend the Bush legacy in foreign policy."[20] She was a refreshing figure on the podium that summer in the Houston Astrodome. Mary McGrory of the *Washington Post* said that Condi "gave a cogent, rational review of our international successes, without suggesting as others did, that George Bush had singlehandedly done a Joshua on the Berlin Wall."[21] The *San Francisco Chronicle* named Condi the best of the "rising stars" at the convention: "The brainy Stanford professor was perhaps the most impressive figure off the Republican bench. Breaking the mold of second-string speakers, she provided a clear, crisp, and compelling articulation of the rationale for Bush's foreign policy. If Pete Wilson was watching, he was probably kicking himself for passing over Rice in favor of [John] Seymour for a U.S. Senate appointment."[22]

University of Chicago provost Gerhard Casper went to Stanford to interview for the university presidency in 1991, but it could just as well be said that he went to Stanford to interview his prospect for the number two job of provost. Condi was one of fifteen members of a search committee to identify the next president of Stanford.[23] As with most jobs throughout her career, Condi impressed the right people, and she never had to submit an application. They came to her as soon as they were in a position to hire.

Gerhard Casper got the job. After his inauguration, he called Condi into his office. In his statement about Condi's appointment to provost, Casper said that when he met Condi, he was "greatly impressed by her academic values, her intellectual capacity, her eloquence. Since then, I've come to admire her judgment and persuasiveness as well."[24]

Condi's appointment won national attention for Stanford. She was the youngest provost in Stanford's 102-year history, the first black, and the first woman. Casper "made a politically shrewd choice," observed the *San Francisco Chronicle,* "and may have hinted at who might be the next president of the university." Indeed, the previous two presidents of Stanford had served as provost prior to becoming president.[25]

Controversy also surrounded Provost Rice: she was connected with the Republican party and its foreign policy leaders; she was a fellow at the Hoover Institution, a leading think tank situated within Stanford campus, and possibly symbolized a university shift toward conservatism; she had never led an academic department; and the office of provost was traditionally reserved for a person of long experience and seniority.

Casper hired Condi in part for her youth. She was of "a generation I would like to see play an expanded role in education." Michael W. Kirst, emeritus professor of education and business administration, saw Condi's youth as an asset, since she "hasn't been socialized into the ways of academic administration" and could approach her new work "with an open mind."[26]

Condi got to work immediately, canceling a month-long research trip to the oilfields of Kazakhstan in order to "get her hands around the budget," as she told the *New York Times.* Stanford faced a deficit of $20 million in its $1 billion budget, and Condi was the one who would have to balance the budget. But fortunately, not only was her master's degree from Notre Dame in international relations but also economics, and she was now able to put it to good use, along with the business experience she had gathered from her work on the various boards. She knew that the job would be difficult, but she was ready for it—ready, indeed, for the controversies. "I tell my students, 'If you find yourself in the company of people who agree with you, you're in the wrong company.'"[27]

So Condi walked into her first meeting of the faculty senate with confidence. She was ready. "She just walked into the job kind of like she had been doing it all her life," said Stephen Krasner, a political scientist and a faculty senator. "I thought that if that was me, I'd be dripping sweat on the desk. She just walked into it like the job fit her."[28]

Condi quickly learned the dynamics of the provost's office. "I had never been a department chair before," she said. "And suddenly I found myself doing everybody else's job and thought there are two problems with that. First of all, if you do everybody else's job, you won't do it very well. Secondly, good people won't work for you." Men and women of experience and talent want to have responsibility, and it would come as an insult if Condi were to usurp their responsibility. She learned that she had to delegate and share authority as much as possible, a lesson that she carried with her to the White House.[29]

Condi also knew that sometimes a leader has to take charge and be tough. "I am direct," she said. Often it was necessary to work slowly to build consensus with the faculty. "But sometimes someone has to draw a line between informing, consulting, and deciding."[30]

By November of 1993, Condi was ready with her cost-reduction strategy. In letters to division deans and administrative vice presidents, Condi asked that faculty cut back on administrative overhead and prepare for budget cuts. Departments and offices would have to plan their budgets and revenues in advance. Specific top-down reductions would follow at a later time, perhaps including staff positions and student services. In the end, Condi hoped to slow the rate of tuition increases. "I actually don't think of this as a budgetary crisis," Condi told a campus newspaper. "This is just managing in the '90s. Every American institution out there is going through the same questions."[31]

But under Condi's leadership, Stanford was not just another American institution. "There was a sort of conventional wisdom that said it couldn't be done . . . that [the deficit] was structural, that we just had to live with it," Condi's friend Chip Blacker told the *Stanford Report*. "She said, 'No, we're going to have to balance the budget in two years.' It involved painful decisions but it worked, and communicated to funders that Stanford could balance its own books and had the effect of generating additional sources of income for the university. . . . It was courageous."[32]

Over the next couple of years, Condi announced several major cost reductions, each with angry opponents. First, the university would outsource its legal affairs to top outside law firms while retaining only limited in-house legal counsel. Stanford's legal bills had lately been as high as $8 million a year, and it was time to save money. That meant pink slips for at least eight lawyers and several other employees.[33]

Second, Condi and President Casper fired a fundraising director for the student affairs office whose job was no longer needed. Because the administrator, Cecilia Burciaga, was Latina, Latino activists on campus launched a pressure campaign to have the firing reversed. Four Latina students began a hunger strike on May 5, 1994, demanding that Burciaga be rehired. "We will not eat again until all the demands are met," said junior Tamara Alvarado as she rallied with her fellow hunger strikers on the campus quad. Condi and President Casper met with the students to explain that Burciaga had been a casualty of "budget realities" that were affecting dozens of other jobs as well.[34] Some students made personal attacks on Condi during the crisis, calling her a traitor for firing Burciaga. "You can't pull that on me," she replied. "I've been black all my life."[35]

Although she wasn't without critics when she became provost, to Condi it was a challenge. "I love this university, and I thought I had a chance to do something good for it."[36]

Condi dreaded firing people, but she thought it was an important part of getting the budget balanced. "I always feel bad for the dislocation it causes in people's lives," she said. "When I had to lay people off, I eased the transition for them in any way I could. But sometimes you have to make difficult decisions, and you have to make them stick."[37]

"Get over it, and move on" is one of Condi's favorite phrases. To her way of thinking, worrying and concentrating on struggles in the past is not productive. Rather than using your energy and thoughts focusing on a bad situation, see what you can learn from it and then use your energy to move on to the road right before you. Condi spoke about dealing with struggles in life one day at her church when she was provost:

> Struggle is not to be worn as a badge of honor. Perhaps this is why in describing his personal struggle, the apostle Paul felt it necessary to say to the Philippians, "Forgetting those things which are behind and reaching forward to those things which are ahead, I press toward the goal for the prize of the upward call of God in Christ Jesus"(Philippians 3:13–14). Struggle can only be turned to the good of others if we can let go of the pain, bad memories, and the sense of unfairness of the, "Why me?" that inevitably accompanies personal turmoil.[38]

Finally, during these challenging times for Condi and the school, she launched a review of an expensive perk that provided more than $10,000 a year for college tuition for the children of full-time university employees who had worked at Stanford for at least five years. "The days are long gone when we can simply, without examination, bear costs in the university budget," Condi declared at the faculty senate meeting as she announced the review of the tuition perk.[39] In the end, the faculty decided to phase out the benefit by retaining it for currently qualified employees and capping it at $2,000 for future beneficiaries.[40]

One issue facing Condi from the beginning was the controversy between liberals and conservatives on campus over political correctness. When two conservative Stanford graduates lambasted Stanford's multicultural curriculum in the *Wall Street Journal*, Condi and President Casper replied, "Like it or not, the role of women and questions of race and ethnicity are a part of our national debate and that of many countries." Furthermore, "The classroom is not a bad place to gain a deeper understanding of the history and development of these issues."[41]

Condi was committed to multiculturalism, but she was no fanatic about it. She brought reason and calm to the politically charged campus environment. "What's the opposite of multiculturalism?" she asked. "There's no place in the world for monoculturalism. I would like to think a student leaving Stanford appreciates Duke Ellington and Beethoven with the same fervor. I don't see culture as a prison where you are born and have to stay."[42] She voiced further views on the subject:

> Human history has been the story of clashes of civilizations, and that is the interesting part about it. It is absolutely true that our political structures, our civic structures, come more from Western history than from almost anything else. But I think it is important to teach about clashes of civilizations and how they infected and affected each other and how certain civilizations have won out at certain times.
>
> On the other hand, I've never much liked the representational argument or . . . the "I need to know about my culture" argument. . . . I think that you need to be able to cross cultural lines . . . my view is that Africans and Europeans landed here together and built this country together, and the separation of African culture and African history from American culture and American history is just ahistorical. If you're going to read and understand Frederick Douglass, then you'd better understand Thomas Jefferson, because that is who he was referencing.[43]

Besides that, there was the controversy regarding affirmative action. Condi believed that affirmative action was appropriate when it came to hiring, but not in consideration of tenure. That was Condi's own story; her race put her at an advantage when she was first hired in 1981. But when a faculty group came forward in 1998 to call for affirmative action for women in hiring and promotions, Condi could go along with the first part but not the second. Promoting faculty or granting tenure based on gender was a "real slippery slope," she said.[44] Condi acknowledged the importance of promoting and measuring progress in faculty gender equality, and she pointed to real advances that had been made in recent years (in 1992, there were two female department chairs; in 1999, there were thirteen).[45] But she also added her trademark caution: "It's hard to change one hundred years of academic practices, especially when a lot of the decision-making is done at the departmental level."[46]

Condi continued to defend the university's ban on affirmative action in tenure decisions even after the U.S. Labor Department began investigating the university's practices (at the request of several professors) and declared that affirmative action does apply to tenure.[47] Condi wasn't intimidated. "After you've talked the Ukrainians out of their nuclear missiles, this stuff is just child's play," she said.[48]

Ultimately, Condi knew that excellence transcended race or gender. That had been her firm conviction from the time she was a little girl in Birmingham. She knew that character and human relationships were the bedrock of excellence. Quotas were a bad idea because they made human beings into numbers instead of real people. Condi rejected this model.

Condi never allowed herself to be driven by impersonal bureaucratic rules. She often overruled her daily planner, and she never allowed the university to be driven unbendingly by long-term plans and projections, at least not under her watch. "The danger in a university is that you can over-structure or over-predict what the future is going to look like rather than create the conditions in which the future emerges rather naturally."[49]

When there was a problem on campus, Condi couldn't always address it from her office. She had to go to the scene and make herself visible. She would field questions in the faculty senate, or meet one on one with a professor, or get to know the students. That required flexibility in her schedule. When students staged a campus rally for additional on-campus graduate housing, Condi personally went to the rally in the evening to talk with students and get to know their concerns. She asked questions, and she answered questions. She clarified misunderstandings and pointed out campus limitations, but she resolved that the university would do more, reviewing options like temporary trailer houses on campus or acquiring off-campus housing. Stanford would also offer new loans and grants to help graduate students with their housing needs, she said.[50]

Condi not only proved to be a skilled administrator but also a respected public spokesperson for the university. The press often turned to her for honest and accurate assessments of campus issues. When President Gerhard Casper held press conferences or briefings, he made sure to have Condi on hand.

Stanford audiences looked forward to hearing speeches by the provost. Condi delivered a powerful sermon at Stanford Memorial Church on Founders' Day 1994, calling on her listeners to find their strength in the midst of hardship. She said that another seed of faith was planted in her life shortly after she was appointed provost. The story of how Stanford University originated had touched her deeply, and she shared it with those in attendance.

In 1891, with more than five hundred students, the school opened its doors: "Stanford University was founded out of the grief and anguish of two incredible people: Senator Leland Stanford and his wife, Jane," said Condi. Their son, Leland Jr., had died at the age of fifteen from typhoid fever while traveling in Europe. The couple, "having lost their only child, decided in their pain that they would do something good for other people's children, so they started the university."

The university became successful years later after Senator Stanford had died. His passing almost led to the university's closure because of a financial crisis caused by the government. Over the years, Senator Stanford had paid the expenses for the university, but upon his death, "the United States government seized his assets in a dispute over his railroad. The university was suddenly penniless." Mrs. Stanford rejected the advice of those who told her that her only recourse was to close the school. Instead, she "reduced her personal staff from seventeen to three, kept $350 a month out of the $10,000 permitted her by the courts, and placed the faculty on her personal payroll."

Condi noted how thousands of individuals have attained their education over the years "because of the sacrifice of these two people in the midst of their personal heartache." She went on to say, "As I reflect on those acts of faith and courage, first at the original founding after the death of their son Leland, then again after Senator Stanford died, I realize that Senator and Mrs. Stanford were testament to a belief that we have all but lost in modern life—the conviction that struggle and sorrow are not a license to give way to self-doubt, self-pity, and defeat," she said, "but rather an opportunity to find a renewed spirit and strength to press on."[51] Those acts of self-sacrifice in the midst of heartache are perfect examples that today's defeat can be turned into tomorrow's victory."

Condi was the speaker at a lunch for incoming freshmen in September 1997. Parents and students sat outdoors munching on turkey sandwiches while Condi explained college life to nervous freshmen and emotional parents. Every year, Condi made a bet to the incoming freshmen: "that 30 percent of them will end up studying something here which they did not even know existed when they arrived." Of course, that was Condi's own story when she was at the University of Denver. "That is the nature of higher education."[52] Among the listeners at the freshman convocation in 1997 was a young history major named Chelsea, along with her parents, Bill and Hillary Clinton.[53]

And many in the political world kept an eye on Condi. "I'd be very surprised if she weren't back in public life in the future," said RAND Corporation president James Thomson. "I think she's an obvious person (that) people would think highly of in a political role or a policy post."[54]

"She has the ability to have a cabinet-level job," Michael Mandelbaum of Johns Hopkins University told *Time* magazine after it listed Condi as one of America's star leaders under the age of forty.

When *Time* asked Condi about her political future, she replied, "I don't know. I'm not a very good long-time planner. I went to college to become a great musician—a concert pianist."[55]

Condi was content with what God had given her to do. "It would be nice to go back to Washington one more time in my lifetime, but I would not regret it if I never go back to Washington," she said.[56]

Elsewhere, she said, "I don't suffer from Potomac fever in the way it afflicts many people who have worked in Washington and spend the rest of their lives wanting to go back. I can say in all honesty that I don't spend a waking moment thinking about whether to go."[57]

Condi embraced the moment, not to live in the shadow of what's past or what may come, but to do her best where she was, by God's grace. "I look at life in quite a linear fashion. I don't look too far ahead," Condi said. "If you try to plan what your next adventure is going to be, it is a sure bet you are not going to enjoy or do a good job with whatever you are doing now."[58]

Just because Condi wasn't working in a foreign policy job didn't mean she wasn't involved in diplomatic activities. In the fall of 1998, Hua Di, a Chinese-born Stanford scholar who had worked with Condi at the school, traveled to China for family memorial services and was arrested by Chinese officials. They alleged that he had disclosed Chinese military secrets in his writings. Condi, along with other international security figures, wrote to the Chinese government defending Hua's innocence and asking for his liberation. "Stanford values Hua Di as a colleague and scholar, and we hope for his immediate release," Condi said in a public statement.[59] After a series of appeals, the innocent scholar was convicted in 2001 and sentenced to ten years in prison.[60]

Condi also continued to write and speak about Russia, Eastern Europe, and foreign policy issues in articles, speeches, interviews, and even a book. With her old NSC colleague Philip Zelikow, she coauthored the 1995 book *Germany Unified and Europe Transformed: A Study in Statecraft* (Harvard University Press). Documenting the ten months between the fall of the Berlin Wall and the completion of

German reunification, Condi and Zelikow were rewarded with praise and distinction for producing what Josef Joffe of *Foreign Affairs* called "a standard textbook" on reunification.[61] With 370 pages of text and 104 pages of endnotes, the book earned numerous prestigious awards. The *Washington Post* said that the book was "the policy wonk's 'Cinderella'" for its portrayal of the stunning German transformation. "This is the closest thing to reliable instant history we are likely to get."[62]

Condi's accomplishments earned her a growing list of honors and distinctions. For members of a search committee seeking a new chancellor at the University of California Berkeley, Condi was a top choice until it became clear that she wouldn't leave Stanford.[63] And in March 1999, Condi returned to the University of Denver for its 135th anniversary awards dinner, to be awarded the prestigious Evans alumni award.[64]

Condi stepped down from the provost's office in 1999 to work on the presidential campaign of George W. Bush. She ended up playing key roles in historical events within his administration. Of course, she had made more than her share of history already. As *Boston Globe* columnist Ale Beam wrote around his forty-fifth birthday, "I maintain a stiff upper lip when reading that my contemporary Condoleezza Rice is retiring from the third of three successful careers. . . . Comparing lives with Rice, who is also a concert-quality pianist, prompts me to paraphrase Tom Lehrer's wistful observation that by the time Mozart was my age, he had been dead for nine years."[65]

In Condi's final days at Stanford, she was invited by the Senior Class of 1999 to deliver the annual Class Day Address at Kennedy Grove on campus. This was the fourth time she was chosen to speak at a Class Day while at Stanford. Typically, three or four professors delivered strings of advice for the occasion, but the senior-class officers wanted to honor Condi alone, and Condi's speech was more than a list of axioms. Speaking just before commencement to graduates and their families, Condi talked about the personal challenges of living in a multicultural society.

Culture is important to identity, she explained. "On the one hand, what it is to be human is to have a memory of the past and to proceed from it with expectations of one's future. One who is not grounded in his own culture is most assuredly lost." On the other hand, understanding other cultures and the relationships that can be formed among different cultures is important, as well as knowing one's own roots. Condi said that she was not only an African American Southerner, "but it is also true that I have never felt more at home, more fulfilled, than in my adopted culture, which is that of Russia. To be multicultural is not just to have many cultures represented within an institution; it is to recognize that individuals themselves can be and often are."[66]

The crowd was hushed as she continued.

The challenge of living in a world with different races, creeds, and cultures is to find "a set of values and beliefs" that could unite people across their differences. This can be done politically on the grand scale, but it can also be done personally on the day-to-day scale of human relationships.

> The next time you marvel at how hard it is for "those people" to get along, when you think about the hatred between Serbs and Albanians or Tutsi and Hutu, ask yourself what you have done lately to cross cultural lines. Do you hold to the notion that you must find role

> models only in people who look like you, or that you can be a role model only to your own? Do you want to help them or do you really believe that they can help you? Are you really committed to living in accordance with all that you say about the value of diversity? Are you just tolerant of them, or are they among your friends?[67]

Multiculturalism was not an abstraction or a slogan; it was the life story of Condi Rice.

Gerhard Casper, the university's president, was one of the many who were sad to see Condi leave. At the end of a farewell address for Condi, he presented her with a special going-away gift. Friends from the school had bought her a first-edition Russian-language copy of the novel *War and Peace*. Condi was touched as she received this rare book, printed in 1868.

A student sang two of Condi's favorite gospel songs at a farewell party with more than one hundred guests. Condi and many of the guests were moved to tears upon hearing the woman sing "His Eye Is on the Sparrow" and "I Need Thee Every Hour."

As a reminder of her huge accomplishment as provost for six years, Condi proudly keeps a paperweight saying that Stanford met its budget during her tenure. After those two long, arduous years, she balanced the budget at Stanford. Not only had the $20 million deficit been reduced, the university now was $14.5 million ahead. The surplus money, deposited in a special account, was to be used for emergencies and unexpected expenses.

When asked by the school newspaper what she learned from her experiences as provost, Condi replied, "That I'm able to make tough decisions."[68]

Naysayers said it couldn't be done, but later had to admit the university was better off from her strong leadership in the number two position at Stanford. Condi still regards balancing Stanford's budget as one of her greatest achievements. With pride, she says, "We were never in the red."

While having done a wonderful job as provost by focusing on the job at hand and making some tough decisions, it was now time for Condi to end another chapter in her life. New doors were opening, and it was time to move on to her new job as a top foreign policy adviser for Texas Governor George W. Bush's 2000 presidential campaign. As usual she was optimistic about her future. She said around the time she left Stanford, "I have a very, very powerful faith in God. I'm a really religious person, and I don't believe that I was put on this earth to be sour, so I'm eternally optimistic about things."[69]

Chapter Eleven

Condi the Campaigner

"He is very much his own person . . . I think of myself as an option quarterback."[1]

—Condoleezza Rice

"Without counsel purposes are disappointed: but in the multitude of counsellors they are established."

—Proverbs 15:22, KJV

On the 1988 campaign trail, George H. W. Bush made the mistake of saying that he wasn't very good at "the vision thing." If the first President Bush wasn't a visionary while he was president, he at least seems to have had a vision for his son.

Condi was in Houston in 1995 visiting George and Barbara Bush. The former president had a request for her. Before she went back to Stanford, he wanted her to go up to Austin and introduce herself to the governor. George W. Bush had only recently been sworn in as governor of Texas, but he was doing well so far, and if he kept at it, he might be presidential material in 2008 or 2004—maybe as early as 2000. Whether or not that was what the elder Bush had in mind when he asked Condi to go to Austin, we don't know. What we know is that the meeting proved to be pivotal for the future of Condi's career.

The topic of that first meeting was not foreign policy, or Texas politics, or university politics. They talked baseball. Governor Bush was part-owner of the Texas Rangers. He showed off his signed baseball collection. Condi told Willie Mays stories, since Mays had been one of her mother's students at Birmingham's Fairfield Industrial High School. "Governor Bush was very impressed," Condi later said.[2]

After Condi left Texas, she kept in close touch with the Bushes, both father and son. In the spring of 1998, former Secretary of State George Shultz, one of Condi's Stanford colleagues, invited her across campus for cookies and tea at his home with a few former Ford, Reagan, and Bush administration officials who worked at the Hoover Institution. Their special guests were Governor Bush and his chief political advisor, Karl Rove. Bush wanted to test the waters for a possible 2000 presidential race by holding a "policy salon" with these eminent Stanford scholars. "You're my professors," he explained when they had all arrived. "I'm the Econ. 1 student, and I'm taking it again because I didn't do it well in college." The professors had a good laugh, and then they spent the next several hours going back and forth with the governor of Texas about all of the issues. He asked questions, and they asked questions.[3]

Early in the evening, Bush and Rove got up to leave, and Shultz walked out to the car with Rove. "I hope the good fortune of this place rubs off," he said.

"What do you mean?" Rove asked.

"Well," he said, "Ronald Reagan's Kitchen Cabinet had its first meeting right in my living room." Shultz said goodbye to his guests, and returned to the living room to debrief with Condi and the other colleagues. They all agreed that Bush was good, solid presidential material. Meanwhile, Rove and Bush were debriefing on the road; Bush said he was surprised by how well the meeting had gone. A lot of his earlier doubts suddenly cleared. Over the next several months, Rove would arrange for about six hundred political veterans, scholars, consultants, prospective donors, and policy experts to make the "pilgrimage" to Austin to meet with the governor for lunch. Many went in skeptical and came out ready for the 2000 campaign.[4]

That summer, the Bushes included Condi for the family retreat at Kennebunkport, Maine. It was an intensive few days of mental and physical exercise and foreign policy talk. They talked about it on side-by-side treadmills, on the tennis court, and in a fishing boat. While the former president and the Texas governor were fishing, Dr. Rice sat in the boat fielding questions about national defense, missile defense, China, Russia.[5] "We talked a lot about America's role in the world," she told *Texas Monthly.* "He was doing due diligence on whether or not to run for president."[6]

In December 1998, Condi announced that she would take a leave of absence from her responsibilities at Stanford, with plans to step down in June. Her e-mail and phone line were becoming busy with campaign business, making it increasingly clear how much Governor Bush trusted Condi as an advisor. He would send urgent e-mails to Condi with questions like, "What is going on in East Timor?"[7] Amid all her other responsibilities, she had to make quick responses. Her father told her not to step down from Stanford. He valued educational work and didn't want to see her abandon the university for the political world.[8] But she was confident that George W. Bush could be the next president, and she insisted on doing what she could to serve him. Besides, she considered her new work the political version of football, as she told the *Stanford Weekly:* "I tell my students that policy-making is 90 percent blocking and tackling and 10 percent intellectual."[9] The month she closed the door on the office of provost, Governor Bush announced that he was a candidate for president of the United States. Condi would serve as coordinator of the foreign policy advisory team. "If you're called upon by your country to do public service," she was known to tell others, "it's your obligation to do so."[10]

Through the summer, Condi was a teacher and a personal tutor to Governor Bush. She helped to provide all of the information he needed to set his foreign policy compass, much as she would do if Bush appointed her as his national security advisor should he win. Condi and her Stanford colleagues who originally met with Bush agreed that "he had to lead from his own instincts, not from someone else's. It's important for anybody who is going to be president to have a foreign policy that is organic to one's self."[11] And as Bush's advisor, Condi was not in charge of the show; she was working for the next president of the United States, and she let him lead. "He is very much his own person," she said. "I think of myself as an option quarterback."[12] Condi's job was to provide information and analysis of a situation so that he could make a final decision about where he stood.

She went along on his campaign trips, always teaching, clarifying, and preparing Bush for the White House. She flew between San Jose Airport and Austin Airport every week and a half or so.[13]

Condi was in the car with George and Laura Bush in the heat of late July as they pulled into the little farm town of Crawford, Texas, to look for real estate. Bush wanted a plot of ground that he could make his Western White House if he were elected, much like Ronald Reagan's legendary Rancho del Cielo, where the fortieth president had retreated for weekends and hosted foreign dignitaries. The Bushes and Condi looked at two properties, one at Coryell Canyon, and the other a 1,500-acre plot owned by B. F. Engelbrecht.[14] As far as Condi could tell, the Engelbrecht ranch was covered with grasshoppers—"there were just grasshoppers everywhere," she recalled. "I couldn't quite get it, and I could tell that they loved it. I thought, *Oh, boy.*"[15] In fact, as eighty-two-year-old Mr. Engelbrecht told the *New York Times,* it was Laura Bush who sealed the purchase. "She liked it more than he did."[16]

It didn't take long for Condi to see the charms of the property. "Once we got in the truck and started going down in the canyons, I could see why [the Bushes liked it]."[17] The ranch featured two hundred acres of canyons and woods around a creek, with grand old oak trees and a place where George W. Bush could install a pond for bass fishing.[18] From that day on, the place grew on Condi. "Now I really love being out there," she said in an interview with *Vogue.*[19]

As the 2000 campaign got underway, pundits wondered whether Governor Bush had the skill and experience that was required to lead in the category of defense and foreign policy. "Bush gets an F in foreign affairs," Salon.com headlined after Bush was unable to answer a reporter's questions about foreign heads of state. On PBS, Paul Gigot said that Bush had to prove his ability to lead in foreign policy and to "surround himself with smart people."[20]

Condi publicly defended Bush against charges that he wasn't ready to lead in foreign policy: "Governor Bush has not spent the last ten years of his life at Council on Foreign Relations meetings. He's spent the last ten years of his life building a business and being governor of a state," she said.[21] Behind the scenes, Condi was still busy teaching the next president. And Condi herself had some learning to do. She had been an expert on Russia, and now she was being looked to by the leading Republican contender for the most powerful office in the world as an expert on the entire world. "I've been pressed to understand parts of the world that have not been part of my scope," she explained.[22] She would quickly prove her ability to learn, adapt, and lead.

As early as the summer of 1999, it became clear to observers of the Bush campaign that the forty-four-year-old professor from Stanford was likely to be a major player in the diplomatic arena in the years ahead. But she would be more than a typical high government official, more than an older man in a gray suit. "If she becomes secretary of state or even something lesser, she will be big. Rock-star big,"

Jay Nordlinger wrote for *National Review* in August 1999. "A major cultural figure, adorning the bedroom walls of innumerable kids and the covers of innumerable magazines."[23]

After one of his first major policy speeches on foreign affairs, Bush had Condoleezza Rice on hand to answer questions from reporters.[24] As Americans saw more and more of Condi during that campaign, their confidence in her made them confident in Bush. "Whatever happens to Bush, you'll be hearing more of Condoleezza Rice," a *Washington Post* reporter commented.[25]

For the January 2000 issue of *Foreign Affairs,* Condi spent just two days penning a masterful outline of the prospective Bush administration's foreign policy.[26] She began with a scathing review of the Clinton administration. Clinton had "assiduously avoided" the demands of the post-Cold War period for "a disciplined and consistent foreign policy." Instead, Clinton had uttered empty threats against America's enemies while sending troops to obscure corners of the world on "humanitarian missions."

She echoed Clinton's undersecretary of defense who had called the conflicting troop buildups and defense spending cuts a "death spiral." "It was simply unwise to multiply missions in the face of a continuing budget reduction." This was "an extraordinary neglect," she said. America's credibility in the world had suffered, and the influence of dangerous enemy forces was on the rise. By failing to establish clear "priorities and intent"—by failing to lead in the critical transition from the Cold War to the new challenges of a new century—Clinton had left the free world vulnerable to its worst enemies.[27]

Clinton's successor "will be confronted with a prolonged job of repair," she wrote, transitioning to Bush's foreign policy platform.

Three principles seem to stand out in that platform: defend, deter, and fight to win. America's military had lost its focus while it was off on humanitarian missions in places like Somalia, Haiti, Bosnia, and Kosovo. It was important to have clear goals directly related to America's national interests, to have a clear mission, and to have the clear capability to carry out that mission. After all, "the military cannot be involved everywhere."

At the same time, Condi felt it was necessary to redefine a number of key strategic relationships throughout the world. In her opinion, many of these had been neglected or mishandled by Clinton. She felt China was a "strategic competitor, not the 'strategic partner' the Clinton administration once called it." It was time for serious talks with Russia about security and nuclear policy. America had to strengthen its alliance with Israel while strengthening its watch over the fundamentalist Islamic regime in Iran. And though Clinton had failed to deal with North Korea "resolutely and decisively," it was necessary in a new administration to deter and defend against North Korea's weapons of mass destruction. And then there was Saddam Hussein, the madman in Iraq. Saddam "has no useful place in international politics," Rice declared. "The United States must mobilize whatever resources it can, including support from his opposition, to remove him."[28]

Condi listed five "key priorities" to "refocus the United States on the national interest":

1. To ensure that America's military can deter war, project power, and fight in defense of its interests if deterrence fails;
2. To promote economic growth and political openness by

extending free trade and a stable international monetary system to all committed to these principles, including in the western hemisphere, which has too often been neglected as a vital area of U.S. national interest;

3. To renew strong and intimate relationships with allies who share American values and can thus share the burden of promoting peace, prosperity, and freedom;
4. To focus U.S. energies on comprehensive relationships with the big powers, particularly Russia and China, that can and will mold the character of the international political system; and
5. To deal decisively with the threat of rogue regimes and hostile powers, which is increasingly taking the forms of potential for terrorism and the development of weapons of mass destruction (WMD).[29]

When it came to specifics, Governor Bush said that as president he would want to withdraw U.S. peacekeeping forces from the Balkans, sparking controversy in the Clinton administration and abroad. But Condi was ready with the full explanation. "The U.S. is the only power that can handle a showdown in the Gulf, mount the kind of force that is necessary to protect Saudi Arabia, and deter a crisis in the Taiwan Strait," she said. "And extended peacekeeping detracts from our readiness for these kinds of global missions.

"This comes down to function," she continued. "Carrying out civil administration and police functions is simply going to degrade the American military capability to do the things America has to do. We don't need to have the 82nd Airborne escorting kids to kindergarten."[30]

For the 2000 Republican National Convention in Philadelphia, Condi was invited to deliver the first keynote address. She explained that she was a Republican because "I found a party that sees me as an individual, not as part of a group." With that, the audience exploded with applause. The Wachovia Center arena shook; Condi had fans. As Jay Nordlinger commented in *National Review*, "Her words were possibly the most thrilling of the whole convention."[31] The editors of *National Review* added, "Condoleezza Rice made it clear that she will be an asset to the Bush administration."[32] She was backing Bush, she said, because he was a man of integrity and strength. "If the time ever comes to use military force, President George W. Bush will do so to win—because for him, victory is not a dirty word."[33] As George Will observed after the speech, Condi had an "economical and lucid way of speaking her formidable mind."[34]

Throughout the convention, the press fell in love with Condi. She became a symbol at the convention of the Republican Party's growing efforts to reach women and minority voters. When Governor Bush gave his speech a few days later, Condi stood in an underground area backstage and watched the speech on a monitor alongside movie actor and economist Ben Stein. "She was extremely friendly and intelligent," he wrote later in the *American Spectator*. "I am glad she's on our side."[35]

During the election season, Condi's father had heart troubles that would soon take his life. He was chatting with Ann Reilly Dowd one day at his home, for an article about Condi in *George* magazine, when he slumped over from a heart arrhythmia. Dowd called 911 and Condi, who was nearby. "When she arrived," Dowd wrote, "the Reverend John Rice was on the floor getting shock treatments. I was trembling, but she was almost serene. 'Thank God you were here,' she told me, putting her arms around my shoulders. 'God works in strange ways.' Then, leaning over her father, she whispered, 'Daddy, it's Condoleezza. I'm here . . . We're going to take good care of you.'"[36]

For the next few days, John Rice was in the hospital on life support. Condi and Clara took turns sleeping in the room. When he came off life support, he remained bedridden. He was weak and debilitated with symptoms of a stroke. Although John wasn't able to speak much in sentences, he was able to sing hymns and praise songs. Condi and Clara would join in and the three often sang together his favorite hymn, "In the Garden," before ending in prayer.[37] Some days were better than others.[38]

Condi called her father every day during the campaign. He couldn't say much more than "Hi, darling," but Condi knew there was strength in her father's spirit, even if his heart was weak.[39]

Condi went to Dearborn, Michigan, in the month leading up to the election to speak to Arab American voters, a quickly growing segment of the American electorate.[40] She joined a nationwide "W Stands for Women" bus tour, along with Laura Bush, Lynne Cheney, former first lady Barbara Bush, and Senator John McCain's wife, Cindy. The tour included stops in Michigan, Pennsylvania, and Wisconsin.[41]

The presidential elections of 2000 were hotly contested. Two nights after the election, Condi was at the Bush campaign headquarters in Austin, watching the Florida recount returns with Bush's chief pollster Matthew Dowd. "It's just weird," she told *Newsweek,* as Bush continued to lose more and more votes.[42] For weeks, the election recounts, court battles, uncertainty, and media frenzy dragged on. On December 12, the U.S. Supreme Court handed down its decision in the case *Bush v. Gore*, determining the Florida election had gone in Bush's favor. The following day, Vice President Gore called Governor Bush to concede.

As the president-elect assembled his cabinet and senior official roster, the *Economist* remarked, "The big uncertainty is whether the team is imaginative enough to respond successfully to—or, better still, head off—the threats and crises that will confront it. Youth and brains will certainly be on hand. Condoleezza Rice, as national security advisor, can supply both."[43] Despite her youthfulness, she had probably the best résumé of any previous national security advisor, or at least the broadest. As Philip Zelikow remarked, "It is unusual for someone in her position to have government, academic, and managerial experience."[44] This set of transferable skills would prove critical in the unique position she was to fill. "Most people learned in the affairs of state can't screw in a light bulb, and most people who can screw in a light bulb cannot restore American authority in the world," commented Fareed Zakaria, former editor of *Foreign Affairs*. "She can do both."[45] On December 18, Governor Bush held a press conference in Austin to announce that Condi was to fill the top security post in his administration.

Back in Palo Alto, Clara Rice helped to prop her husband up in his hospital bed to see the television as the president-elect of the United States made his announcement. John Rice's girl was going to be one of the most powerful women in the world. He could only glue his eyes on the television in awe at what God had done through his life.[46] "He just stared," said Clara. "He didn't say a word."[47]

"Dr. Rice is not only a brilliant person, she is an experienced person," Bush said. "She is a good manager. I trust her judgment. America will find that she is a wise person, and I'm so honored you're joining the administration."[48]

As his little daughter was introduced, John Rice sat in his hospital bed and wept. "[He] had tears in his eyes," said Clara.[49]

Condi made some brief remarks as she accepted her new job. "It's a wonderful time for the United States in foreign policy because it's a time when markets and democracy are spreading, when our values are being affirmed around the world, and yet it's a time of great challenge." She reaffirmed her loyalty to Bush. "He will conduct a foreign policy that combines humility with strength," she said. And then she made a personal note about the meaning of her appointment. She had come a long way from the segregation of Birmingham. It was her hope that the Bush administration could "continue the last thirty-plus years of progress toward one America."[50]

The hospital phone rang again and again as friends called to congratulate John Rice and wish him well. Though John couldn't say much, Clara held the phone to his ear for him to listen.[51] Former President George Bush was one of his supporters who had been making regular calls.[52]

Condi left Texas to go back to Palo Alto to spend one last Christmas with her father. He was weak when she got there. John Rice was the one who gave her confidence and made her feel so comfortable in "a man's world." He had taught her the power of hope and determination from the time she first walked and talked and played a key on the piano; he had stood up against racism and prejudice; he had centered his mortal existence on Condi, and now her number one supporter was slipping into eternity. His "Little Star" was there at his bedside on Christmas Eve, when at seventy-seven years of age, John Rice breathed his last breath.

It was one of the only times that Clara Rice ever saw Condi weeping, but Condi wept then. She wept with all of the sorrow of a daughter who had lost a father and with all the joy of a believer whose dearest teacher and friend had gone to courts far higher even than the grandest palaces and halls she would visit in the coming years. Through tears, she said to her father, "Tell Mom that I love her."[53]

The "homegoing service" for Reverend John Rice was packed to overflowing at Clara's Baptist church. Clara and Condi planned the funeral together. The two sang a duet of "In the Garden," Condi with her beautiful soprano and Clara singing alto, accompanied by a musician. A band played "When the Saints Go Marching In."[54]

In March, the memorial service for John Rice filled the sanctuary of his church in Alabama, Westminster Presbyterian Church. Retired teachers who knew Dr. Rice as a colleague, community servants, volunteers, congregants old and young who sat under Rice's preaching—all were there to celebrate a man whose greatest legacy was his only daughter. Condi walked up the aisle with members of the extended family as "A Mighty Fortress" resounded from the organ Angelena Rice once played. She wore a dark taupe suit with a long jacket and black heels.[55]

A former teacher spoke of John Rice's commitment to education. A forty-nine-year-old attorney who grew up with Condi listed some of the occupations the children of Westminster had pursued: "We are now chemists, reporters for major newspapers around the world, president of a university, college professors and administrators, government workers, computer analysts, politicians, doctors, lawyers, musicians, a meteorologist, ministers, and even the national security adviser for the president of the United States."

Condi was in tears as she sat in the pew, but when it came her turn to speak, she was strong. She explained that her father had three passions: God, family, and education. "It didn't matter where you came from. What mattered was where you were going. Even if Birmingham was a place of limited horizons for black children, it should still be a place of unlimited dreams."[56]

Chapter Twelve

Advising a President

"We can only do so much to protect ourselves at home, and so the best defense is a good offense. We have to take the fight to the terrorists."[1]

—Condoleezza Rice

"To every thing there is a season, and a time to every purpose under heaven: . . . a time of war, and a time of peace."

—Ecclesiastes 3:1, 8, KJV

Early in January 2001, Condi met with Bill Clinton's National Security Council counter-terrorism coordinator Richard Clarke and National Security Advisor Sandy Berger to discuss the national security threat from al Qaeda and other terrorist organizations. Given the sensitivity of the threat, Condi decided to keep Clarke on as the chief counter-terrorism point man in the Bush administration because of his experience. She also kept his entire staff.[2] "We understood that the [al Qaeda] network posed a serious threat to the United States," Condi said a few years later.[3]

When the new administration moved in, Condi settled into her sunny corner office in the West Wing, first occupied by Henry Kissinger during the Nixon administration. She would joke that the office was Kissinger's gift to her.[4]

She bought two condominiums at the Watergate, the second one a guest residence for her friends and relatives. She moved the Steinway Grand piano into the central area of her living room, and before long she was holding chamber groups there on Sunday afternoons. Having reupholstered some of her mother's furniture, Condi now used these keepsakes in her own home. Her mornings began at 4:30 exercising at home, and then she was into the office by 6:30, ready for the day. A speed reader, she read six newspapers.[5] At quarter past seven, she checked in with Secretary of Defense Donald Rumsfeld and Secretary of State Colin Powell by telephone and discussed any matters in need of attention.[6] By 8:00 she was ready for her daily security briefing with the president, Vice President Cheney, Chief of Staff Andy Card, and CIA director George Tenet.[7] During these meetings, Tenet updated the president on any important intelligence information, and the four officials fielded questions from

Bush.[8] After that, Condi held meetings in fifteen- or twenty-minute blocks of time until 7:00 p.m. Her long-time assistant, Ruth Elliott, said, "She doesn't like idle time."[9] Preferring phone conversations, Condi didn't bother with e-mail, since it could be misinterpreted.

Her job as NSA was to serve as a mediator between the different cabinet members and advisors who comprised the National Security Council: Vice President Cheney, Secretary of State Colin Powell, Secretary of Treasury Paul O'Neill, Secretary of Defense Donald Rumsfeld, Chairman of the Joint Chiefs of Staff General Richard Meyers, CIA Director Tenet, and several other senior officials. She had to gather information from these men and relay it to the president in a clear and concise manner while allowing him room to make a final decision on a matter. It was not her job to present her own opinion, but to organize the various opinions within the administration. Of course, the president trusted Condi so much that he doubtless sought her opinion at times. Clearly, he trusted her enough to make her a public representative on national security matters to a greater extent than any previous NSA.

As the administration got underway, tensions were growing in the Middle East. Peace talks between Israel and Palestine were broken off and Israeli-Palestinian relations declined further. In the following months, the president would call on leaders of both sides to quell the violence and embrace diplomatic solutions.

Crisis with China

There were also problems in the Far East. In her 2000 *Foreign Affairs* article, Condi asserted that China was a "strategic competitor."

"Cooperation should be pursued," she wrote, "but we should never be afraid to confront Beijing when our interests collide."[10]

A literal collision happened in the skies over international waters off China on April 1, 2001. A Chinese fighter jet trying to intimidate a U.S. Naval reconnaissance plane accidentally collided with it over Hainan Island. The navy crew made an emergency landing of the wounded plane on the island and destroyed the surveillance equipment per U.S. Navy protocol. The Chinese jet dropped into the ocean after the crash, and the pilot was missing. China would not release the twenty-four naval crew members and demanded a formal apology, causing one of the most heated situations between the two countries in three decades. Condi and the White House had difficulty communicating with Chinese officials; President Zemin was traveling, and when Condi called her Chinese equivalent, foreign policy advisor Qian Qichen, she couldn't reach him.[11] Finally, after weeks of difficult negotiations about apologies and compensation for the lost plane and pilot, the navy crew was able to return to its home base in Whidbey Island, Washington.

During this tense time—her first major crisis as national security advisor—Condi remained calm and confident. Her friend Chip Blacker, who had served on Bill Clinton's National Security Council, was chatting casually with Condi in her apartment one day when the phone rang. "The president called, and there was no stiffening of the spine. She was respectful and responsive, but then she put the phone down and said, 'What do you think of the NBA?'"[12] As much as this story demonstrates Condi's iconic demeanor, it also indicates a unique trust with the president. "That's the way to tell there's a real special relationship there," said Blacker. "I was always very comfortable with President Clinton, but he never called me at home, and if he had, I'm sure that I would have stood up."

President Bush so trusted Condi as his national security advisor that he gave her unprecedented responsibilities on the public relations front. NSA was a duty traditionally kept behind scenes, but already, Condi was representing the president in the press on a regular basis. During the standoff with China, Condi made several media appearances on behalf of the president. "It's not business as usual just yet with China," she said.[13] She defended the spy plane's mission as a legitimate operation in the cause of global security. "We're happy to talk to the Chinese government about how we might avoid such an accident in the future," she explained. "But we're going to continue to do what is most effective for our national security strategy."[14] Philip Zelikow suggested that Condi's top priority as NSA was to see to it "that people feel the country is safe."[15] Thus Condi was seen and heard frequently, and Americans loved her.

"She appears impeccably organized and prepared, with a great mass of detail in her head which she has reduced to a simple clear form," Nicholas Lemann wrote in a profile of Condi for the *New Yorker*. "She is gracious, poised, and charming, and isn't stiff or puffed up with her own officialdom. She has a wide, easy smile and a comfortable manner. No question ever seems to catch her unaware or to set off a rambling, disjointed answer. She ties everything up in a neat package of certainty and conviction."[16] The *Financial Times* headlined that Condi was "Political Punch in a Package of Charm."[17]

They called her "Warrior Princess" at the White House.[18] The president of the United States called her "Mother Hen."[19] One time he called her "Martha Stewart with access to nuclear codes."[20]

Vision Becomes Reality in Poland

In June, the president went to Poland, where his father had gone twelve years before to celebrate Polish independence. By 2001, Poland was on the road to prosperity. "Our fathers—yours and mine—struggled and sacrificed to make this vision real," Bush said to the students and faculty of Warsaw University. "Now it is within our grasp. Today, a new generation makes a new commitment: a Europe and an America bound in a great alliance of liberty—history's greatest united force for peace and progress and human dignity. The bells of victory have rung. The Iron Curtain is no more."[21]

As Bush looked down from the platform where he was speaking, he saw the faces of ambitious, hopeful students who had come of age in a free society. He saw teachers who could live and work with freedom of speech and freedom of the press. There were the dignitaries of the Polish government, and then the American delegation, which included Secretary Colin Powell and Condi. Condi's eyes were filled with tears as she realized the significance of the moment. She understood how far Poland had come in so short a time. It was largely because of her diplomatic work in the first Bush administration, when so much uncertainty surrounded Poland, that the young democracy was strong. The president knew why Condi was so moved. Seeing her, he too became emotional. Before long, the whole arena was filled with the tearful emotions of people who loved freedom.

When Bush had finished, the crowd rose to a standing ovation and an orchestra accompanied the drama. Tears streamed down Condi's face. The president approached her and scolded himself, "I shouldn't have looked at you, you know."[22] As Condi told *Vogue* magazine, "I was teary-eyed the whole time we were in Poland."[23] Seeing the Polish flag waving proudly with the NATO flag, listening to the playing of the American national anthem at the Polish palace, seeing the palace itself that had been in disrepair in 1989—all of it brought tears to her eyes. The scene was, as she told reporters at a briefing in Warsaw, "really extraordinarily moving."[24]

Terrorists Attack America

But while the Cold War was over, a new kind war was quietly taking shape. A corps of Middle Eastern terrorists had come into the United States, where they were making their final plans for the destruction of major American economic, government, and military landmarks. As unspecific intelligence about terrorist threats came into the CIA, pointing especially toward the al Qaeda network, the threats became a topic at dozens of the president's Oval Office morning briefings. Richard Clarke's panel of counterterrorism officials from the CIA, FBI, Secret Service, and several cabinet departments met more and more frequently, and yet, as Condi noted, the terrorist chatter they were getting "was frustratingly vague."[25]

"Unbelievable news in coming weeks."

"Big event . . . there will be a very, very, very, very big uproar."

"There will be attacks in the near future."

The administration took several immediate steps. Federal agencies and departments were moved to a high state of alert. At least five times, the Defense Department warned the military that al Qaeda might be planning an attack, and in certain regions it set troops on high alert. The State Department warned American embassies, while the FBI warned law enforcement officials at every level across the country, and the CIA began a new campaign to disrupt al Qaeda.

Beginning in the spring of 2001, Condi and her staff assembled "a new and comprehensive strategy to eliminate the al-Qaida [sic] terrorist network," as she later told Congress. Through the summer, the National Security Council worked under highly classified terms to craft what would be the Bush administration's first major national security policy directive to agency and department heads. In stark contrast with President Clinton's directive to transport terrorists to the United States for trial, the Bush administration directive called on Secretary of Defense Rumsfeld to make plans for the destruction of Taliban and al Qaeda operations within Afghanistan. It also directed the CIA to aggressively increase its covert efforts against al Qaeda, and it asked the Treasury and State Departments to work through diplomatic means to cut off al Qaeda's finances and national sanctuaries. The plan was approved by the administration on September 4, 2001.[26]

Exactly one week later, September 11, Condi was scheduled to be at Johns Hopkins University. She was to speak at the School of Advanced International Studies on the topic of missile defense. There were particular gaps in the nation's long-range missile defense capabilities that had to be filled if America was to be strategically effective and safe. "We need to worry about the suitcase bomb, the car bomb, and the vial of sarin released in the subway [in Tokyo, 1995]," *Washington Post* quoted in an excerpt of her prepared remarks. "[But] why put deadbolt locks on your doors and stock up on cans of mace and then decide to leave your windows open?"[27]

The windows were open in the skies over America that morning of September 11, but it wasn't a long-range missile that came flying in. Because of the national security crisis that developed that day, Condi never gave the speech. She postponed her speaking engagement by several months.

No Safe Harbor for Terrorists

The next day, on September 12, Karen Hughes, counselor to the president, and Condi met with President Bush in the Oval Office. "Let's get the big picture," Bush told them. "A faceless enemy has declared war on the United States, so we are at war. We are going to wage this war; it requires a strategy, a plan, a vision, a diplomatic effort, and the complete understanding of the American people. . . . This will require complete focus; the command structure in the White House has to coordinate the response of the government." He told Hughes, "You're in charge of communicating this war." Then he turned to Condi: "This Saturday, have everybody come to Camp David; we'll develop the plan."[28]

Karen Hughes writes in her book, *Ten Minutes from Normal*, about the president's meeting on Thursday, September 13th with congressional leaders from both parties. "'These guys [the terrorists] are like rattlesnakes; they strike and go back in their holes; we're not only going to go after the holes, we're going to go after the ranchers," he told them, explaining the new Bush doctrine to go after those who harbor terrorists as well as the terrorists themselves. "There will be no safe harbor for terrorism," the president told the congressional leaders. "Who knows where this will lead. . . . we're talking to Pakistan in a way we've never talked to them before . . . Afghanistan, maybe Iraq."[29]

On September 20, the president addressed a joint session of Congress to declare a global war on terrorism. He enunciated formally for the first time what would become known as the Bush Doctrine: "Every nation, in every region, now has a decision to make. Either you are with us, or you are with the terrorists."[30]

Liberation of Afghanistan

The American military began air strikes against the Taliban over Afghanistan on October 7 in "Operation Enduring Freedom." But before the strikes began, a great amount of ingenuity and planning occurred first. Besides having working weekends at Camp David, the Bushes' ranch in Texas became another place to discuss pressing issues. One day Condi and Karen Hughes were sitting around the kitchen table at the ranch discussing the complex situation in Afghanistan with First Lady Laura Bush. The Taliban had forced the people into poverty and starvation.

As the women talked, they came up with a creative idea to help deal with the scarcity of food facing the oppressed citizens of Afghanistan. Soon the world watched their plan executed as U.S. military hit al Qaeda terrorist training camps and Taliban military targets. At the same time, brightly colored yellow packages filled with food, medicine, and supplies were dropped from planes to the starving people of Afghanistan.[31]

Exactly two months later, the Taliban abandoned its final outpost at Kandahar, effectively ending Taliban rule in Afghanistan.[32] Condi spoke about what the world saw following the Taliban's desertion: "I've watched over the last year and a half how people want to have human dignity worldwide," she said.

> We forget that when people are given a choice between freedom and tyranny, they will choose freedom. I remember all the stories before the liberation of Afghanistan that they wouldn't "get it," that they were all warlords and it would just be chaos. Then we got pictures of people dancing on the street of Kabul just because they could listen to music or send their girls to school.[33]

Still, al Qaeda terrorists were very much at large in the mountains and deserts of Afghanistan and throughout the world. The new war would not be short.

Truths that September 11th Reinforced

When Condi finally took the podium at the School of Advanced International Studies at Johns Hopkins on April 29, 2002, the topic was not missile defense. "It's going to take years to understand the long-term effects of September 11th," she said. "There are certain verities that September 11th reinforced and brought home to us in the most vivid way."[34] Rice suggested that America had woken up to old truths about the world. George Washington knew that democracies can grow lazy and forgetful without occasional reminders of reality. Washington often observed that democratic people "must *feel,* before they will see."[35] On September 11, America felt, and America saw.

Condoleezza Rice saw five things, which she shared at Johns Hopkins. First, war is real. "There has been an end to innocence about international politics and about our own vulnerability," she said. War is a part of human nature, and nature does not change. If men and women are to be free in such a world, they must sometimes fight. Indeed, America had "a special responsibility to help make the world more secure" through "robust military power."[36]

Second, "the events of September 11th underscored the idea that a sound foreign policy begins at home." The Bush administration was improving "airport security, visa requirements, protection of nuclear power plants, and other physical and cyber security infrastructure," as well as working with Mexico and Canada "to construct smart and modern borders—borders that protect us from those who would harm us, but facilitate the trade and human interchange that enrich us."

The third truth was that "we can only do so much to protect ourselves at home, and so the best defense is a good offense. We have to take the fight to the terrorists." Echoing the Bush Doctrine, Rice declared that "there can be no distinction between terrorists and those who harbor them."

Fourth, September 11 taught America "the need to deny terrorists and hostile states the opportunity to acquire weapons of mass destruction." Terrorist regimes sought to acquire WMDs, she warned. "The world's most dangerous people simply cannot be permitted to obtain the world's most dangerous weapons."

Fifth, allies were critically important. "Global terror demands a global solution," she said. Since terrorism was a global problem, America needed every friend and partner it could get in its pursuit of the terrorists.

And there was another lesson from September 11. Condi said that "an earthquake of the magnitude of 9/11 can shift the tectonic plates of international politics. The international system has been in flux since the collapse of Soviet power. Now it is possible—indeed, probable, that that transition is coming to an end." If the fall of the Berlin Wall and the fall of the World Trade Center "bookend a major shift in international politics," she said, "then this is a period not just of grave danger, but of enormous opportunity." Though the free world was confronted with a new danger, it could rise to the challenge, seeking "not merely to leave the world safer, but to leave it better."

A Better Future

She shared the administration's vision of a better world. "Our goal today is what President Bush has called a balance of power that favors freedom. . . . Nations must decide which side they are on in the fault line that divides civilizations from terror. They must decide whether to embrace the paradigm of progress: democracy and freedom and human rights and clean, limited government. Together, with others, we can help people and nations make positive choices as they seek a better future, and we can deter those who want to take away a better future for others." And, she concluded, the work of maintaining freedom "is the work of every generation."[37]

The remarkable thing about Condi's message is that it had noticeably shifted away from the realist position she had taken in the past, toward idealism. Instead of limiting America's involvement in the world, Condi and the president wanted to expand America's involvement in places where it could advance democracy and freedom. Pundits speculated about this shift, and many believed that Condi's position was a reflection of her loyalty to the commander in chief rather than an independent change of personal philosophy.

Condi articulated the new direction of American foreign policy in a landmark December 2002 document called *U.S. National Security Strategy: A New Era*. Condi wrote in her lead article that the new challenges of the post-9/11 world could require the use of preemptive military force. In a world where the tools of war ranged from suitcase bombs, anthrax packages, and box-cutters to weapons of mass destruction—all in the hands of terrorist thugs—"the risks of waiting must far outweigh the risks of action."[38]

Underlying the new strategy was the idea that all men and women yearn for freedom, and that any culture may adapt to freedom. "We do not seek to impose democracy on others," Condi wrote, "we seek only to help create conditions in which people can claim a freer future for themselves. We recognize as well that there is no 'one size fits all' answer."[39] That means that other nations wouldn't have a government identical to the United States. Instead, if freedom and democracy were truly universal ideals, they were not contingent on a particular cultural setting. They could thrive anywhere.

Dealing with Hardships

Condi's early morning routine on Sundays started the same as other days, with exercise, but instead of going to the White House, she often appeared on political talk shows. She made an excellent guest presenting the administration's point of view in a clear, eloquent manner with her pleasant self-assurance. But that's not all that Condi did on Sunday mornings. Before spending the afternoon playing her piano or visiting with friends and family, following the television shows, Condi would head over to National Presbyterian Church for services. White House staff were instructed not to page or disturb her at church.

Condi spoke about the spiritual challenges of September 11th in a Sunday school class at her church in Washington in August 2002. She reflected on her own spiritual journey, and then she spoke about the terrorist attacks. "When you go through something like that, you have to turn to faith because you can rationalize it, you can make an intellectual answer about it but you can't fully accept it until you can feel it here." She tapped her chest.

Later in 2003, at the National Prayer Breakfast in Washington, DC, Condi spoke about lessons learned from September 11, both for individuals and our country. She also told how she deals with hardships. Her speech was given a few days after the Columbia Space Shuttle tragedy in which seven astronauts died. One of Condi's favorite Bible passages is found in the fifth chapter of the book of Romans. She refers to it in the following speech:

> [It] is at times like these that we are reminded of a paradox, that it is a privilege to struggle. A privilege to struggle for what is right and true. A privilege to struggle for freedom over tyranny. A privilege, even, to struggle with the most difficult and profound moral choices.
>
> In the Bible in Romans 5, where we are told to "rejoice in our sufferings, knowing that suffering produces endurance, and endurance

produces character, and character produces hope, and hope does not disappoint us, because God's love has been poured into our hearts through the Holy Spirit which has been given to us."

For me, this message has two lessons.

First, there is the lesson that only through struggle do we realize the depths of our resilience and understand that the hardest of blows can be survived and overcome. . . . Yet it is through struggle that we find redemption and self-knowledge. In this sense it is a privilege to struggle because it frees one from the idea that the human spirit is fragile, like a house of cards, or that human strength is fleeting. . . .

We learn in times of personal struggle—the loss of a loved one, illness, or turmoil—that there is a peace that passeth understanding. When our intellect is unequal to the task—the spirit takes over; finding peace in the midst of pain is the true fulfillment of one's humanity.

Struggle doesn't just strengthen us to survive hard times—it is also the key foundation for true optimism and accomplishment. Indeed, personal achievement without struggle somehow feels incomplete and hollow. It is true too for humankind—because nothing of lasting value has ever been achieved without sacrifice.

There is a second, more important, lesson to be learned from struggle and suffering. We can use the strength it gives us for the good of others. . . . I believe this lesson applies not only to individuals, but to nations. America emerged from the losses of September 11th as a nation that is not only stronger, but hopefully better and more generous. Tragedy made us appreciate our freedom more—and [become] more conscious of the fact that God gives all people, everywhere, the right to be free. It made us more thankful for our own prosperity, for life, and health—and more aware that all people, everywhere deserve the opportunity to build a better future.[40]

After Operation Enduring Freedom, the people of Afghanistan were now working toward building a better future. Though Afghanistan was in transition to democracy, the Bush Doctrine suggested that the war was much larger than just Afghanistan. While Condi was busy preparing the National Security Strategy, the men and women at the Pentagon and Vice President Cheney were thinking about the next war: Iraq.[41] The goal was to take out Saddam

Condi has gone to visit the troops in Iraq on a number of trips.

Hussein, who presented a danger to the United States and the world. In order to do that, the president and administration would have to build a popular argument about the relationship between Iraq and the September 11 attacks.

Condi was not one to diminish the impact of September 11. "No less than December 7, 1941, September 11, 2001, forever changed the lives of every American and the strategic perspective of the United States," she told the Veterans of Foreign Wars after receiving an award. "That day produced an acute sense of our vulnerability to attacks hatched in distant lands that come without warning, bringing tragedy to our shores." She articulated the link between the soldiers serving in the war on terror and those who had served in previous wars. "There is no higher calling," she told the veterans.[42]

But unlike Operation Enduring Freedom, war in Iraq was not an easy sell. There was a growing divide between the old realist school and the new idealism of the Bush Doctrine.[43]

In the coming months, the military began deployments to the Middle East in preparation for its work in Iraq. Some 250,000 American troops were shipped out throughout the winter, joined by 45,000 British and 2,000 Australian troops. Condi held to the belief that removing Saddam Hussein from power was a risk worth taking.[44]

On March 17, American attempts to gain support from the United Nations fell short, and the president went on television to demand that Saddam and his sons surrender power within forty-eight hours or face invasion. When the deadline arrived, American forces began dropping carefully guided bombs over strategic targets in Baghdad. On April 9, Marines marched into Baghdad as jubilant

Iraqi citizens tore down symbols of the Baathist regime, including a massive statue of Saddam Hussein in Baghdad's central square.[45] With the Iraqi dictator in hiding, the Baathist regime had been toppled in a matter of a few weeks. On May 1, the president personally landed a Navy 3-SB Viking on the deck of the aircraft carrier USS *Abraham Lincoln* before announcing that major combat in Iraq was completed.[46]

But the war was far from over. As Iraqi citizens made strides toward free elections and democratic government, terrorists took up arms in villages throughout Iraq. American soldiers patrolled the violent streets of Fallujah. Sunni insurgents mounted attacks against the Americans, then against the Shia, in a struggle for political control. American troops found themselves at the center of a growing international controversy. The president and Condi stood firm.

Surprise Visit to Baghdad

The day before Thanksgiving, 2003, Condi was at the Bush ranch in Crawford, Texas. As far as almost everybody around the president knew, he would spend Thanksgiving with his family on the ranch. But after dinner on Wednesday night, a plain vehicle with tinted windows pulled up to the driveway in front of the Bush ranch house. Only Condi and the president knew what was going on. Dressed in casual clothes, they pulled on baseball caps and headed out the door to get in the waiting car. Without a motorcade of security, press, and staff that usually has right of way in traffic, the car got into some holiday evening traffic on the Waco freeway. Then Bush and Rice boarded Air Force One on a secluded tarmac at Texas State Technical College and they were off to Iraq.

Fearing the security crisis that could erupt if it were known Bush was to be in Baghdad, the trip was top secret.[47]

En route, the small delegation switched to a second Air Force One at Andrew's Air Force Base in Maryland before resuming the flight under the cover of night across the world. The plane adopted a false call sign, but that didn't stop a British Airlines pilot from looking out of his cockpit and radioing over to the nearby Boeing 747, "Did I just see Air Force One?" From the Air Force One pilot came the reply, "Gulfstream 5." "Oh," said the British pilot, as if to commit himself to keep a secret.[48]

Meanwhile, Paul Bremer, the Presidential Envoy to Iraq, had joined six hundred American servicemen and women for Thanksgiving dinner and what was billed as a "USO show" at Baghdad International Airport.[49]

As Bush entered the mess tent at Baghdad International Airport, the massive roar of the six hundred troops filled the tent: "Hoo-ah!" For several minutes, the tent was filled with the noise of jubilant soldiers. Bush went to the podium and said a few words. "I was just looking for a warm meal somewhere," he joked. "Thank you for inviting me to dinner."[50] More than a few cheers and tears of thanksgiving were given that evening in Baghdad. The president himself had tears in his eyes as he spoke, and he couldn't stop smiling as he worked the chow line for the men and women in uniform. What was going to be another meal away from home and family for the armed forces became a tremendous morale booster. "It turned a holiday meal into a holiday party," said Spec. Andrew Meissner.[51]

The Struggle Against Terror

A couple weeks later, Condi was scheduled to be at the Reagan Presidential Library in Simi Valley, California, to deliver the eighth annual Ronald Reagan lecture, about the war on terror. In the middle of the night before her trip, she received a call informing her that Saddam Hussein had been captured. Without firing a shot, U.S. troops from the Fourth Infantry Division had seized the Iraqi dictator on December 14 in the cellar of a farmhouse near Tikrit.[52]

Like her Johns Hopkins speech, Condi had a good reason to postpone this one. When she went to Simi Valley two months later, she joked, "Mrs. Reagan and I agreed that the only reason that I wouldn't make it this time was if somehow we'd gotten Osama bin Laden." In her speech, she drew a parallel between the Soviet ideologies with which Ronald Reagan had contended and Islamic terrorism. "The terrorist ideology is the direct heir to Communism, and Nazism, and fascism—the murderous ideologies of the 20th century. The struggle against terror is fundamentally a struggle of vision and values. The terrorists offer suicide, and death, and pseudo-religious tyranny. America and our allies seek to advance the cause of liberty and defend the dignity of every person."[53]

Most Anticipated Testimony of the Year

Back in the nation's capital, a panel of distinguished public servants had convened at the request of the Congress and the president to investigate the events of September 11. The National Commission on Terrorist Attacks Upon the United States, known as the 9/11 Commission, invited Condi to testify on behalf of the administration at a public hearing.[54]

On April 8, Condi went before the 9/11 Commission. CNN's Anderson Cooper heralded his network's coverage of Condi as "the most anticipated testimony of the year."[55] She wore a simple gray suit with gold earrings and necklace, and an American flag lapel pin. In her prepared remarks, she recounted the counter-terrorism activities the Bush administration had launched in its earliest days before September 11. "Yet, as your hearings have shown," she said, "there was no silver bullet that could have prevented the 9/11 attacks." Echoing the rhetoric of Abraham Lincoln in his second inaugural address, Condi transitioned to the hard reality of the past few years, and the work remaining. "So the attacks came," she said.

"Now we have an opportunity and an obligation to move forward together," she continued. "Bold and comprehensive changes are sometimes only possible in the wake of catastrophic events—events which create a new consensus that allows us to transcend old ways of thinking."[56] As World War II had given rise to the reorganization of America's defense structure, September 11 made possible the creation of the Department of Homeland Security, the Patriot Act, and an offensive war on terrorism "to find and defeat the terrorists wherever they live, hide, and plot around the world."[57]

Condi explained the policy decision that the administration faced after September 11. "We could fight a narrow war against al-Qaida [sic] and the Taliban, or we could fight a broad war against a global menace. We could seek a narrow victory, or we could work for a lasting peace and a better world. President Bush chose the bolder course."[58]

Following Condi's prepared remarks, each of the five Democrats and five Republicans on the commission had ten minutes to ask questions. Tony Snow of FOX News, soon to become White House press secretary, had predicted that Condi's appearance would be "a very prim and tame hearing for the most part."[59] Not so. Democrat commission members hammered Condi with questions about the administration's pre-9/11 counter-terrorism efforts, apparently hoping that she would say the attacks were preventable. When Condi insisted on explaining herself fully to former Senator Bob Kerrey, he interrupted as though he were the one testifying. "Please don't filibuster me," Condi continued in her even manner.

"It's not fair," Kerrey added. "I have been polite, I've been courteous."[60]

Actually, Kerrey was not a model of courtesy; he kept referring to Condi as "Dr. Clarke," somehow mixing her up with the former counter-terrorism chief. Condi was the exemplar that day, asserting herself against the Democrats with measured coolness and control. "She probably could have done the whole thing with a teacup and saucer balanced on her head," remarked the *Washington Post.*[61] Never raising her voice, she disarmed anti-war critics with her sharp memory and polished arguments. For example, Condi reminded Bob Kerrey of "a brilliant speech" he had given after the bombing of the USS *Cole.* His point, she explained: "go after Saddam Hussein."[62]

Condi, said the *Washington Post,* is "easily one of the administration's most effective communicators. She's also among the least likely to come off as fanatical, cranky, intemperate, or possessed by the delusion that she and God are on a first-name basis."[63]

President Bush was reelected in 2004. Condi's role in the campaign was smaller than it had been four years earlier. In the final weeks of the campaign, she made a nationwide tour to campaign for the president in several "battleground states."[64] When she stopped at the University of Washington, the *Seattle Times* reported, "Rice sounded at times like a candidate, and a friendly crowd of several hundred rewarded her with rousing ovations as she recounted victories in Afghanistan and Iraq and listed steps she says the administration has taken to make America safer."[65]

Surprise Birthday Party

The week after the election, Condi Rice turned fifty years old. She was with her Aunt G on the evening of her birthday, dressed casually in a suede jacket and slacks, en route to a small, informal birthday dinner with some friends. But the Secret Service driver made an unexpected turn onto Embassy Row, pulling into the drive of the British Embassy. Ambassador David Manning was waiting outside, and he approached the car. "G," Condi said to her aunt, "something is going on here, and we're not dressed."

Aunt G laughed. "That's right, babe. Get out of the car." Aunt G, Ambassador Manning, and Condi walked into the embassy building. There, lining both sides of a grand double staircase, were more than one hundred of Condi's friends. Secretary of State Colin Powell was there, and former Secretary of State George Shultz, former Clinton NSA Sandy Berger, NFL executive Gene Washington, Bush's advisor, Karen Hughes, and relatives. Everybody was dressed for a gala—

in gowns and tuxedoes. And as Condi looked up at them standing there, they broke into singing "Happy Birthday."[66]

When they had finished, Condi stood in delighted embarrassment and shouted, "Look what I'm wearing!" Everybody laughed and cheered. For secretly, Ambassador Manning had obtained intelligence on Condi's measurements and had shared that intelligence with the Spanish designer Oscar de la Renta who prepared a red, bare-shouldered, strapless, floor-length gown for the occasion. Condi was ushered upstairs, where the gown and her hairdresser were ready for her. By the time Condi emerged down the stairs, George and Laura Bush, fresh off the campaign trail, had arrived to celebrate Condi's birthday. The pianist Van Cliburn played the national anthem. Dinner was served at tables labeled with the names of football stars. Afterward there was dancing.[67] As NFL executive Gene Washington, who has been Condi's date at several parties, told the *Washingtonian* about Condi's social presence: "Condi doesn't work the room. The room works Condi."[68]

Becoming America's Top Diplomat

Secretary of State Colin Powell had not seen eye to eye with other administration officials on some important issues, and it was time for him to retire. There was little question about who would replace him.

Only Condi had doubts. During a weekend at Camp David, the president offered her the world's top diplomatic job, fourth in line of succession to the presidency. She wasn't sure that she was adequate for the task. "You know, Mr. President, you probably need new people," she said. Then Bush laid out his second-term agenda and explained how vital her role in that agenda would be.

When they left Camp David that weekend, the president had his nominee for secretary of state.[69]

Chapter Thirteen

The Most Powerful Woman in the World

"When I look at my own story or many others that I have seen, I think, 'How could it possibly be that it has turned out this way?' Then my only answer is it's God's plan. And that makes me very optimistic that this is all working out in a proper way if we all stay close to God and pray and follow in His footsteps."[1]

—Condoleezza Rice

"For we are His workmanship, created in Christ Jesus for good works, which God prepared beforehand that we should walk in them."

—Ephesians 2:10, NKJV

On the seventh floor of the State Department in the nation's capital is the office of the woman *Forbes* has called the most powerful woman in the world.[2]

The office is located down a long, red-carpeted hall lined with portraits of former secretaries of state. In this office, she follows in the footsteps of those whose résumés contain things like founding father, president, or Nobel Peace Prize recipient; people like Thomas Jefferson, James Madison, James Monroe, John Quincy Adams, Daniel Webster, William Seward, William Jennings Bryan, George Marshall, Dean Acheson, John Foster Dulles, and Henry Kissinger. And then there's Condi.

Before her confirmation in the U.S. Senate, Condi went to speak before the Senate Foreign Relations Committee on January 18, 2005. She laid out her ideas for her next four years as secretary of state. It was time, she said, to build on the accomplishments the Bush administration made following September 11. "We must use American diplomacy to help create a balance of power in the world that favors freedom," she said. Reflecting on the path that brought her to the nomination hearing that day, she spoke of how her story, "the story of the triumph of universal values over adversity," was a promise for all Americans and all people everywhere. America's values included "a belief in democracy, and liberty, and the dignity of every life, and the rights of every individual."

Drawing a parallel with the Cold War, Condi said that in America's new "long-term struggle against an ideology of tyranny and terror," American diplomacy faced three great tasks. "First, we will unite the community of democracies in building an international system that is based on our shared values and the rule of law. Second, we will strengthen the community of democracies to fight the threats to our common security and alleviate the hopelessness that feeds terror. And third, we will spread freedom and democracy throughout the globe."[3]

Because of Iraq War tensions that were building in the Senate, debate over Condi's confirmation lasted for hours on January 26. Ted Kennedy of Massachusetts, Robert Byrd of West Virginia, and Barbara Boxer of California led the Democrats who opposed Condi's confirmation. When the vote was called, only thirteen Democrats voted against Condi becoming secretary of state. The votes for Condi numbered eighty-five.[4]

On the morning of January 28, 2005, Condi was at her condominium with her Aunt G, Aunt Connie, and Uncle Alto Ray, and cousin Lativia, getting ready for the big day. Condi was wearing a white, button-down suit jacket and skirt. Just as Condi was about to go out the door, Lativia looked over at her and proclaimed, "Who would have thought a little girl from Birmingham, Alabama?"

"I know," said Condi.

"Today you'll make a country proud," said Lativia.[5]

Later that morning, accompanied by her Uncle Alto, Condoleezza Rice took the oath of office as America's sixty-sixth secretary of state. Supreme Court Justice Ruth Bader Ginsburg administered the oath in a ceremony at the State Department attended by Condi's relatives, members of Congress, State Department officials, and the president and First Lady.[6]

Afterward, President Bush went forward to thank Secretary Powell for his service and to introduce Powell's successor. "Colin Powell leaves big shoes to fill at the State Department," the president said, "but Condi Rice is the right person to fill them. As national security advisor, she has led during a time when events not of our choosing have forced America to the leading edge of history." He expressed his confidence that Condi would "lead by character and conviction and wisdom."[7]

Shaking hands with President Bush, Condi took the lectern and spoke briefly, but movingly, about the significance of the moment. She was the first black woman to serve as secretary of state. Moreover, she saw herself in the light of an old vision of freedom. It took "impatient patriots—like Frederick Douglass, and Abraham Lincoln, and Martin Luther King—to move us ever closer to our founding ideals." But those ideals are not limited to America, she said.

> September 11, 2001, made us see more clearly than ever how our values and our interests are linked and joined across the globe. That day of fire made us see that the best way to secure a world of peace and hope is to build a world of freedom. We do not simply seek the absence of terrorism. We seek a world where the aspirations for freedom of men and women triumph. Today, it is more fitting than ever that our nation should pursue a foreign policy that is grounded in democratic principles and aligns itself with the efforts of all those around the globe who share our love of liberty.[8]

Condi moved into her new seventh-floor office, where the windows look out over the great Potomac River. High-backed lavender chairs surrounded a coffee table. In time, she would fill the shelves with football memorabilia, a Torah from former Israeli Prime Minister Ariel Sharon, and some rubble from the bombed-out house where Iraqi al Qaeda leader Abu Musab al-Zarqawi was killed in 2006. There is a photograph of her with all the living secretaries of state: Henry Kissinger, Alexander Haig, George Shultz, James Baker III, Lawrence Eagleburger, Warren Christopher, Madeleine Albright, Colin Powell.[9] She had a portrait of Dean Acheson put on the wall, a man who was secretary of state at the outset of the Cold War. Condi sat in Acheson's chair, figuratively, at the outset of a new global war.[10]

In her first six months on the job, Condi met with NATO leaders in Brussels; conferred with European Union officials in Luxembourg; made stops in Paris, Rome, and Jerusalem; and met with British Prime Minister Tony Blair at Ten Downing Street. Subsequently, she toured Eastern Europe and South America, in addition to visiting New Delhi, Seoul, Islamabad in Pakistan, and Kabul in Afghanistan.

The visit to Afghanistan was Condi's first, and visiting hostile and war-torn countries is not without danger. Seeing the country was a moving experience for her. "I probably knew every piece of territory in Afghanistan by map and by history," she said of her Soviet studies. After September 11, Condi was struck by the reality that Afghanistan was the center of the war on terror. When she visited there in 2005, she was excited about the growing promise of stability and democracy.[11]

Before going to Beijing, Condi stopped at a university in Tokyo, calling on China to "embrace some form of open, genuinely representative government."[12] In Beijing, she went to the Great Hall of the People to see Chinese President Hu Jintao. She told the leader of communist China that there were conditions on American trade investments in China: the United States expected a conversation about moving toward democracy and freedom. Condi called on Hu to explore the possibilities and promises of strengthened civil and religious liberty.[13] When talking about the Chinese leaders, she said, "They will see that freedom of religion and respect for human rights are part of the foundation of decent and successful societies."[14]

Indicating her personal concern for religious freedom, Secretary Rice took time after her meeting with Hu to visit an officially recognized Christian church in an alleyway not far from Tiananmen Square where young anti-communists held a massive demonstration in 1989. It was Palm Sunday. Though she went to Gangwashi Protestant Church without cameras, and though the visit was not part of her official business, people in China and around the world saw Condi's church attendance as a symbolic diplomatic gesture. Sitting in the front row, she listened to the pastor, using headphones. When the five hundred congregants sang "Constantly Abiding," Condi sang along in English. "There's a peace in my heart that the world never gave," she sang. She signed a visitor's book: "Thank you for allowing me to share Palm Sunday with you. Yours in Christ, Condoleezza Rice." As she left the church, the congregation broke into applause.[15]

Condi also made a surprise visit to Iraq in May 2005. Seeing the signs of progress and change in Baghdad was encouraging for a woman whose efforts had been so critical to the successes thus far. In Baghdad, Condi held a joint press conference with Iraqi interim prime minister Iyad Allawi. She explained that America's role in Iraq was to help secure the people until they could be self-sufficient. "Our promise to the Iraqi leadership is that the multinational forces are here to help Iraq defend itself until it can defend itself." At one of Saddam's former palaces, Condi was cheered loudly by U.S. troops and diplomats, whom she rallied to continue their work. Condi's visit to Iraq reassured her after seeing the progress the Iraqis have made.[16]

In April, shortly before her trip to Iraq, Condi said in a briefing, "Liberty is forgiving of many feelings, but it forgives neither apathy nor neglect. Its continued health makes demands on us all, and its greatest victories are won over decades."

Once again Condi was back in the Middle East, this time in Jordan, Saudi Arabia, and Egypt, to talk about the possibilities of democracy. But after holding a tense meeting with the Egyptian foreign minister at the State Department, she postponed her scheduled appearance at a conference in Cairo, Egypt, because of the arrest, on trumped-up charges, of pro-democracy activist Ayman Nour.[17] A few weeks later, Nour was bailed out of prison by his supporters, launching his candidacy for president of Egypt.[18]

When Condi went to Cairo in May, she met with Nour. And she spoke at the postponed conference of government officials and academics in Cairo. No one there could doubt that she was serious about democracy. "The ideal of democracy is universal," she said, distancing herself from past American diplomacy in the Middle East as much as she challenged Egyptian leaders. For sixty years, the United States pursued stability at the expense of democracy in the Middle East—"and we achieved neither. Now, we are taking a different course. We are supporting the democratic aspirations of all people."

Condi addressed several misconceptions about democracy. Instead of promoting chaos and conflict, democracy promotes "listening, and debating, and cooperating with one another." Instead of eroding morality, democracy is built on "public character and private virtue." She argued that there can be no progress without "free minds and free markets." And she commended the rights of women as an indispensable component of democracy.

Across the Middle East, from Jordan to Iraq to Lebanon, men and women were voluntarily choosing democracy, she said. Without mentioning Ayman Nour, Condi spoke in no uncertain terms about America's expectations for Egypt: "The Egyptian government must fulfill the promise it has made to its people—and to the entire world—by giving its citizens the freedom to choose. . . . Opposition groups must be free to assemble, and to participate, and to speak to the media. Voting should occur without violence or intimidation."[19]

U.S. News and World Report later called her speech "perhaps the sternest public lecture ever by a visiting American diplomat on the need for Egypt to move toward full democracy."[20] Frank Gardner of the BBC called Condi's diplomatic approach "immensely risky."[21] Similar things were said of Ronald Reagan's words about the Berlin Wall in 1987.

Sometimes risk-taking is the only way to effect change in the world. Condi knew this important lesson from studying history and living in the midst of it. If Rosa Parks hadn't taken a risk on a bus, which led to the Montgomery Bus Boycott, for instance, the civil rights movement may never have happened. Rosa Parks passed away in October 2005, and Condi went to speak at her memorial service in Montgomery.

"I can honestly say that without Mrs. Parks, I probably would not be standing here today as secretary of state," she said.[22]

Taking her own risky stand for freedom, Condi assumed an approach decidedly different from the "national interest" realism she had begun with during the 2000 campaign. Expanding on the diplomatic aspects of the Bush Doctrine she had helped to craft, Condi began to speak of "transformational diplomacy," a form of diplomacy in which the United States assumes a direct stake in the transformation of regimes to democratic governance.

In a key speech at Georgetown University in January 2006, Condi outlined the principles of transformational diplomacy. Nation-states formerly were characterized by borders and territorial claims, limiting the range of national interest to a particular place. If a country across the world, or even next door, was politically dysfunctional, it was perceived as "merely a burden to their people, or at most, an international humanitarian concern but never a true security threat."

In the new millennium, all that has changed. Instead of just nation-states next door to one another fighting each other, with new technology all the old ways have changed and threatening nations have become much more of an international threat.

Secretary Rice defined the objective of transformational diplomacy this way: "to work with our many partners around the world, to build and sustain democratic, well-governed states that will respond to the needs of their people and conduct themselves responsibly in the international system." Transformational diplomacy, she clarified, "is rooted in partnership, not in paternalism."

"In doing these things with people, not for them; we seek to use America's diplomatic power to help foreign citizens better their own lives and to build their own nations and to transform their own futures."[23] The paradigm of diplomacy had shifted, and Condi Rice was faced with the monumental challenge of first explaining that new paradigm to the world, and then crafting diplomatic practices in line with that paradigm. That meant commissioning a diplomatic corps throughout the world to advance the ideals of democracy.

Condi networked with allied third world countries to provide tools for fighting terrorism. She dispatched Arab-speaking television representatives to the Middle East, since most Middle Easterners got their news on television networks like Al Jazeera instead of in newspapers. She placed individual diplomats at American Presence Posts in important non-embassy cities, so that America could build up its local relationships. And she built the State Department's new Office of Reconstruction and Stabilization to channel emergency resources to unstable hotspots as the need should arise.[24]

Diplomatic reforms like these may not sound so difficult, but in reality they require a great deal of leadership, like trying to turn around an ocean liner. Yet so far, Condi had handled her job smoothly. One day, a Japanese reporter said to her, "Gee, being secretary of state must be really tough." Condi, confident as ever, fired back with a chuckle and replied, "No, it's wonderful." Glenn Kessler of the *Washington Post* asked Condi to elaborate on why it is wonderful to be secretary of state.

"Well, because it's such a remarkable time," she said. "And I think it's the combination of being able to work to effect policy but also to be able to represent those policies for the United States. I enjoy very much the diplomacy. I like the one-on-one diplomacy with other foreign ministers and with other people representing other governments. I really enjoy strategic problem solving, trying to get a solution on difficult issues."[25]

One foreign diplomat Condi has worked with closely is British Foreign Secretary Jack Straw. In spring 2006, Condi returned to Iraq with Straw on her State Department Boeing 757. While flying red eye one night, Condi quietly gave up her cabin to the foreign minister, who was feeling sick from a bad cold, so that he could sleep well in her fold-out bed. Flight attendants discovered the secretary of state asleep on the aisle floor of the galley, and word quickly spread to the press corps in the front of the plane.[26] Straw did not find out until later that Condi had given up her own bed to him and had slept on the floor.

But more than turning a little choice into a special diplomatic gesture, Condi performed an expression of kindness from one person to another. People have noticed things like this about Condi, around the world and back at home. As former Attorney General John Ashcroft attested, "Kindness may not be the currency of Washington," but, "she's taught me kindness. Just being involved with her reminds you of the value of it."[27]

But Condi was accustomed to sleeping on the go. Between January 2005 and June 2007, Condi logged some 1,250 travel hours and nearly 600,000 miles in and between 64 countries.[28] As of August 2007, she's bumped those air miles up to 608,381. The British publication *Times* has done the math and says, "That's the equivalent of flying to the Moon, and back, adding four orbits of the Earth for good measure. In a little over 18 months, Ms. Rice has spent 54 and a half days traveling."[29]

From serving as a key leader in the war on terrorism to dealing with North Korea, from Syria and Iran to China and Russia, and from genocide in Sudan to trade with South America, Condi has had to set priorities and cover a lot of pressing issues as secretary of state.

Given the variety of problems and challenges that face her every day, Condi is serious when she devotes time and words to an issue.

Secretary Rice has also worked to raise global awareness of human trafficking and to provide aid money to relieve women and children who are victims of the sex trade. As the 2006 recipient of the Independent Women's Forum Woman of Valor Award, Condi spoke eloquently about recognizing the human rights of women. From Sudan to Afghanistan to Iraq, the rights of women were at stake.

Condi speaks at the IWF dinner upon receiving the Woman of Valor Award, May 2006.

"When we talk about respect for women, we are referring to a moral truth," she said. "Women are free by nature, equal in dignity and entitled to the same rights, the same protections and the same opportunities as men." It took a while, she said, for women in the United States to be recognized as equals to men. But America is moving ever closer to its ideals, she said. "Those same ideals lead America into the world to combat the dehumanization of women in all its forums, especially the international evil of human trafficking, a modern form of slavery for millions of women."[30]

As support for the war in Iraq has eroded among even staunch Republicans, Condi has maintained her resolve and loyalty to the president. She went before the Senate Foreign Relations Committee on

January 11, 2007, to set forth the administration's "new strategy that speaks both to our stakes in Iraq and to the need to change the way that we are doing things." She said that America must "see Iraq in a regional context" and in the context of the larger war on terrorism.

Ultimately, the goal is to leave Iraq, but to leave it independent, more peaceful, and free. "The most urgent task before us now is to help the Iraqi government . . . establish confidence among the Iraqi population that it will and can protect all of its citizens whether they are Sunni, Shia, Kurds, or others, and that they will in an even-handed fashion punish those violent people who are killing innocent Iraqis, whatever their sect, ethnicity, or political affiliation."[31]

After Condi's testimony the day after the president announced a new deployment of twenty thousand troops to Iraq, Condi was grilled with questions by Republicans and Democrats about the prudence of staying in Iraq.[32] But Condi maintained her confidence and resolve in the face of growing opposition. She has remained the president's most valuable public defender.

In an interview in the *Reader's Digest* in 2006, Condi expressed her gratitude to those heroes fighting the war on terrorism. "It's really hard in Iraq," she said.

> You know, every day, I look at the loss of American life and I am absolutely in awe of what our men and women in uniform are doing, what our men and women who are there as diplomats are doing. . . . And it's extraordinary, but it's in a long line of noble service that Americans have given to the world. . . . And people who are serving in Iraq or in Afghanistan, for that matter, are in that line of heroes who defended freedom not here on our shores, but

to forward defense of freedom so that we don't have more attacks on our territory.[33]

In September 2007, the first party of the army's 3rd Stryker Brigade's 3,800 troops returned to Fort Lewis, Washington. Firsthand accounts from soldiers are encouraging compared to when they first arrived in Iraq in the spring. At first, Lt. Col. Joe Davidson said the missions were challenging, "moving toward the sound of the guns as we did so often." Staff Sgt. William Rose said that after his unit moved from Baghdad to Baqouba in March, "You didn't know what was going to happen day to day to day." But now the area has really improved since he and his men arrived—"much better, ten-fold better," he said.[34] It appears that the "surge" of more troops in early 2007 is having the desired effect.

Despite low poll ratings for President Bush and his administration, one member of the Bush cabinet has received consistently high marks from the American public: Condi. "Most people like Condi," CNN reported in April 2006. "It's those other guys that are making the Bush administration look bad." Indeed, President Bush's favorable ratings in the CNN poll in April 2006 were 40 percent, his lowest yet, while 57 percent had an unfavorable opinion. As for Condi Rice, 57 percent were favorable, and only 22 percent were unfavorable.[35]

Every corner of American culture has a reason to adore her. Music journalists sit stunned in Condi's Watergate apartment as she performs Shostakovich on the Steinway grand piano. At an Asian diplomatic gala, Condi performed Brahms' "Sonata in D Minor" alongside the Malaysian violinist Mustafa Fuzer Nawi.[36] The crowd at Washington's Constitution Center gave a standing ovation following Condi's duet performance of Brahms with the cellist Yo-Yo Ma in April 2002.

Condi first met Ma when he visited Stanford years before. "At a reception, she came up and said: 'I play the piano,' and I answered, 'How lovely.' Then we talked, and I found out she could play." When Yo-Yo Ma learned that he was to be honored with a National Medal of Arts, he called on Condi to join him on stage. The day before, they met to rehearse, and as Ma described the depth of their discussion about the music, "We had a real rehearsal." Condi, he told the *Washington Post*, "is a good musician."[37]

Gilbert Kaplan of New York Public Radio called Condi "the most accomplished musician ever to work in the White House" before interviewing Condi about her musical background and personal talent, Russian composers, Schumann, Artur Rubinstein, and Beethoven.[38] After Anthony Tommasini sat in on one of Condi's chamber orchestra sessions on a Sunday afternoon, he wrote for the *New York Times* music page, "Whatever else she is to political supporters and opponents, Ms. Rice may be the most prominent amateur musician in the world right now, which is big news for classical music."[39]

But her love of music is not restricted to classical music. She enjoys a wide variety of music genres, from Motown to Led Zeppelin.

In the world of fashion, Condi is admired by fashion connoisseurs around the world for her exquisite tastes. When she went back to see Yo-Yo Ma in concert at the Kennedy Center in November 2006, she wore a black Oscar de la Renta dress with a fiery red design along the bottom. (When Yo-Yo Ma finished his performance, Condi broke with her party at intermission and went into a practice room with Ma, where they struck up some Brahms just like old times.)[40] *Washington Post* fashion writer Robin Givhan remarked, "She's steered clear of that cliché, patriotic color palette," noting that Condi has chosen the Swiss designer Akris for many of her outfits. "She's not going to leave her femininity or sense of style in a closet because of what she does."[41]

Condi's cousin Lativia makes frequent trips up from Atlanta and arranges private after-hours shopping trips with Condi to get around security limitations. They mostly search for shoes. The shoe-shopping excursions become the highlights of Condi's calendar for weeks in advance. "We'll call each other constantly and say, 'Only five weeks left!' And then, 'Only four weeks left!'" says Lativia.[42] Former Clinton administration National Security Council staffer Chip Blacker jokes, "She may have more shoes than Imelda Marcos."[43]

The troops are happy to see Secretary of State Condoleezza Rice during her visit to Germany, February 2005.

Condi is a star celebrity in the fashion world, hailed on *Vanity Fair* magazine's 2006 "Best Dressed" list. "Condoleezza is immaculately groomed and formidably dignified—but with an audacious renegade streak," said the magazine. "The black dominatrix boots she wore in Germany kicked up an international controversy the likes of which we haven't seen since Nancy Reagan flashed her satin Galanos knickers in Paris. Even *Foreign Policy* was stunned into declaring that Condi's fetishy knee-high stilettos punted a message around the planet that 'the United States is a force to be reckoned with.'"[44]

Indeed, as Condi stepped off the plane at Weisbaden Airfield in Germany in February 2005, she grabbed people's attention dressed in a black skirt to just above her knees, a flowing black coat down to her mid-calves, and stunning, shining, high black boots with tall, narrow heels. With seven gold buttons descending along the front of the coat, Condi's outfit resembled the outfit worn by Keanu Reeves in *The Matrix.* As she greeted military personnel at the airfield, they stood and cheered with gaping mouths. "Rice challenges expectations and assumptions," Givhan observed in the *Washington Post.* "There is undeniable authority in her long black jacket with its severe details and menacing silhouette. The darkness lends an air of mystery and foreboding. Black is the color of intellectualism, of abstinence, of penitence. If there is any symbolism to be gleaned from Rice's stark garments, it is that she is tough and focused enough for whatever task is at hand."[45]

Despite unfavorable attitudes toward America in Spain, Condi visited Spain around the time of her Weisbaden appearance and won over the place with "the Condi flip." That's how the Spanish described Condi's special hairstyle, with the lightly flipped hair in the back.[46]

Sports fans love Condi because she is a fellow die-hard who schedules time every Sunday afternoon during football season to watch a game. She talked with ESPN.com about the history of athletics, the

Yankees, the NFL, and sports diplomacy. Sports, she said, "is a great icebreaker. Everyone knows how much I love it. So it's just part of the conversation. The president and I share a love of sports. . . . I love to go in and give him a hard time about the Texas Longhorns. Of course, they've been pretty good lately."[47] Not only is she a spectator, she also is an avid tennis player, and she took up golf not too long ago.

Condi's best friend at Stanford is a documentary filmmaker and fellow football lover named Randy Bean. Like Condi, Randy is a preacher's daughter who grew up on football. Unlike Condi, Randy is a Democrat. "People ask how we became friends, and I always say, 'God and football,'" said Bean. "I could forgive Condi her politics because she loved football, and likewise she could forgive mine."[48] That's a big clue to why Condi transcends the political poll-tides of the Bush administration. Almost everybody loves Condi. She appeals to a wide variety of people from different walks of life.

As I was waiting to meet her at an event in May 2006, a woman about fifty years old pushed her way up through the crowd to talk to Secretary Rice. The lady reached out to shake hands with Condi, saying, "See, Rice, I'm a Democrat, but I love you and think you should run for president."

Oprah Winfrey profiled Condi on her show "Secrets of Women Who Rule," featuring behind-the-scenes video of Condi's day and an interview on the couch with Oprah, for which Condi wore an elegant black pantsuit with a striking gold necklace. And Oprah was also interested in Condi's talent for cooking. "I love to cook—it's one of my favorite things to do," Condi said. "I make really good fried chicken. I'm a good southern girl, and in the south, it's not food if it's not fried."[49]

Not only did *Time* magazine have a short article on Condi in 2006 in its special edition highlighting "The 100 People Who Shape Our World," but *Time* also asked Condi to write about Oprah. One can pick up clues on what is important to people by what they focus on when they speak or write about other people. Saying that Oprah's story is America's story, Condi shows she is always inspired by people who raise themselves up, despite struggles and challenges, through education and hard work in the liberty that America offers. Just like she and her family did. Condi opened a window into her own philosophy when describing Oprah.

"I believe influence is the union of power and purpose," wrote Condi. "As a TV star, magazine founder, businesswoman and celebrity, Oprah Winfrey certainly has power. But most important, she has purpose—an abiding commitment to the principles of goodness and generosity that transcend any one individual. I have sat with Oprah in interviews and in my home. I have felt her warmth, and I am always moved by her deep love for others."

These values are what are important to Condi: to have a life where whatever gifts, talents, or opportunities she has are used for a good purpose. She promotes that which she believes in: optimism; individualism; liberty; freedom; treating others with respect, dignity, and love; and inspiring people to become the best they can be using the gifts that God has given them for Him.

Condi explains herself this way: "Well, first, my faith is a part of everything that I do . . . and it's not something that I can set outside of anything that I do because it's so integral to who I am."[50]

Along the same vein, friend Randy Bean says, "Her faith is absolutely fundamental to who she is. It's part of her fiber."[51] A couple of years ago, when Condi was asked about the possibility of marrying, she responded by saying that she hasn't met the right person yet. But then the next words she spoke about marriage went to the heart of her long-held optimistic beliefs about life in general, including her faith in God. "It doesn't mean it won't happen some day," she said. "But I'm a deeply religious person, and my life has, I think, unfolded as it was supposed to." When asked if she would be open to meeting "Mr. Right," with a laugh she said, "I don't have much time right now, but sure. Who wouldn't be?"

Besides faith, another strong theme in Condi's life is the notion of hope. Faith and hope are tightly intertwined themes in Condi's life, and she often gives hope to others as inspiring leaders have in the past. Many of her speeches and interviews speak of hope. She speaks words of hope to others and paints a picture of what is possible to a nation weary of war and those who are enslaved and living in despair in other parts of the world.

Condi has seen changes in her lifetime that many said would never happen, including the end of segregation in the South and the tearing down of the Berlin Wall that had separated Germany for twenty-eight years. She looks back to examples in history, such as the founding of our nation by a few people who believed that freedom and liberty were the keys to a democratic nation.

Much of the secret to understanding Condi is to look at her viewpoint and attitude in life. Because she is a visionary and an optimist, she is willing to take on a challenge and work to change the world for the better. Condi believes that democracy is possible for people living in parts of the world in oppressive situations.

For Condi Rice, eternal perspective is everything. "I think people who believe in a creator can never take themselves too seriously," she said. Condi had seen the problem with ideologies that took this life too seriously, particularly Soviet communism. She believed that such ideologies were destined to fail, because they could not cope with the reality of human existence and the need for human freedom.

> I feel that faith allows me to have a kind of optimism about the future. You look around you and you see an awful lot of pain and suffering and things that are going wrong. It could be oppressive. But when I look at my own story or many others that I have seen, I think, "How could it possibly be that it has turned out this way?" Then my only answer is it's God's plan. And that makes me very optimistic that this is all working out in a proper way if we all stay close to God and pray and follow in His footsteps.[52]

Condi says she tries to say in her prayers, "'Help me to walk in Your way, not my own.' To try to walk in a way that is actually trying to fulfill a plan and realize you are a cog in a larger universe."[53] This optimism, hope, and faith in God's providence is in all aspects of Condoleezza Rice's life story, from the seeds planted in her childhood in segregated Alabama and the loss of her parents, to her struggles while professor and provost at Stanford University, all the way to her most challenging jobs as NSA and secretary of state of the United States.[54] But one thing is for sure; she's not worried about her future: "Ambiguity has never bothered me at all. I think that part of it is that I'm pretty religious, and that probably helps to make one less fearful and more optimistic about what's possible. I rather like living with ambiguity."[55]

The world is watching to see where God leads this "Steel Magnolia" next on her life's journey.

Epilogue

Winter 2008

Ever since Condi was in the first Bush administration, observers have pointed back to that day in 1965 when she stood in front of the White House and told her parents that she would work there someday. She worked there under two presidents, and then she was promoted to the State Department, where she is fourth in the line of succession to the Oval Office. It wouldn't be difficult to imagine a day when Condi was elected as president of the United States.

When Tim Russert of NBC's *Meet the Press* asked Condi in March 2005 if she would run, she replied, "Tim, I don't want to run for president of the United States." Russert continued to probe for a final answer, and she said, "I will not run for president of the United States. How is that? I don't know how many ways to say 'no' in this town. I really don't."[1]

For a moment, Condi fueled speculation about a possible run for the White House when, at a conference of young Latinos in May 2006, she was asked whether "a Latino or Latina person or an African

American person or a person from any other minority" will someday be president. "Yes," she said, followed by audience laughter and applause. Realizing the reason for the crowd's tremendous reaction, Condi clarified. "I think it will happen, and I think it will happen in my lifetime"—provoking more laughter—"but it won't be me."[2]

When polls in August 2006 were showing Condi as one of the top three potential presidential contenders for 2008, the *Salt Lake Tribune* asked her reaction. "It's flattering but that's not for me," she replied. "I know what my strengths are and I know what I want to do with my life and I'm hoping that in these last two and a half years as secretary of state that I can help to advance the president's vision for democracy."[3]

There's an old tradition in America, dating back to George Washington, that men—and now women—of presidential quality don't seek the presidency. But with the exception of General William T. Sherman, who famously said that if he was nominated he would not run, and if elected he would not serve, saying "no" to the White House has pretty assuredly meant "yes." In recent years, the act of declining the presidential race is more a political calculation than a sign of magnanimity. But with Condi, there is a record of magnanimity that suggests she may be different. Condoleezza Rice doesn't seek positions. She lets them find her.

For now, she plans to return to teach at Stanford. As she told a classroom of schoolchildren in California, "I hope to see some of you at Stanford when I get back."[4] As her stepmom Clara says, "Condi's coming home."[5]

At the time of this writing, it is unlikely that Condi will mount a presidential campaign. But it is quite likely that the Republican nominee will ask Condi to serve as a candidate for vice president. Not only has Condi proven herself a loyal member of the Bush team, a skilled diplomat, a fine teacher and administrator, a lady of glamour, and a woman of character and faith, she has the rare and priceless ability to lead and inspire nations. Of course, she's a black woman too. If she were elected, it would be a triumph of the principles on which the nation was founded.

Who would have thought, when Condi was growing up in Birmingham in the 1950s and 1960s, that one day a little black girl would grow up to be presidential or vice presidential material? In 1776, it would have been almost unthinkable.

But the principles of 1776 outlasted the prejudices of the day. The central idea of the Declaration of Independence, that all human beings are "created equal" and "endowed by their Creator with certain unalienable rights," has survived, and thrived. The success of Condi Rice is a testimony to the resilience of America's principles, principles that Condi believes are true for all people in the world. Condi also believes that America is not on a mission to remake the world in its image but to advance the ideals common to all men and women that America was founded on in the first place.

At the end of the day, it is not because of one's racial group or socioeconomic class or creed that he or she is entitled to the rights that come from God. "Who you are is who you are as an individual," Condi told a group of black journalists in 2002.[6] Condi has demonstrated that all her life. As an individual, Condi has risen above the odds and achieved amazing things. Few people could better personify the American Dream.

Today, the American Dream is still alive, despite the immense challenges from within and without. Condi has reckoned with those challenges, and in the midst of them she has seen the source of human strength. It comes from the infinite strength of Almighty God. For Condoleezza Rice, strength is to be found in Jesus Christ.

And when Condi finally goes back to California, the effects of her work in the early years of the millennium will go on. "No one," she has written, "will be able to know the full scope of what our statecraft has achieved. But I have an abiding confidence that we will have laid a firm foundation of principle—a foundation on which future generations will realize our nation's vision of a fully free, democratic, and peaceful world."[7]

Bibliography

Allen, Mike. "Inside Bush's Top-Secret Trip," *Washington Post,* November 28, 2003.

American Academy of Arts and Sciences. "About the Academy," http://www.amacad.org/about.aspx.

American Academy of Arts and Sciences. *Records of the Academy,* No. 1986/1987.

Baer, Donald, Michael Barone, Peter Cary, Gary Cohen, Matthew Cooper, Miriam Horn, Thomas Moore, and Eva Pomice. "People to Watch," *U.S. News and World Report,* 25 Dec. 1989/1 Jan. 1990.

Barbour Publishing. *Light for My Path for Grandparents: Illuminating Selections from the Bible.* Uhrichsville, OH: Humble Creek, 2002.

Barrett, Ted. "GOP Senator: Bush Plan Could Match Vietnam

Blunder," CNN, 11 Jan. 2007, http://www.cnn.com/2007/POLITICS/01/11/iraq.congress/index.html, accessed 20 June 2007.

BBC News. "Rice Calls for Mid-East Democracy," 20 June 2005, http://news.bbc.co .uk/1/hi/world/middle_east/4109902.stm, accessed 5 June 2007.

BBC News. "White House U-turn on 9/11 Inquiry," 31 March 2004, http://newsvote.bbc .co.uk/mpapps/pagetools/print/news.bbc.co.uk/2/hi/americas/3583639.stm, accessed 20 June 2007.

Beam, Ale. "Playing, and Losing, at Agemanship," *Boston Globe,* 3 Feb. 1999.

Bee, Helen. *The Developing Child*, Third Edition. New York: Harper & Row, 1981.

Bennet, James. "Chelsea and 1,649 Other Freshmen Arrive at Stanford," *New York Times,* 20 Sept. 1997.

Blunt, Sheryl Henderson. "'The Privilege of Struggle,'" *Christianity Today,* 1 Sept. 2003, http://www.christianitytoday.com/ct/article_print.html?id=10883, accessed 4 Nov. 2006.

———. "The Unflappable Condi Rice," 22 Aug. 2003, http://www.ctlibrary.com/ct /2003/september/1.42.html, accessed 4 June 2007.

Boomer, Rachel. "'People of America Will Never Forget,'" *Halifax Daily News,* 12 Sept. 2006, http://www.hfxnews.ca/index.cfm?sid=8104&sc=1, accessed 12 Sept. 2006.

Booth, Robert. "Jack Becomes Embedded While Condi Loses Sleep," *The Guardian,* 3 April 2006, http://politics.guardian.co.uk/print/0,,329448821-110481,00.html, accessed 13 June 2007.

Bremer, L. Paul. *My Year in Iraq: The Struggle to Build a Future of Hope.* New York: Simon and Schuster, 2006.

Brinkley, Joel. "Rice Sounds a Theme in Visit to Beijing Protestant Church," *New York Times,* 21 March 2005.

British Monarchy, "Mailbox," *Royal Insight,* Nov. 2003, http://www.royal.gov .uk/output/Page2682.asp, accessed 13 Aug. 2007.

Broder, David S. "The Future Is—Futures?" *Washington Post,* 20 June 1984.

Brown, Fred, and Susan Greene, "Adviser Condi Rice Launched Career in Denver," *Denver Post,* 2 Aug. 2000.

Brumas, Michael. "Bush's 'Vulcans' Iron out Foreign Policy," *New York Times,* 30 June 2000.

Burdman, Pamela. "Search for Chancellor Winding Up," *San Francisco Chronicle,* 31 Jan. 1997.

Bush, George H. W. "Remarks to the Polish National Assembly in Warsaw," 10 July 1989, http://bushlibrary.tamu.edu/research/papers/1989/89071002.html, accessed 6 June 2007.

Bush, George W. Address to a Joint Session of Congress and the American People, 20 Sept. 2001, http://www.whitehouse.gov/news/releases/2001/09/20010920-8.html, accessed 21 June 2007.

———. "Bush makes historic speech aboard warship," CNN, 1 May 2003, http://www .cnn.com/2003/US/05/01/bush.transcript/, accessed 25 June 2007.

———. "President Bush Meets With Troops in Iraq on Thanksgiving," 27 Nov. 2003, http://www.whitehouse.gov/news/releases/2003/11/20031127.html, accessed 6 June 2007.

———. "President Proclaims National Day of Prayer and Remembrance for the Victims of the Terrorist Attacks on September 11, 2001," http://www.whitehouse.gov/ news/releases/2001/09/20010913-7.html, accessed 13 Aug. 2007.

———. "Remarks by the President in an Address to Faculty and Students of Warsaw University," 15 June 2001, http://www.whitehouse.gov/news/releases/2001/06 / 20010615-1.html, accessed 7 June 2007.

———. "Remarks at the Announcement of Appointments," *New York Times,* 18 Dec. 2000.

Canadian Press. "Rice Brings Message of Thanks to Halifax," 11 Sept. 2006, http://www .theglobeandmail.com/servlet/story/RTGAM.20060911.wrice0911/BNStory/National, accessed 13 Aug. 2006.

Carman, Diane. "Rice Has Gone Far Since DU," *Denver Post*, 9 April 2004.

CBC News. "Rosa Parks Lies in State in Washington," 30 Oct. 2005, http://www.cbc .ca/world/story/2005/10/30/parks-remembered051030.html, accessed 25 June 2007.

———. "The Days After," 10 Sept. 2003, http://www.cbsnews.com/stories/2002/09 /11/60II/main521684.shtml, accessed 3 Aug. 2007.

———. "The President's Story," 11 Sept. 2002, http://www.cbsnews.com/stories/2002/ 09/10/60II/main521483.shtml, accessed 7 Aug. 2007.

———. "The President's Story," 10 Sept. 2003, http://www.cbsnews.com/stories/2002/ 09/11/60II/main521718.shtml, accessed 3 Aug. 2007.

Cheng, Helen. "Hua Di Convicted by Chinese a Second Time," *Stanford Daily*, 6 Feb. 2001, http://daily.stanford.edu/article/2001/2/6/huaDiConvictedByChineseA SecondTime, accessed 28 June 2007.

CNN. "Chronology of Terror," 12 Sept. 2001, http://edition.cnn.com/2001/US/09/11 /chronology.attack/, accessed 7 Aug. 2007.

———. "Poll: We like Condi, but who's Karl?" 26 April 2006, http://www.cnn.com /politics/04/26/poll.administration, expired link 4 June 2007.

——— "Saddam Statue Toppled in Central Baghdad," 9 April 2003, http://www.cnn .com/2003/WORLD/meast/04/09/sprj.irq.statue/, accessed 25 June 2007.

Collins, Amy Fine. "Vanity Fair Presents the 67th Annual Best-Dressed List 2006," *Vanity Fair,* Sept. 2006.

Cook, John. *The Book of Positive Quotations.* Minneapolis: Fairview Press, 1997.

Coolican, J. Patrick. "Despite Violence, Iraqi Elections Will Occur as Scheduled, Rice Says," *Seattle Times,* 8 Sept. 2004.

Curiel, Jonathan. "Rice Still Stretching Her Horizons," *San Francisco Chronicle,* 9 Feb. 1993.

Davidson, Joanne. "DU friends and Alums Rise to the Occasion," *Denver Post,* 18 March 1999.

Dennis, Mark. "Bush Channels Reagan on Foreign Policy,"

Salon.com, 20 Nov. 1999, http://www.salon.com/news/feature/1999/11/20/foreign/index.html, accessed 1 June 2007.

Del Guidice, Vinny. "Attack on the Pentagon, September 11, 2001," *Arlington Fire Journal*, March 18, 2005, http://arlingtonfire journal.blogspot.com/2005/03/attack-on-pentagon-sept-11-2001.html, accessed 7 Aug. 2007.

Der Spiegel. Inside 9-11: What Really Happened. New York: St. Martin's Press, 2002.

Devroy, Ann. "Black Woman Called Favorite to Fill Wilson's Senate Term," *Washington Post,* 30 Nov. 1990.

Ditchfield, Christin. *Condoleezza Rice: National Security Advisor.* New York: Franklin Watts/Scholastic, 2003.

Dowd, Ann Reilly. "What Makes Condi Run," *AARP Magazine,* Sept. and Oct. 2005, http://www.aarpmagazine.org/people/condoleeza.html, accessed 12 June 2007.

The Economist. "Bush's World," 6 Jan. 2001.

The Economist. "The Birth of an Arab-American Lobby," 14 Oct. 2000.

Elyot, Sir Thomas. *The Boke Named Governor.* New York: Dutton, 1962.

Felix, Antonia. *Condi: The Condoleezza Rice Story.* New York: Newmarket Press, 2005.

Flower, Kevin, Enes Dulami, and Kianne Sadeq, "Rice Makes Surprise Visit to Iraq," CNN, 15 May 2005, http://www.cnn.com/2005/WORLD/meast/05/15/iraq.main/, accessed 5 June 2007.

Foster, Brooke Lea. "Being Condi," *Washingtonian,* March 2007.

Gegax, T. Trent, Evan Thomas, Peter Goldman, et. al. "What a Long, Strange Trip," *Newsweek,* 20 Nov. 2000.

Gerstenzang, James. "Shoving of Bush Staffer Investigated," *The Washington Post,* 7 June 1990.

Getler, Michael. "Black Journalists and the New Era," *Washington Post,* 18 Aug. 1991.

Givhan, Robin. "Condoleezza Rice's Commanding Clothes," *Washington Post,* 25 Feb. 2005.

Goodenough, Patrick. "Rice Attends Church in Country Where Religious Freedom Is Relentlessly Restricted," CNS News, 21 March 2005, http://www.cnsnews.com /ViewForeign Bureaus.asp?Page=%5CForeignBureaus%5Carchive%5C200503 %5CFOR20050321b.html, accessed 5 June 2007.

Gordon, Tom, and Mary Orndorff. "Condoleezza Rice: Defying the Stereotypes," *Birmingham News,* 22 Jan. 2001.

Gottfried, Kurt, Richard L. Garwin, Condoleezza Rice, et. al. "Crisis Stability and Nuclear War," *Bulletin of the American Academy of Arts and Sciences,* Vol. 40, No. 8, May 1987.

Graham, Billy. Address at the National Cathedral, 14 Sept. 2001, http://www.american rhetoric.com/speeches/billygraham911memorial.htm, accessed 3 Aug. 2007.

Greene, Marilyn. "Summit Specialist Cold-Shouldered in San Francisco," *USA Today,* 6 June 1990.

Harnden, Toby, and Simon Davis, "Americans Welcome 'Valiant' Spy Crew," *The Daily Telegraph,* 13 April 2001.

Haygood, Wil. "'Honored to Have the Chance,' To Her Parents, Failure in Life Was Never an Option for 'Condi' Rice," *Boston Globe,* 21 Dec. 2000.

Henry, Ed. "Rice Confirmed as Secretary of State," CNN, 26 Jan. 2005, http://www.cnn .com/2005/ALLPOLITICS/01/26/rice.confirmation/, accessed 25 June 2007.

Herspring, Dale R. Book review, *The American Political Science Review,* Vol. 79, No. 3, Sept. 1985.

Hoagland, Jim. "This Year's Cinderella," *Washington Post,* 24 Dec. 1995.

Hughes, Karen. *Ten Minutes from Normal.* New York: Viking Penguin, 2004.

Jet. "Rice Appointed to National Council on the Humanities," 27 April 1992.

Johnson, Richard. "Hindsights," Book review, *Denver Post,* 15 Feb. 1994.

Johnson-Elie, Tannette. "A lesson from Rice in Individuality," *Milwaukee Journal Sentinel,* 20 Nov. 2002.

Jones, Christopher. Book review, *Soviet Studies,* Vol. 38, No. 4, Oct. 1986.

Kalvoda, Josef. Book review, *The American Historical Review,* Vol. 90, No. 5, Dec. 1985.

Keen, Judy. "Barbara Bush to Captain 'Women Tour,'" *USA Today,* 16 Oct. 2000.

Kennedy, James H. "City Native and Bayou La Batre Doctor Among 'Time' Promising Young Leaders," *Birmingham News,* 1 Dec. 1994.

Kershner, Vlae. “Remap Plan Challenges Demos,” *San Francisco Chronicle,* 12 Oct. 1991.

Kessler, Glenn. “Rice Drops Plans for Visit to Egypt,” *Washington Post,* 26 Feb. 2005.

———. “Rice Hitting the Road to Speak,” *Washington Post,* 20 Oct. 2004.

Kralev, Nicholas. “Political Punch in a Package of Charm,” *Financial Times,* 26 Feb. 2000.

Kranish, Michael. “Bush Cramming Before Campaigning,” *Boston Globe,* 6 June 1999.

La Ganga, Maria L. “In Race for White House, the ‘Cult of Condi’ Plays Growing Role,” *Los Angeles Times,* 28 May 2000.

Lee, Jessica. “She’s Bush’s Top Expert on Soviets; Grasp of Issues Impresses Colleagues,” *USA Today,* 30 May 1990.

Leman, Kevin. *The Birth Order Book: Why You Are the Way You Are.* Grand Rapids: Revell, 1998.

Lemann, Nicholas. “Her Brilliant Career,” *The New Yorker,* 14 Oct. 2002, http://www .newyorker.com/printables/online/0201014on_onlineonly02, accessed 2 May 2006.

——— "Without a Doubt: Has Condoleezza Rice Changed George W. Bush, or Has He Changed Her?" *The New Yorker,* 14 Oct. 2002.

Lindlaw, Scott. "Rice Lays Groundwork for Calif. Return," *San Jose Mercury News,* 25 May 2007, http://www.mercurynews.com/search/ci_5984022?nclick_check=1, accessed 5 June 2007.

Los Angeles Times photo. "Condoleezza Rice, Soviet and East European," *The Sunday Oregonian,* 16 April 1989.

Luther, Martin. "Preface to Romans," Scroll Publishing, http://www.scrollpublishing.com /store/Luther-Romans.html, accessed 3 Aug. 2007.

Mann, James. *Rise of the Vulcans: The History of Bush's War Cabinet.* New York: Viking, 2004.

Mann, Paul. "Soviet Economic Reform May Force Transformation of Entire Military," *Aviation Week/Space Technology,* 2 May 1988.

Mabry, Marcus. *Twice as Good: Condoleezza Rice and Her Path to Power.* New York: Rodale Books, 2007.

Maraniss, David. "September 11, 2001," *Washington Post,* 16 Sept. 2001.

McCombs, Phil. "Secret Weapon at the NSC; Condoleezza Rice,

Breaking Barriers on Bush's Team," *Washington Post,* 17 March 1989.

McDonald, Hamish. "Rice Talks Democracy, Religion in China," *The Age,* 22 March 2005, http://www.theage.com.au/news/World/Rice-talks-democracy-religion-in-China/2005/03/21/1111253953601.html, accessed 5 June 2007.

McGrory, Mary. "Please Pass the Oxygen Masks," *Washington Post,* 25 Aug. 1992.

McIntyre, Jamie. "U.S. Reconnaissance Planes Take Flight Again Near China," CNN, 7 May 2001, http://cnnstudentnews.cnn.com/2001/fyi/news/05/07/us.china /index.html, accessed 1 June 2007.

Meeker, Meg. *Strong Fathers, Strong Daughters: 10 Secrets Every Father Should Know.* Washington, DC: Regnery Publishing, 2006.

Meet the Press, "Transcript for March 13," NBC, 13 May 2005 update; http://www .msnbc.msn.com/id/7173024/, accessed 4 June 2007.

Mishra, Raja, and Bryan Bender, "Hussein Captured," *Boston Globe,* 15 Dec. 2003.

Morgenthau, Hans. "Alone With Himself and History," *New York Times,* 13 Nov. 1960.

Morgenthau, Hans. "World Politics in the Mid-Twentieth Century," *The Review of Politics,* University of Notre Dame, 1948.

Murray, A. J. H. "The Moral Politics of Hans Morgenthau," *The Review of Politics,* University of Notre Dame, 1996.

.

National Commission on Terrorist Attacks upon the United States. *9/11 Commission Report.* New York: W.W. Norton and Company, 2004.

National Review. "Philadelphia II: Winners & Losers," 28 Aug. 2000, Vol. LII, No. 16.

NBC, MSNBC, news services. "Senate Opposition to Bush Plan Grows," MSNBC, 11 Jan. 2007, http://www.msnbc.msn.com/id/16579285/, accessed 20 June 2007.

Newsweek. "Pumping Iron, Digging Gold, Pressing Flesh," 20 Nov. 2000.

New York Times. "From 'Not College Material' to Stanford's No. 2 Job," 23 June 1993.

New York Times. "Summit in Washington: Faces of the Summit," 1 June 1990.

Niemeyer, Paul V. "Obituary for Gerhart Niemeyer," Philadelphia

Society, 1997, http://www.phillysoc.org/gerhart.htm, accessed 15 June 2007.

Nordlinger, Jay. "The GOP's Burden: The Color of the Convention," *National Review,* 28 Aug. 2000, Vol. LII, No. 16.

Nordlinger, Jay. "Star-in-Waiting," *National Review*, 30 Aug. 1999/17 Nov. 2004, http://www.nationalreview.com/flashback/nordlinger200411170605.asp, accessed 1 June 2007.

Oberdorfer, Don. "U.S. Secretly Studied Possibility of Gorbachev Coup, Soviet Collapse," *The Washington Post,* 17 Jan. 1993.

Oil & Gas Journal. "Tankers," PennWell Publishing Company, 30 Aug. 1993.

Online Newshour. "Bush on Foreign Affairs," PBS, 19 Nov. 1999, http://www.pbs.org /newshour/shields&gigot/november99/sg_11-19_bush.html, accessed 1 June 2007.

The Oprah Winfrey Show. "Secrets of Women Who Rule," Oct. 2003, http://www.oprah .com/tows/slide/200310/20031017/tows_slide_20031017_women_03.jhtml, accessed 6 May 2006.

Orin, Deborah. "The Anxious Days Before Bush Flight," *New York Post,* 29 Nov. 2003.

Ostrom, Mary Anne. "Condoleezza Rice Tours Silicon Valley

During a 'Home Visit,'" *San Jose Mercury News,* 24 May 2007, http://www.mercurynews.com/search /ci_5978431?nclick_check=1, accessed 27 June 2007.

O'Toole, Kathleen. "Rice Implores Graduates to Reap Benefits of Crossing Cultural Boundaries," *Stanford Report,* 16 June 1999, http://news-service.stanford.edu /news/1999/june16/classday2-616.html, accessed 7 Sept. 2006.

——— "Rice: War Stories no Teaching Tool, But Role Playing Works," *Stanford Report,* 28 Oct. 1998, http://new-service.stanford.edu/news/1998 /october28/riceteach1028.html, accessed 7 Sept. 2006.

Overholser, Geneva. "Profile of a Heavy Hitter," *Washington Post,* 7 Sept. 1999.

Page, Clarence. "Why Condi's Star Is Rising," *Jewish World Review,* 10 Jan. 2006, http://jewishworldreview.com/0106/page011006.php3, accessed 4 June 2007.

Parkes, Christopher. "Leaders for a New Millennium: Package Still Under Wraps—Condoleezza Rice," *Financial Times,* 28 Dec. 1995.

Quayle, Dan. *Standing Firm.* New York: HarperCollins, 1995.

Randolph, Eleanor. "NBC's Coup on Gorbachev Interview Sends

Rival Journalists Scrambling; Summit Is Expected to Draw 6,000 to Washington," *Washington Post,* 1 Dec. 1987.

Randolph, Laura B. "Black Women in the White House," *Ebony,* Oct. 1990, http://find articles.com/p/articles/mi_m1077/is_n12_v45/ai_8904380, accessed 7 June 2007.

Ratnesar, Romesh. "Condi Rice Can't Lose," *Time,* 20 Sept. 1999, http://www.time.com /time/magazine/article/0,9171,1101990927-31242,00.html, accessed 1 June 2007.

The Record (Bergen County, N.J.). "About the Photo," 2001, http://www.arlington cemetery.net/fireman-01.htm, accessed 9 Aug. 2007.

Reed, Julia. "The President's Prodigy," *Vogue,* October 2001.

The Review of Politics, http://www.nd.edu/~rop/, accessed 15 June 2007.

Rice, Condoleezza. "A Balance of Power that Favors Freedom," *U.S. National Security Strategy: A New Era..* Washington, DC: U.S. Department of State, Dec. 2002.

———. "Acknowledge That You Have an Obligation to Search for the Truth," Stanford News Service, 16 June 2002, http://news-service.stanford.edu/news/2002/june19 /comm_ricetext-619.html, accessed 3 July 2007.

———. "America's Unique Opportunity," PBS Online NewsHour, 1 August 2000, http://www.pbs.org/newshour/election2000/gopconvention/condoleezza_rice.html, accessed 1 June 2007.

———. "Campaign 2000: Promoting the National Interest," *Foreign Affairs,* January/February 2000, http://www.foreign affairs.org/20000101faessay5 /condoleezza-rice/campaign-2000-promoting-the-national-interest.html, accessed 1 June 2007.

———. "Dr. Condoleezza Rice's Opening Remarks to Commission on Terrorist Attacks," 8 April 2004, http://www.whitehouse.gov/news/releases/2004 /04/20040408.html, accessed 19 June 2007.

———. "Interview with Essence Magazine," 25 May 2006, http://www.state.gov /secretary/rm/2006/71813.htm, accessed 27 June 2007.

———. "Interview with Rebecca Walsh, Salt Lake Tribune," 29 Aug. 2006, http://www.state.gov/secretary/rm/2006/71637.htm, accessed 5 June 2007.

———. "Interview with Robin Wright and Glenn Kesler of the Washington Post," 26 July 2005, http://www.state.gov/secretary/rm/2005/50414.htm, accessed 28 June 2007.

———. "Iraq: A New Way Forward," 11 Jan. 2007, http://www.state.gov/secretary /rm/2007/78605.htm, accessed 20 June 2007.

———. Letter to the editor, *The American Historical Review*, Vol. 91, No. 4, Oct. 1986.

———. "National Security Advisor Condoleezza Rice Remarks to Veterans of Foreign Wars," 25 Aug. 2003, http://www.white-house.gov/news/releases/2003/08/2003 0825-1.html, accessed 6 June 2007.

———. "National Security Advisor Dr. Condoleezza Rice Discusses War on Terror at Reagan Library and Museum," 28 Feb. 2004, http://www.whitehouse.gov/news /releases/ 2004/02/20040228-1.html, accessed 6 June 2007.

———. Opening Remarks at Senate Foreign Relations Committee, 18 Jan. 2005, http://www.state.gov/secretary/rm/2005/40991. htm, accessed 1 June 2007.

———. "The Party, the Military, and Decision Authority in the Soviet Union," *World Politics*, Vol. 40, No. 1, Oct. 1987.

———. "The Politics of Client Command: Party-Military Relations in Czechoslovakia, 1948–1975," abstract, Ph.D. Dissertation, University of Denver, DAI, 43, no. 05A, 1981.

———. "Press Briefing by National Security Advisor Condoleezza Rice," 15 June 2001, http://www.whitehouse.gov/news/ releases/2001/06/20010615-2.html, accessed 7 June 2007.

———. "The Promise of Democratic Peace," *Washington Post,* 11 Dec. 2005.

———. "Remarks at the American University in Cairo," 20 June 2005, http://www-.state.gov/secretary/rm/2005/48328.htm, accessed 5 June 2007.

———. "Remarks at Espacio USA Conference," 5 May 2006, http://www.state.gov /secretary/rm/2006/65936.htm, accessed 5 June 2007.

———. "Remarks at the Independent Women's Forum Upon Receiving Woman of Valor Award,"10 May 2006, http://www.state.gov/secretary/rm/2006/66139.htm, accessed 5 June 2007.

———. Remarks at Paul H. Nitze School of Advanced International Studies at Johns Hopkins, 29 April 2002, http://www.whitehouse.gov/news/releases/2002/04 / 20020429-9.html, accessed 30 May 2007.

———. "Remarks by National Security Advisor Dr. Condoleezza Rice at the National Prayer Breakfast," 6 Feb. 2003, http://www.luthersem.edu/rnysse/OT2116-Prophets/ Rice-NationalPrayerBreakfast.htm, accessed 3 Aug. 2007.

———. "Remarks to Halifax International Airport Officials and Staff," 11 Sept. 2006, http://www.state.gov/secretary/rm/2006/72041.htm, accessed 13 Aug. 2007.

———. *The Soviet Union and the Czechoslovak Army, 1948–1983: Uncertain Allegiance.* Princeton, N.J.: Princeton University Press, 1984.

———. "Transform America, one by one," *Birmingham News,* 22 May 1994.

———. "Transformational Diplomacy," 18 Jan. 2006, http://www.state.gov/secretary/rm /2006/59306.htm, accessed 4 June 2007.

———. "Walking in Faith: Rice Finds Strength in Religion," *Washington Times,* 27 Aug. 2002.

———. "The White House and the Wall," *Newsweek,* 15 Nov. 1999.

Roberts, Jerry. "Best and Worst of the GOP Convention," *San Francisco Chronicle,* 22 Aug. 1992.

Robinson, James. "Changes Proposed in Tuition Benefits for Employees," *Stanford Report,* 9 Dec. 1998, http://news-service. stanford.edu/news/1998/december9 /emptuition129.html, accessed 28 June 2007.

Robinson, James. "'Velvet-Glove Forcefulness,'" *Stanford Report,* 9 June 1999, http://news-service.stanford.edu/news/1999/june9/rice-69.html, accessed 27 July 2006.

Rockwell, Keith M. "Gorbachev Reforms Deemed Insufficient to Help Economy," *The Journal of Commerce,* 14 Sept. 1987.

Rumsfeld, Donald. "A Force for Good," *Wall Street Journal*, 11 Sept. 2006, A14.

Russakoff, Dale. "How football Helped Shape Condoleezza the Strategist," *The Standard*, 7 Feb. 2005, http://www.eastandard.net/archives/cl/hm_news /news.php?articleid=12571&date=7/2/2005, 4 June 2007.

Russakoff, Dale. "Lessons of Might and Right," *Washington Post Magazine,* 9 Sept. 2001.

Ryan, Bernard. *Condoleezza Rice: Secretary of State.* New York: Ferguson/Facts on File, 2004.

Sammon, Bill. *Fighting Back: The War on Terrorism—from Inside the Bush White House.* Washington, DC: Regnery Publishing, 2002.

San Francisco Chronicle. "Chevron Proposals at Meeting," 8 May 1991.

———. "Chief named to Search for Stanford President," 29 Oct. 1991.

———. "Stanford Scholar Held Prisoner in China for Past 10 Months," 29 Oct. 1998.

Serafin, Tatiana. "#1 Condoleezza Rice," *Forbes,* Nov. 2005, http://www.forbes.com /lists/2005/11/MTNG.html, accessed 8 June 2007.

Schuller, Robert H. *Move Ahead with Possibility Thinking.* Old Tappan, N.J.: Fleming H. Revell Company, 1973.

Shales, Tom. "Cool, Calm Condoleezza Rice," *Washington Post,* 9 April 2004.

Simon, Mark. "An Astute Choice for Stanford," *San Francisco Chronicle,* 20 May 1993.

———. "Soviet Expert Rice Gets Stanford Provost Post," *San Francisco Chronicle,* 19 May 1993.

———. "Stanford May Cut Tuition Perk," *San Francisco Chronicle,* 21 Oct. 1996.

Smyth, Patrick, and Joe Carroll, "U.S. Presence in Balkans Becomes Election Issue," *Irish Times,* 23 Oct. 2000.

Stanford Magazine. "Rice on Students, Tough Decisions, and Her Oil Tanker," May/June 1999, http://www.stanfordalumni.org/news/magazine/1999/mayjun/farm_report/condi_full_text.html, accessed 3 July 2007.

Stanford University News Service. "Provost Rice at Founders' Day Calls for Strength in Adversity," 8 March 1994, http://news-service.stanford.edu/pr/94/940308Arc4392 .html, accessed 27 June 2007.

Stein, Ben. "Prime Stein," *The American Spectator*, Oct. 2000.

Tanber, George J. "Rice Sees Wide World of Sports," ESPN.com, 27 Feb. 2007 http://sports.espn.go.com/espn/blackhistory 2007/news/story?id=2780487, accessed 4 June 2007.

Texas Monthly. "Fantastic Four," Aug. 1999.

Thomas, Evan, John Barry, Richard Wolffe, Martha Brant, Daniel Klaidman, and Nadine Joseph. "The Quiet Power of Condi Rice," *Newsweek*, 16 Dec. 2002.

Thomas, Evan, with Karen Breslau, Ron Nordland, Ron Moreau. "Their Faith and Fears," *Newsweek*, 9 Sept. 2002.

Time. "For National Purposes," 9 May 1932, http://www.time.com/time/printout/0,8816, 743719,00.html, accessed 7 Aug. 2007.

———. "For the Record," 24 Sept. 2001, http://www.time.com/time/magazine/article /0,9171,1000886,00.html?promoid=googlep, accessed 13 Aug. 2007.

Tommasini, Anthony. "Condoleezza Rice on Piano," *New York Times*, 9 April 2006, http://www.nytimes.com/2006/04/09/

arts/music/09tomm.html?ex=1302235200&en=9b7986206bf57c24&ei=5088&partner=rssnyt&emc=rss, accessed 5 June 2007.

Trescott, Jacqueline. "High-Powered Duet for Arts Medalists: Yo-Yo Ma Teams With Condoleezza Rice," *Washington Post,* 23 April 2002.

Ullmann, Walter. Book review, *Russian Review,* Vol. 45, No. 3, July 1986.

U.S. Department of Justice. "Troy A. Eid, United States Attorney," http://www .usdoj.gov/usao/co/eid_bio_new.pdf, accessed 18 June 2007.

U.S. Department of State. "Condoleezza Rice Sworn in as 66th U.S. Secretary of State," 28 Jan. 2005, http://usinfo.state.gov/special/Archive/2005/Jan/28-638748.html, accessed 4 June 2007.

———. "President Thanks Secretary of State Rice at Swearing-in Ceremony," 28 Jan. 2005, http://www.whitehouse.gov/news/releases/2005/01/20050128-2.html, accessed 4 June 2007.

———. "Secretary Rice Plays Brahms at ASEAN Gala Dinner," 27 July 2006, http://www.state.gov/r/pa/ei/pix/2006/69691.htm, accessed 4 June 2007.

———. "Terrorist Attacks have Transformed Nation, Rice says," Office of International Information Programs, 14 Sept. 2001, http://www.globalsecurity.org/military /library/news/2001/09/mil-010914-usia04.htm, accessed 7 Aug. 2007.

———. "Travels with the Secretary," http://www.state.gov/secretary/trvl/, accessed 13 June 2007.

U.S. News and World Report. "America's Best Leaders: Condoleezza Rice," 31 Oct. 2005, http://www.usnews.com/usnews/news/articles/051031/31rice.htm, accessed 5 June 2007.

Van Natta, Don and Lizette Alvarez, "A Hijacked Boeing 757 Slams into the Pentagon, Halting the Government," *New York Times,* 12 Sept. 2001, A5.

Washington, George. Letter to Henry Knox, 8 March 1787. *George Washington: A Collection,* William B. Allen, ed. Indianapolis: Liberty Fund, 1988.

Washington National Cathedral, "Scientists and Technicians Window," http://www .cathedral.org/cathedral/discover/spacewindow.shtml, accessed 7 Aug. 2007.

Washington Post, "Sense and Security: Condoleezza Rice's Journey from an All-Black World to the White House," 31 March 2004.

Watson, Lloyd. "Stanford Professor's Busy Off-Campus Schedule," *San Francisco Chronicle,* 9 Oct. 1991.

Weiss, LeAnn. *Heartlifters for Mom.* West Monroe, La.: Howard Publishing, 2000.

Wells, Jennifer. "World Awaits Rice's Definition of Danger," *Toronto Star,* 4 April 2004.

Wilkerson, Isabel. "The Most Powerful Woman in the World," *Essence,* Feb. 2002, http://findarticles.com/p/articles/mi_m1264/is_10_32/ai_94044128/pg_2, accessed 3 Aug. 2007.

Will, George. "Why Condoleezza Rice Is a Republican, and Why More African Americans Will Be," *Pittsburgh Post-Gazette,* 7 Aug. 2000.

Williams, Daniel. "Egypt Frees an Aspiring Candidate," *Washington Post,* 13 March 2005.

Winter, Laura J., and Tracy Connor, "I Was Just Looking for a Warm Meal Somewhere," *New York Daily News,* 28 Nov. 2003.

WNYC. "Mad About Music: Condoleezza Rice," 2 Jan. 2005, http://www.wnyc.org /shows/mam/episodes/2005/01/02, accessed 3 July 2007.

Woodward, Bob. *State of Denial: Bush at War, Part III.* New York: Simon and Schuster, 2006.

Workman, Bill. "Female Faculty Say Stanford Has Promotion Bias," *San Francisco Chronicle,* 14 May 1999.

———. "Housing Shortage Protested at Stanford," *San Francisco Chronicle,* 28 May 1998.

———. "New Stanford Report on Minority Recruiting," *San Francisco Chronicle,* 28 Oct. 1994.

———. "Stanford Chief Defends Hiring, Tenure Policy," *San Francisco Chronicle,* 5 Feb. 1999.

———. "Stanford Chief Hits Wall Street Journal Piece," *San Francisco Chronicle,* 11 Oct. 1995.

———. "Stanford Cuts Budget Third Straight Year," *San Francisco Chronicle,* 11 Nov. 1993.

———. "Stanford Goes Off Campus For Legal Aid," *San Francisco Chronicle,* 4 May 1994.

———. "Stanford Students Rally, Begin Hunger Strike," *San Francisco Chronicle,* 6 May 1994.

———. "Women Acting to Advance Their Cause at Stanford," *San Francisco Chronicle,* 14 May 1998.

Wright, Robin. "Top Focus on 9/11 Wasn't on Terrorism," *Washington Post,* 1 April 2004.

Yardley, Jim. "Eyes of Texas Are on a Ranch Bush Wants," *New York Times,* 8 Aug. 1999.

Zelikow, Philip, and Condoleezza Rice, *Germany Unified and Europe Transformed: A Study in Statecraft.* Cambridge, Mass.: Harvard University Press, 2002.

Notes

Prologue

1. Dale Russakoff, "Lessons of Might and Right," *Washington Post*, September 9, 2001, W23.
2. Ibid.
3. LeAnn Weiss, *Heartlifters for Mom* (West Monroe, LA: Howard Publishing, 2000), 29.
4. Ann Reilly Dowd, "Is There Anything This Woman Can't Do?" *George*, June 2000, 102.
5. Condoleezza Rice, interview by Elizabeth Farnsworth, "What's Next?" *PBS Online Newshour*, PBS, July 4, 1996, http://www.pbs.org/newshour/bb/europe/july96/runoff_results3_7-4.html (accessed October 25, 2007).
6. Ibid.
7. Antonia Felix, *Condi: The Condoleezza Rice Story* (New York: Newmarket Press, 2005), 144–45.
8. Dowd, "Is There Anything?"
9. James Robinson, "Velvet-Glove Forcefulness: Six years of provostial challenges and achievements" *Stanford Report*, June 9, 1999, http://news-service.stanford.edu/news/1999/june9/rice-69.html (accessed October 25, 2007).

Chapter 1

1. Condoleezza Rice, "Remarks by National Security Advisor Dr. Condoleezza Rice at the National Prayer Breakfast" (National Prayer Breakfast, Washington, DC, February 6, 2003) http://www.luthersem.edu/rnysse/OT2116-Prophets/Rice-NationalPrayerBreakfast.htm (accessed October 25, 2007).
2. George W. Bush, interview by Scott Pelley, "The President's Story," *60*

Minutes II, CBS, September 10, 2003, http://www.cbsnews.com/stories/2002/09/11/60II/main521718.shtml (accessed October 25, 2007).

3. Leslie Montgomery, *The Faith of Condoleezza Rice* (Wheaton, IL: Crossway Books, 2007), 172.
4. National Commission on Terrorist Attacks upon the United States, *9/11 Commission Report* (New York: W. W. Norton and Company, 2004).
5. Ibid.
6. Condoleezza Rice, interview by Oprah Winfrey, "Oprah Talks to Condoleezza Rice," *O: The Oprah Magazine*, February 2002.
7. Bill Sammon, *Fighting Back: The War on Terrorism—from Inside the Bush White House* (Washington, DC: Regnery Publishing, 2002), 42.
8. Condoleezza Rice, interview by Oprah Winfrey, "Oprah Talks to Condoleezza Rice."
9. Bush, interview by Scott Pelley, "The President's Story."
10. Bernard Ryan, *Condoleezza Rice: Secretary of State* (New York: Ferguson/Facts on File, 2004), 67-68.
11. Ibid., 68.
12. Condoleezza Rice, interview by Oprah Winfrey, "Oprah Talks to Condoleezza Rice."
13. Bush, interview by Scott Pelley, "The President's Story."
14. Sammon, *Fighting Back*, 93.
15. Condoleezza Rice, interview by Oprah Winfrey, "Oprah Talks to Condoleezza Rice."
16. George W. Bush, interview by Scott Pelley, "The President's Story."
17. Condoleezza Rice, interview by Oprah Winfrey, "Oprah Talks to Condoleezza Rice."
18. Sammon, *Fighting Back*, 101.
19. Bush, interview by Scott Pelley, "The President's Story."
20. Der Spiegel, *Inside 9-11: What Really Happened* (New York: St. Martin's Press, 2002).
21. National Commission on Terrorist Attacks upon the United States, *9/11 Commission Report*, 16.
22. Vinny Del Guidice, "Attack on the Pentagon, September 11, 2001," *Arlington Fire Journal*, 18 March 2005, http://arlingtonfirejournal.blogspot.com/2005/03/attack-on-pentagon-sept-11-2001.html (accessed October 25, 2007).
23. David Maraniss, "September 11, 2001," *Washington Post*, September 16, 2001, A01.
24. Donald Rumsfeld, "A Force for Good," *Wall Street Journal*, September 11, 2006, A14.
25. Del Guidice, "Attack on the Pentagon."
26. Rumsfeld, "A Force for Good," A14.

27. Don Van Natta and Lizzette Alvarez, "A Hijacked Boeing 757 Slams into the Pentagon, Halting the Government," *New York Times*, September 12, 2001, A5.
28. Sammon, *Fighting Back*, 104.
29. Ibid., 106.
30. Karen Hughes, *Ten Minutes from Normal* (New York: Viking Penguin, 2004), 240.
31. CNN, "Chronology of Terror," 12 September 2001, http://edition.cnn.com/2001/US/09/11/chronology.attack/ (accessed October 25, 2007).
32. Christin Ditchfield, *Condoleezza Rice: National Security Advisor* (New York: Franklin Watts/Scholastic, 2003), 85.
33. Bush, interview by Scott Pelley, "The President's Story."
34. CNN, "Chronology of Terror."
35. National Commission on Terrorist Attacks Upon the United States, *9/11 Commission Report*, 14.
36. Bush, interview by Scott Pelley, "The President's Story."
37. Sammon, *Fighting Back*, 106–7.
38. Hughes, *Ten Minutes from Normal*, 243–44.

Chapter 2

1. Isabel Wilkerson, "The Most Powerful Woman in the World," *Essence*, February 2002.
2. Leslie Montgomery, *The Faith of Condoleezza Rice* (Wheaton, IL: Crossway Books, 2007), 63.
3. Evan Thomas, John Barry, Richard Wolffe, Martha Brant, Daniel Klaidman, and Nadine Joseph, "The Quiet Power of Condi Rice," *Newsweek*, December 16, 2002, 24.
4. U.S. Department of State, "Terrorist Attacks Have Transformed Nation, Rice says," news release, September 14, 2001, http://usinfo.state.gov/is/Archive_Index/NSCs_Rice_on_Terrorist_Attacks.html (accessed October 25, 2007).
5. "Sense and Security: Condoleezza Rice's Journey from an All-Black World to the White House," *Washington Post*, March 31, 2004, C16.
6. Royal Household at Buckingham Palace, "Mailbox, November 2003," *Royal Insight*, http://www.royal.gov.uk/output/Page2682.asp (accessed October 25, 2007).
7. Office of the Press Secretary, "President Proclaims National Day of Prayer and Remembrance for the Victims of the Terrorist Attacks on September 11, 2001," news release, September 13, 2001, http://www.whitehouse.gov/news/releases/2001/09/20010913-7.html (accessed October 25, 2007).
8. "For National Purposes," *Time*, May 9, 1932,

http://www.time.com/time/printout/0,8816,743719,00.html (accessed October 25, 2007).
9. George W. Bush, interview by Scott Pelley, "The President's Story," *60 Minutes II*, CBS, September 10, 2003, http://www.cbsnews.com/stories/2002/09/11/60II/main521718.shtml (accessed October 25, 2007).
10. Karen Hughes, *Ten Minutes from Normal* (New York: Viking Penguin, 2004), 251.
11. Bill Sammon, *Fighting Back: The War on Terrorism—from Inside the Bush White House* (Washington, DC: Regnery Publishing, 2002), 167.
12. Hughes, *Ten Minutes from Normal*, 252.
13. Condoleezza Rice, interview by Scott Pelley, "The Days After," *60 Minutes II*, CBS, September 10, 2003, http://www.cbsnews.com/stories/2002/09/11/60II/main521684.shtml (accessed October 25, 2007).
14. Wilkerson, "The Most Powerful Woman in the World."
15. Condoleezza Rice, "Remarks to Halifax International Airport Officials and Staff" (keynote address, Halifax International Airport, Halifax, NS, September 11, 2006) http://www.state.gov/secretary/rm/2006/72041.htm (accessed October 25, 2007).

Chapter 3

1. Condoleezza Rice, "Remarks at African American History Month Celebration" (keynote address, Dean Acheson Auditorium, Washington, DC, February 18, 2005) http://www.state.gov/secretary/rm/2005/42488.htm (accessed October 25, 2007).
2. Leslie Montgomery, *The Faith of Condoleezza Rice* (Wheaton, IL: Crossway, 2007), 118; and Leslie Montgomery, *Were It Not for Grace: Stories from Women After God's Own Heart* (Nashville: Broadman and Holman, 2005), 10.
3. Condoleezza Rice, "Transform America, One by One," *Birmingham News*, May 22, 1994, 1.
4. Rice, "African American History Month Celebration."
5. Ibid.
6. Condoleezza Rice, "America's Unique Opportunity," PBS Online NewsHour, 1 August 2000, http://www.pbs.org/newshour/election2000/gopconvention/condoleezza_rice.html (accessed October 25, 2007).
7. Ibid.
8. Rice, "African American History Month Celebration."
9. Antonia Felix, *Condi: The Condoleezza Rice Story* (New York: Newmarket Press, 2005), 24.
10. Ibid., 23–24.
11. Marcus Mabry, *Twice as Good: Condoleezza Rice and Her Path to Power* (New York: Rodale Books, 2007), 18–19.

12. Felix, *Condi*, 24.
13. Mabry, *Twice as Good*, 19.
14. Ibid., 19–20.
15. Felix, *Condi*, 33.
16. Ibid.
17. Rice, "America's Unique Opportunity."
18. Montgomery, *Faith of Condoleezza Rice*, 30.
19. Mabry, *Twice as Good*, 21.
20. Felix, *Condi*, 28.
21. National Park Service. "Building a University," American Visionaries: Booker T. Washington, http://www.nps.gov/history/museum/exhibits/tuskegee/btwuniv.htm (accessed October 25, 2007).
22. Booker T. Washington, "An Address at the Metropolitan A.M.E. Church," 22 May 1900, *The Booker T. Washington Papers*, ed. Louis R. Harlan, Raymond W. Smock, Barbara S. Kraft (Champaigne, IL: Univ. of Illinois Press, 1976), 533.
23. John Cook, *The Book of Positive Quotations* (Minneapolis: Fairview Press, 1997), 445.
24. William Addams Reitwiesner, "The Ancestors of Condoleezza Rice" (William Addams Reitwiesner Genealogical Services, U.S. Decennial Census records), http://www.wargs.com/political/rice.html (accessed October 25, 2007).
25. Rice, "Transform America," 1.
26. Mabry, *Twice as Good*, 21.
27. Ibid., 22.
28. Dale Russakoff, "Lessons of Might and Right," *Washington Post*, September 9, 2001, W23.
29. Condoleezza Rice, "Condoleezza Rice on the American Dream," *Forbes*, March 29, 2007, http://www.forbes.com/2007/03/29/condoleezza-rice-dream-oped-cx_bw_dream0307_0329rice.html (accessed October 25, 2007).
30. Russakoff, "Lessons of Might."
31. Ibid.
32. Julia Reed, "The President's Prodigy," *Vogue*, October 2001, 399.
33. Mabry, *Twice as Good*, 22.
34. Nicholas Kralev, "Political Punch in a Package of Charm," *Financial Times*, February 26, 2000.
35. Mabry, *Twice as Good*, 22.
36. Russakoff, "Lessons of Might."
37. Ibid.
38. Ibid.
39. Reed, "The President's Prodigy."
40. Montgomery, *Faith of Condoleezza Rice*, 31.

41. Mawbry, *Twice as Good*, 22–23.
42. Mabry, *Twice as Good*, 23.
43. Ibid.
44. Rice, "Transform America," 1.
45. Viktor Frankl, *Man's Search for Meaning: An Introduction to Logotherapy* (Boston: Beacon Press, 1992), 110.
46. Ibid., 75.
47. Rice, "African American History Month Celebration."

Chapter 4

1. Christin Ditchfield, *Condoleezza Rice: National Security Advisor* (New York: Franklin Watts/ Scholastic, 2003), 9.
2. Condoleezza Rice, "Remarks at the Southern Baptist Convention Annual Meeting" (keynote address, Greensboro Coliseum, Greensboro, NC, June 14, 2006) http://www.state.gov/secretary/rm/2006/67896.htm (accessed October 25, 2007).
3. Marla Lehner, "Condi Rice: From Intern to Secretary of State," *People*, January 27, 2005, http://www.people.com/people/article/0,26334,1021460, 00.html (accessed October 25, 2007).
4. Marcus Mabry, *Twice as Good: Condoleezza Rice and Her Path to Power* (New York: Rodale Books, 2007), 24.
5. Tom Gordon and Mary Orndorff, "Condoleezza Rice: Defying the Stereotypes," *Birmingham News*, January 22, 2001, 01-A
6. Wil Haywood, "'Honored to Have the Chance,' To Her Parents, Failure in Life was Never an Option for 'Condi' Rice," *Boston Globe*, December 21, 2000.
7. LeAnn Weiss, *Heartlifters for Mom* (West Monroe, LA: Howard Publishing, 2000), 1.
8. Ditchfield, *Condoleezza Rice*, 15.
9. Rice, "Remarks at the Southern Baptist Convention."
10. Kevin Chappell, "Ebony Interview with Secretary of State Condoleezza Rice: The Country's Top Diplomat Talks About Race, the President, and Embracing Her Blackness," *Ebony*, November 2005, http://findarticles.com/p/articles/mi_m1077/is_1_61/ai_n15770854 (accessed October 25, 2007).
11. Martha Brant, Evan Thomas, Christian Caryl, and Roy Gutman, "A Steely Southerner," *Newsweek*, August 6, 2001, 28.
12. Julia Reed, "The President's Prodigy," *Vogue*, October 2001.
13. Henry David Thoreau, *Walden* (New York: Houghton, Mifflin and Company, 1897), 142. [[Does pg number reflect 1897 edition?]]
14. Dale Russakoff, "Lessons of Might and Right," *Washington Post*, September 9, 2001, W23.

15. Anthony Tommasini, "Condoleezza Rice on Piano," *New York Times*, April 9, 2006, http://www.nytimes.com/2006/04/09/arts/music/09tomm.html?ex=1302235200&en=9b7986206bf57c24&ei=5088&partner=rssnyt&emc=rss (accessed October 25, 2007).
16. Haywood, "Honored to Have the Chance."
17. Tommasini, "Condoleezza Rice on Piano."
18. Russakoff, "Lessons of Might."
19. Antonia Felix, *Condi: The Condoleezza Rice Story* (New York: Newmarket Press, 2005), 37.
20. Phil McCombs, "Secret Weapon at the NSC; Condoleezza Rice, Breaking Barriers on Bush's Team," *Washington Post*, March 17, 1989.
21. Felix, *Condi*, 39.
22. Ann Reilly Dowd, "What Makes Condi Run," *AARP The Magazine*, September/October 2005.
23. Reed, "The President's Prodigy," 399.
24. Sheryl Henderson Blunt, "The Privilege of Struggle: How Rice understands suffering and prayer," *Christianity Today*, September 1, 2003, http://www.christianitytoday.com/ct/article_print.html?id=10883 (accessed October 25, 2007).
25. Kevin Leman, *The Birth Order Book* (Grand Rapids, MI: Fleming H. Revell, 1998), 130.
26. Ibid., 135.
27. Ibid.
28. Ibid., 130, 135.
29. Condoleezza Rice, interview by Gilbert Kaplan, *Mad About Music: Condoleezza Rice*, WNYC, January 2, 2005, http://www.wnyc.org/shows/mam/episodes/2005/01/02 (accessed October 25, 2007).
30. Ibid.
31. Tommasini, "Condoleezza Rice on Piano."
32. Condoleezza Rice, "The Privilege of Struggle" (lecture, Menlo Presbyterian Church, Menlo Park, CA, 1993).
33. Mike Knepler, "Aunt G.'s Favorite Niece: Condoleezza Rice," *The Virginian-Pilot* (Norfolk, VA), March 6, 2002.
34. Mike Knepler, "Condoleezza Rice and Aunt G: National Security Adviser Enjoys Family Time with Norfolk Aunt," *The Virginian-Pilot* (Norfolk, VA), March 6, 2002.
35. Sheryl Henderson Blunt, "The Unflappable Condi Rice: Why the world's most powerful woman asks God for help," *Christianity Today*, August 22, 2003, http://www.ctlibrary.com/ct/2003/september/1.42.html (accessed October 25, 2007).
36. Knepler, "Condoleezza Rice and Aunt G."

37. Nicholas Lemann, "Without a Doubt: Has Condoleezza Rice Changed George W. Bush, or Has He Changed Her?" *The New Yorker*, October 14, 2002, 164.
38. Rice, interview by Gilbert Kaplan, *Mad About Music*.
39. Ibid.
40. Blunt, "The Unflappable Condi Rice."
41. Evan Thomas, John Barry, Richard Wolffe, Martha Brant, Daniel Klaidman, and Nadine Joseph, "The Quiet Power of Condi Rice," *Newsweek*, December 16, 2002.
42. Blunt, "The Unflappable Condi Rice."
43. Mabry, *Twice as Good*, 105.
44. Helen Bee, *The Developing Child* (New York: Harper & Row, 1981), 375.
45. Meg Meeker, *Strong Fathers, Strong Daughters* (Washington, DC: Regnery Publishing, 2006).
46. Condoleezza Rice, interview by Oprah Winfrey, "Secrets of Women Who Rule," *The Oprah Winfrey Show*, NBC, October 2003.
47. Condoleezza Rice, interview by Oprah Winfrey, "Oprah Talks to Condoleezza Rice," *O: The Oprah Magazine*, February 2002.
48. Russakoff, "Lessons of Might."
49. Isabel Wilkerson, "The Most Powerful Woman in the World," *Essence*, February 2002.
50. George J. Tanber, "Rice Sees Wide World of Sports," *ESPN.com*, February 27, 2007, http://sports.espn.go.com/espn/blackhistory2007/news/story?id=2780487 (accessed October 25, 2007).
51. Ibid; and Skip Wood, "NFL Commissioner Tagliabue to Retire in July," *USA Today*, 20 March 2006, http://www.usatoday.com/sports/football/nfl/2006-03-20-tagliabue-retires_x.htm (accessed October 25, 2007).
52. Dale Russakoff, "How Football Helped Shape Condoleezza the Strategist," *The Standard*, February 7, 2005 http://www.eastandard.net/archives/cl/hm_news/news.php?articleid=12571&date=7/2/2005 (accessed October 25, 2007).
53. Ibid.
54. Ibid.
55. Leslie Montgomery, *The Faith of Condoleezza Rice* (New York: Newmarket Press, 2007), 44.
56. Condoleezza Rice, "Walking in Faith: Rice Finds Strength in Religion," *Washington Times*, August 27, 2002, A02.
57. Blunt, "The Privilege of Struggle."
58. Ditchfield, *Condoleezza Rice*, 9.

Chapter 5

1. Condoleezza Rice, "Dr. Rice Speaks at Vanderbilt" (Commencement address,

Vanderbilt University, Nashville, TN, May 13, 2004) http://www.whitehouse.gov/news/releases/2004/05/20040517.html (accessed October 25, 2007).

2. "Academic Style: Stanford's New Provost Brings a Different Perspective to Campus," *Chicago Tribune*, August 15, 1993.
3. Rice, "Dr. Rice Speaks at Vanderbilt."
4. Jessica McElrath, "Creation of the Jim Crow South," *About.com*, http://afroamhistory.about.com/od/jimcrowlaw1/a/creationjimcrow.htm (accessed October 25, 2007); Interpretive Staff. "'Jim Crow' Laws," Martin Luther King, Jr., National Historic Site, January 5, 1998, http://www.nps.gov/malu/documents/jim_crow_laws.htm (accessed October 25, 2007).
5. Rice, "Dr. Rice Speaks at Vanderbilt."
6. Condoleezza Rice, "Walking in Faith: Rice Finds Strength in Religion," *Washington Times*, August 27, 2002, A02.
7. Elaine Sciolino, "Compulsion to Achieve: Condoleezza Rice," *New York Times*, December 18, 2000.
8. Warren Merrill, "John W. Rice," *Palo Alto Weekly*, May 6, 1998, http://www.paloaltoonline.com/weekly/morgue/cover/1998_May_6.COVER6.html (accessed October 25, 2007).
9. Ibid.
10. Peter Stothard, "What Condi Did First," *Times Online* (London), April 1, 2006, http://women.timesonline.co.uk/tol/life_and_style/women/celebrity/article699653.ece (accessed October 25, 2007).
11. Dale Russakoff, "Lessons of Might and Right," *Washington Post*, September 9, 2001, W23.
12. Ibid.
13. Kevin Chappell, "Ebony Interview with Secretary of State Condoleezza Rice: The Country's Top Diplomat Talks About Race, the President, and Embracing Her Blackness," Ebony, November 2005, http://findarticles.com/p/articles/mi_m1077/is_1_61/ai_n15770854 (accessed October 25, 2007).
14. "Connor Behind Bill Banning 'Rides,'" *Birmingham Post-Herald*, August 25, 1961.
15. Stanford University News Service, "Soviets Face Hard Choices in Arms Control, Rice Says," *Stanford Report*, December 2, 1983.
16. Julia Reed, "The President's Prodigy," *Vogue*, October 2001.
17. Marcus Mabry, *Twice as Good: Condoleezza Rice and Her Path to Power* (New York: Rodale Books, 2007), 48.
18. Reed, "The President's Prodigy."
19. Ibid.
20. Russakoff, "Lessons of Might."
21. Ibid.

22. Rice, "Dr. Rice Speaks at Vanderbilt."
23. "Pastor Says—All Was Calm—Then Chaos," *Birmingham Post-Herald*, September 16, 1963.
24. Ibid.
25. Lillian Foscue, "Dead and Injured Taken to Hospital," *Birmingham Post-Herald*, September 16, 1963.
26. Rice, "Dr. Rice Speaks at Vanderbilt."
27. Condoleezza Rice, "Acknowledge That You Have an Obligation to Search for the Truth" (Commencement address, Stanford University, Stanford, CA, June 16, 2002 May 13, 2004) http://news-service.stanford.edu/news/2002/june19/comm_ricetext-619.html (accessed October 25, 2007).
28. Condoleezza Rice, interview by Jon Sopel, *The Politics Show*, BBC1, October 22, 2005, http://www.state.gov/secretary/rm/2005/55425.htm (accessed October 25, 2007).
29. Condoleezza Rice, "Remarks with United Kingdom Foreign Secretary Jack Straw" (address, Gallery of Distinguished Citizens Induction Ceremony, Birmingham, AL, October 22, 2005), http://www.state.gov/secretary/rm/2005/55427.htm (accessed October 25, 2007).
30. Ibid.
31. CITATION MISSING
32. Russakoff, "Lessons of Might."
33. Ibid.
34. Condoleezza Rice, interview by Steve Weisman, *New York Times*, October 20, 2005, http://www.state.gov/secretary/rm/2005/55437.htm (accessed October 25, 2007).
35. Condoleezza Rice, "Joint Press Availability with the Foreign Secretary of the United Kingdom Jack Straw" (address, Oak Mountain Hurrican Katrina Relief Site, Birmingham, AL, October 23, 2005), http://www.state.gov/secretary/rm/2005/55435.htm (accessed October 25, 2007).
36. Chappell, "Ebony Interview with Condoleezza Rice."
37. U.S. Conference of Mayors, "Proclamation Announcing February 28, 2001 as 'Dr. Dorothy Irene Height Day,'" http://www.usmayors.org/uscm/us_mayor_newspaper/documents/04_02_01/HeightResolution.pdf (accessed October 25, 2007).
38. National Social Work Pioneers, "Dorothy Height," National Association of Social Workers Foundation, http://www.naswfoundation.org/pioneers/h/height.htm (accessed October 25, 2007).
39. George W. Bush, "Remarks on Presenting the Congressional Gold Medal to Dorothy Height" (address, Capitol Rotunda, Washington, DC, March, 24 2004), http://www.presidency.ucsb.edu/ws/print.php?pid=72586 (accessed October 25, 2007).

40. Northrop Grumman, "Dorothy Height Shares History at Northrop Grumman," http://www.northropgrumman.com/diversity/022005_height.html (accessed August 16, 2007; site now discontinued).
41. Condoleezza Rice, "Remarks at Naturalization Ceremony" (address, Benjamin Franklin Room, Washington, DC, April 23, 2007), http://www.state.gov/secretary/rm/2007/apr/83402.htm (accessed October 25, 2007).
42. Condoleezza Rice, "Transform America, One by One," *Birmingham News*, May 22, 1994, 1.
43. Stanford University News Service, news release, December 2, 1983.
44. Condoleezza Rice, "Remarks at the Southern Baptist Convention Annual Meeting" (keynote address, Greensboro Coliseum, Greensboro, NC, June 14, 2006) http://www.state.gov/secretary/rm/2006/67896.htm (accessed October 25, 2007).

Chapter 6

1. Author, "The Top of Her Game," *Essence Magazine*, February 2002, #.
2. Wil Haywood, "'Honored to Have the Chance,' To Her Parents, Failure in Life was Never an Option for 'Condi' Rice," *Boston Globe*, December 21, 2000.
3. Marcus Mabry, *Twice as Good: Condoleezza Rice and Her Path to Power* (New York: Rodale Books, 2007), 70.
4. Ibid.
5. Warren Merrill, "John W. Rice," *Palo Alto Weekly*, May 6, 1998, http://www.paloaltoonline.com/weekly/morgue/cover/1998_May_6.COVER6.html (accessed October 25, 2007).
6. Condoleezza Rice, "The Privilege of Struggle" (lecture, Menlo Presbyterian Church, Menlo Park, CA, 1993).
7. Antonia Felix, *Condi: The Condoleezza Rice Story* (New York: Newmarket Press, 2005), 64.
8. Julia Reed, "The President's Prodigy," *Vogue*, October 2001, 399.
9. Felix, *Condi*, 66-67.
10. Ibid., 67-68
11. Condoleezza Rice, interview by Gilbert Kaplan, *Mad About Music: Condoleezza Rice*, WNYC, January 2, 2005, http://www.wnyc.org/shows/mam/episodes/2005/01/02 (accessed October 25, 2007).
12. "From 'Not College Material' to Stanford's No. 2 Job," Campus Journal, *New York Times*, sec. B, June 23, 1993.
13. Reed, "The President's Prodigy," 399.
14. Ibid.
15. Ibid.

16. Condoleezza Rice, "Acknowledge That You Have an Obligation to Search for the Truth" (Commencement address, Stanford University, Stanford, CA, June 16, 2002 May 13, 2004) http://news-service.stanford.edu/news/2002/june19/comm_ricetext-619.html (accessed October 25, 2007).
17. Sheryl Henderson Blunt, "The Unflappable Condi Rice: Why the world's most powerful woman asks God for help," *Christianity Today*, August 22, 2003, http://www.ctlibrary.com/ct/2003/september/1.42.html (accessed October 25, 2007).
18. Leslie Montgomery, *The Faith of Condoleezza Rice* (Wheaton, IL: Crossway Books, 2007), 92.
19. Last name, "The Top of Her Game."
20. Ibid.
21. Rice, *Mad About Music.*
22. Ibid.
23. Condoleezza Rice, interview by Oprah Winfrey, "Oprah Talks to Condoleezza Rice," *O: The Oprah Magazine*, February 2002.
24. Mabry, *Twice as Good*, 75.
25. Maria L. La Ganga, "In Race for White House, the 'Cult of Condi' Plays Growing Role," *Los Angeles Times*, May 28, 2000, 3.
26. Blunt, "The Unflappable Condi Rice."
27. Rice, *Mad About Music.*
28. Ibid.

Chapter 7

1. Condoleeza Rice, "Commencement Address at Boston College" Boston, MA, May 22, 2006.
2. Phil McCombs, "Secret Weapon at the NSC; Condoleezza Rice, Breaking Barriers on Bush's Team," *Washington Post*, March 17, 1989, D1.
3. Ibid.
4. Condoleezza Rice, interview by Oprah Winfrey, "Oprah Talks to Condoleezza Rice," *O: The Oprah Magazine*, February 2002.
5. Mark L. von Hagen, "From 'Splendid Isolation' to 'Fruitful Cooperation': The Harriman Institute in the Post-Soviet Era," *Columbia Magazine*, Summer 1996.
6. University of Notre Dame, http://newsinfo.nd.edu/content.cfm?topicId=32 (accessed October 25, 2007).
7. Paul V. Niemeyer, "Obituary for Gerhart Niemeyer," *Philadelphia Society*, 1997, http://www.phillysoc.org/gerhart.htm (accessed October 25, 2007); Antonia Felix, *Condi: The Condoleezza Rice Story* (New York: Newmarket Press, 2005), 90-91.
8. Felix, *Condi*, 92.

9. Ibid., 93.
10. The Review of Politics, "History," The University of Notre Dame, http://www.nd.edu/~rop/ (accessed October 25, 2007).
11. A. J. H. Murray, "The Moral Politics of Hans Morgenthau," *The Review of Politics*, University of Notre Dame, 1996, 87-88.
12. Condoleezza Rice, "Remarks at the Southern Baptist Convention Annual Meeting" (keynote address, Greensboro Coliseum, Greensboro, NC, June 14, 2006) http://www.state.gov/secretary/rm/2006/67896.htm (accessed October 25, 2007).
13. Jay Nordlinger, "Star in Waiting," *National Review*, August 30, 1999, http://www.nationalreview.com/flashback/nordlinger200411170605.asp (October 25, 2007).
14. Marcus Mabry, *Twice as Good: Condoleezza Rice and Her Path to Power* (New York: Rodale Books, 2007), 87-88.
15. Nicholas Lemann, "Without a Doubt: Has Condoleezza Rice Changed George W. Bush, or Has He Changed Her?" *The New Yorker*, October 14, 2002, 164.
16. Dale Russakoff, "How Football Helped Shape Condoleezza the Strategist," *The Standard*, February 7, 2005, http://www.eastandard.net/archives/cl/hm_news/news.php?articleid=12571&date (accessed October 25, 2007).
17. Leslie Montgomery, *The Faith of Condoleezza Rice* (Wheaton, IL: Crossway Books, 2007), 195.
18. "Former Bronco Starts Ministry in Pueblo," KRDO News 13, December 28, 2004, http://www.krdotv.com/displaystory.asp?id=8725 (accessed June 7, 2006, site now discontinued).
19. Michael Dobbs, "Albright, Rice Share 'Korbellian' Outlook," *Houston Chronicle*, January 7, 2001, A-6.
20. Ibid.
21. Felix, *Condi*, 105.
22. McCombs, "Secret Weapon at the NSC."
23. Michael Dobbs, "Josef Korbel's Enduring Foreign Policy Legacy: Professor Mentored Daughter Albright and Student Rice," *Washington Post*, December 28, 2000.
24. Ann Blackman, *Seasons of a Life: A Biography of Madeleine Korbel Albright* (New York: Scribner, 1998), 16.
25. Mabry, *Twice as Good*, 82.
26. Michael Dobbs, "Madeline Albright: A Twentieth Century Odyssey" (New York: Henry Holt and Company, 2000), 220.
27. Dale Russakoff, "Lessons of Might and Right," *Washington Post*, September 9, 2001, W23.

28. Julia Reed, "The President's Prodigy," *Vogue*, October 2001.
29. Wil Haywood, "'Honored to Have the Chance,' To Her Parents, Failure in Life was Never an Option for 'Condi' Rice," *Boston Globe*, December 21, 2000.
30. McCombs, "Secret Weapon at the NSC."
31. Ann Reilly Dowd, "Is There Anything This Woman Can't Do?" *George*, June 2000.
32. Fred Brown and Susan Greene, "Adviser Condi Rice Launched Career in Denver," *Denver Post*, August 2, 2000, A-19.
33. Ibid.
34. Diane Carman, "Rice Has Gone Far Since DU," *Denver Post*, April 9, 2004, B-03.
35. Felix, *Condi*, 107.
36. McCombs, "Secret Weapon at the NSC."
37. Felix, *Condi*, 95.
38. Condoleezza Rice, *The Soviet Union and the Czechoslovak Army, 1948–1983: Uncertain Allegiance* (Princeton, NJ: Princeton University Press, 1984), 218; Christopher Jones, review of *The Soviet Union and the Czechoslovak Army, 1948–1983: Uncertain Allegiance*, by Rice, *Soviet Studies* 38, no. 4 (October 1986): 603.
39. Dowd, "Is There Anything?"
40. Ibid.
41. Ibid.
42. Ibid.
43. Dale R. Herspring, review of *Uncertain Alliance: The Soviet Union and the Czechoslovak Army, 1948–1983*, by Condoleezza Rice, *The American Political Science Review* 79, no. 3 (September 1985): 905.
44. Walter Ullmann, review of *Uncertain Alliance: The Soviet Union and the Czechoslovak Army, 1948–1983*, by Condoleezza Rice, *Russian Review* 45, no. 3 (July 1986): 314.
45. Josef Kalvoda, review of *Uncertain Alliance: The Soviet Union and the Czechoslovak Army, 1948–1983*, by Condoleezza Rice, *The American Historical Review* 90, no. 5 (December 1985): 1236.
46. Condoleezza Rice, letter to the editor, *The American Historical Review* 91, no. 4 (October 1986): 1051.

CHAPTER 8

1. Condoleezza Rice, "Commencement Address at Boston College" Boston, MA, May 22, 2006.
2. Marcus Mabry, *Twice as Good: Condoleezza Rice and Her Path to Power* (New York: Rodale Books, 2007), 94–95.

3. Ibid., 96
4. Condoleezza Rice, "Quotes," Women in Higher Education, http://www.wihe.com/$spindb.query.NEWlistquotes.wihequotes (accessed October 26, 2007).
5. Stanford University News Service, "Dean's Awards for Distinguished Teaching, 1992–93," *Stanford Report*, 1993.
6. Fred Brown and Susan Greene, "Adviser Condi Rice launched Career in Denver," *Denver Post*, August 2, 2000, A-19.
7. Stanford University News Service, "Dean's Awards for Distinguished Teaching."
8. Brown and Greene, "Adviser Condi Rice."
9. Ibid.
10. Christin Ditchfield, *Condoleezza Rice: National Security Advisor* (New York: Franklin Watts/Scholastic, 2003), 89, 91.
11. Mabry, *Twice as Good*, 97.
12. Antonia Felix, *Condi: The Condoleezza Rice Story* (New York: Newmarket Press, 2005), 119.
13. Mabry, *Twice as Good*, 98.
14. Condoleezza Rice, "Walking in Faith: Rice Finds Strength in Religion," *Washington Times*, August 27, 2002, A02.
15. Ibid.
16. Anthony Tommasini, "Condoleezza Rice on Piano," *New York Times*, April 9, 2006, http://www.nytimes.com/2006/04/09/arts/music/09tomm.html?ex=1302235200&en=9b7986206bf57c24&ei=5088&partner=rssnyt&emc=rss (accessed October 25, 2007).
17. Condoleezza Rice, "National Security Advisor tells Americans about God's call," *The Layman*, October 2002, 15.
18. Rice, "Walking in Faith," A02.
19. Ibid.
20. Ibid.
21. Dale Russakoff, "Lessons of Might and Right," *Washington Post*, September 9, 2001, W23.
22. Brown and Greene, "Adviser Condi Rice."
23. Felix, *Condi*, 116–117.
24. Phil McCombs, "Secret Weapon at the NSC; Condoleezza Rice, Breaking Barriers on Bush's Team," *Washington Post*, March 17, 1989, D1.
25. David S. Broder, "The Future Is—Futures?" *Washington Post*, June 20, 1984, A21.
26. Stanford University News Service, news release, June 18, 1984.
27. James Robinson, "Velvet-Glove Forcefulness: Six years of provostial challenges and achievements" *Stanford Report*, June 9, 1999, http://news-service.stanford.edu/news/1999/june9/rice-69.html (accessed October 25, 2007).

28. Condoleezza Rice, "Title," (Class Day speech, Stanford University, Stanford, CA, June 19, 1985). Rice spoke in 1985, 1988, 1993, and 1999.
29. Hoover Institute, "Overview," http://www.hoover.org/about (accessed October 26, 2007).
30. McCombs, "Secret Weapon at the NSC."
31. Ibid.
32. Felix, *Condi*, 123–24.
33. Ditchfield, *Condoleezza Rice*, 42.
34. Eleanor Randolph, "NBC's Coup on Gorbachev Interview Sends Rival Journalists Scrambling; Summit Is Expected to Draw 6,000 to Washington," *Washington Post*, December 1, 1987, A17.
35. McCombs, "Secret Weapon at the NSC."
36. American Academy of Arts and Sciences, *Records of the Academy*, 1986/1987: 6; American Academy of Arts and Sciences, "About the Academy," http://www.amacad.org/about.aspx (accessed October 26, 2007).
37. Kurt Gottfried, Richard L. Garwin, Condoleezza Rice, et. al. "Crisis Stability and Nuclear War," *Bulletin of the American Academy of Arts and Sciences* 40, no. 8 (May 1987): 19.
38. Rice, Stanford's Class Day speech, 1988 http://fsi.stanford.edu/news/1222.
39. McCombs, "Secret Weapon at the NSC."
40. James Mann, *Rise of the Vulcans: The History of Bush's War Cabinet* (New York: Viking, 2004), 149.
41. Keith M. Rockwell, "Gorbachev Reforms Deemed Insufficient to Help Economy," *The Journal of Commerce*, September 14, 1987, 3A.
42. Paul Mann, "Soviet Economic Reform May Force Transformation of Entire Military," *Aviation Week & Space Technology* (May 2, 1988): 2.
43. McCombs, "Secret Weapon at the NSC."
44. Ibid.
45. Ibid.
46. Ibid.
47. Mabry, *Twice as Good*, 108.
48. Condoleezza Rice, "The Privilege of Struggle" (lecture, Menlo Presbyterian Church, Menlo Park, CA, 1993).
49. Leslie Montgomery, *The Faith of Condoleezza Rice* (Wheaton, IL: Crossway Books, 2007), 129.

Chapter 9

1. Phil McCombs, "Secret Weapon at the NSC: Condoleezza Rice, Breaking Barriers on Bush's Team," *Washington Post*, March 17, 1989, D1.

2. Jacob Heilbrunn, "Condoleezza Rice: George W.'s Realist," *World Policy Journal* 16, no. 9 (Winter 1999): 49–55.
3. Romesh Ratnesar, "Condi Rice Can't Lose," *Time*, September 20, 1999, http://www.time.com/time/magazine/article/0,9171,1101990927-31242,00.html (accessed October 26, 2007).
4. Antonia Felix, *Condi: The Condoleezza Rice Story* (New York: Newmarket Press, 2005), 6.
5. Ibid., 137.
6. Nicholas Lemann, "Without a Doubt: Has Condoleezza Rice Changed George W. Bush, or Has He Changed Her?" *The New Yorker*, October 14, 2002, 164.
7. Ratnesar, "Condi Rice Can't Lose."
8. Heilbrunn, "Condoleezza Rice."
9. McCombs, "Secret Weapon at the NSC."
10. Ibid.
11. Felix, *Condi*, 138. In his official statement on March 16, 1989, Scowcroft said, "Condi brings prodigious expertise, both academic and practical, to her position. She has a broad intellectual conception of the problems and realities of the Soviet Union and Eastern Europe." (McCombs, "Secret Weapon at the NSC.")
12. James Mann, *Rise of the Vulcans: The History of Bush's War Cabinet* (New York: Viking, 2004), 172.
13. Christin Ditchfield, *Condoleezza Rice: National Security Advisor* (New York: Franklin Watts/ Scholastic, 2003), 43.
14. McCombs, "Secret Weapon at the NSC."
15. Mann, *Rise of the Vulcans*, 172.
16. Sheryl Henderson Blunt, "The Privilege of Struggle: How Rice understands suffering and prayer," *Christianity Today*, September 1, 2003, http://www.christianitytoday.com/ct/article_print.html?id=10883 (accessed October 25, 2007).
17. Julia Reed, "The President's Prodigy," *Vogue*, October 2001, 403.
18. Laura B. Randolph, "Black Women in the White House," *Ebony*, October 1990, http://findarticles.com/p/articles/mi_m1077/is_n12_v45/ai_8904380 (accessed October 26, 2007).
19. Jessica Lee, "She's Bush's Top Expert on Soviets; Grasp of Issues Impresses Colleagues," *USA Today*, May 30, 1990, 2A.
20. Los Angeles Times photo, "Condoleezza Rice, Soviet and East European," *The Sunday Oregonian*, April 16, 1989, A22.
21. "Political Punch in a Package of Charm," *The Financial Times* (London), February 26, 2000.
22. "Welcome Back, Professor Rice," Stanford REES Newsletter, Spring 1991.

23. Ibid.
24. George Bush, "Remarks to the Polish National Assembly in Warsaw," July 10, 1989, http://bushlibrary.tamu.edu/research/papers/1989/89071002.html (accessed June 6, 2007; site now discontinued).
25. McCombs, "Secret Weapon at NSC."
26. Ibid.
27. Blunt, "Unflappable Condi Rice."
28. Ibid.
29. Felix, *Condi*, 147.
30. Condoleezza Rice, "The White House and the Wall," *Newsweek*, November 15, 1999, 35.
31. Ibid.
32. Ibid.
33. Lee, "Bush's Top Expert on Soviets," 2A.
34. Randolph, "Black Women in the White House."
35. "Political Punch."
36. Ratnesar, "Condi Rice Can't Lose."
37. Randolph, "Black Women in the White House."
38. Ibid.
39. "Summit in Washington: Faces of the Summit: The Supporting Cast," *New York Times*, June 1, 1990, 7.
40. Marilyn Greene, "Summit Specialist Cold-Shouldered in San Francisco," *USA Today*, June 6, 1990, 2A.
41. James Gerstenzang, "Shoving of Bush Staffer Investigated," *Washington Post*, June 7, 1990, C14.
42. Randolph, "Black Women in the White House."
43. Don Oberdorfer, "U.S. Secretly Studied Possibility of Gorbachev Coup, Soviet Collapse," *Washington Post*, January 17, 1993, A42.
44. Condoleezza Rice to Blackwill, memorandum, 12 January 1990, in *Germany Unified and Europe Transformed: A Study in Statecraft*, Philip Zelikow and Condoleezza Rice (Cambridge, MA: Harvard Univ. Press, 2002), 158-60.
45. Felix, *Condi*, 147.
46. Philip Zelikow and Condoleezza Rice, *Germany Unified and Europe Transformed: A Study in Statecraft* (Cambridge, MA: Harvard University Press, 2002), 370.
47. Zelikow and Rice, *Germany Unified and Europe Transformed*, 2.
48. Leslie Montgomery, *The Faith of Condoleezza Rice* (Wheaton, IL: Crossway Books, 2007).
49. Dan Quayle, *Standing Firm* (New York: HarperCollins, 1995), 301.
50. Ann Devroy, "Black Woman Called Favorite to Fill Wilson's Senate Term," *Washington Post*, November 30, 1990, A4.

51. Brooke Lea Foster, "Being Condi," *Washingtonian*, March 2007, 54–59, 153–155.
52. Rice, "The White House and the Wall," *Newsweek*, November 15, 1999, 35.
53. Foster, "Being Condi," 54–59, 153–155.
54. Reed, "The President's Prodigy," 402.
55. "Condoleezza Rice Leads a Solitary Life, But Surprises the World with her Slim Figure and Determination," *Pravda* (Russia), September 28, 2005, http://english.pravda.ru/opinion/columnists/28-09-2005/8976-condoleezza-0 (accessed October 26, 2007).
56. Donald Baer, Michael Barone, Peter Cary, Gary Cohen, Matthew Cooper, Miriam Horn, Thomas Moore, Eva Pomice, "People to Watch," *U.S. News and World Report*, December 25, 1989/January 1, 1990, 83.
57. Ann Reilly Dowd, "Is There Anything This Woman Can't Do?" *George*, June 2000.

Chapter 10

1. Elaine Sciolino, "Compulsion to Achieve" *New York Times*, Dec. 18, 2000.
2. Christin Ditchfield, *Condoleezza Rice: National Security Advisor* (New York: Franklin Watts/Scholastic, 2003), 53.
3. Brooke Lea Foster, "Being Condi," *Washingtonian*, March 2007, 54–59, 153–155.
4. Kathleen O'Toole, "Rice: War Stories No Teaching Tool, but Role Playing Works," *Stanford Report*, October 28, 1998, http://new-service.stanford.edu/news/1998/october28/riceteach1028.html (accessed September 7, 2006; site now discontinued).
5. Ibid.
6. Ibid.
7. "Chevron Proposals at Meeting," *San Francisco Chronicle*, May 8, 1991, Business, C2.
8. "Tankers," *Oil & Gas Journal* 91, no. 35 (August 30, 1993): 28.
9. Linda Wade, *Condoleezza Rice* (Hockessin, DE: Mitchell Lane Publishers, 2005), 31.
10. Lloyd Watson, "Stanford Professor's Busy Off-Campus Schedule," *San Francisco Chronicle*, October 9, 1991, C3.
11. Jet, "Rice Appointed to National Council on the Humanities," *Magazine/Newspaper Name*, April 27, 1992, 34.
12. Wade, *Condoleezza Rice*, 28-29.
13. Vlae Kershner, "Remap Plan Challenges Demos," *San Francisco Chronicle*, October 12, 1991, A1.
14. Watson, "Stanford Professor's Schedule," C3.

15. Michael Getler, "Black Journalists and the New Era," *Washington Post*, August 18, 1991, C2.
16. Condoleezza Rice, "Interview with *Essence Magazine*," May 25, 2006, http://www.state.gov/secretary/rm/2006/71813.htm (accessed October 26, 2007).
17. Ditchfield, *Condoleezza Rice*, 98-99.
18. Condoleezza Rice, "Interview with *Essence Magazine*."
19. Mary Anne Ostrom, "Condoleezza Rice Tours Silicon Valley During a 'Home Visit,'" *San Jose Mercury News*, May 24, 2007, http://www.mercurynews.com/search/ci_5978431?nclick_check=1 (accessed June 27, 2007).
20. Jonathan Curiel, "Rice Still Stretching Her Horizons," *San Francisco Chronicle*, February 9, 1993, B3.
21. Mary McGrory, "Please Pass the Oxygen Masks," *Washington Post*, August 25, 1992, A2.
22. Jerry Roberts, "Best and Worst of the GOP Convention," *San Francisco Chronicle*, 22 August 1992, A4.
23. "Chief Named to Search for Stanford President," *San Francisco Chronicle*, October 29, 1991, A20.
24. Mark Simon, "Soviet Expert Rice Gets Stanford Provost Post," *San Francisco Chronicle*, May 19, 1993, A13.
25. Mark Simon, "An Astute Choice for Stanford," *San Francisco Chronicle*, May 20, 1993, A17.
26. "From 'Not College Material' to Stanford's No. 2 Job," Campus Journal, *New York Times*, sec. B, June 23, 1993.
27. Ibid.
28. Tom Gordon and Mary Orndorff, "Condoleezza Rice: Defying the Stereotypes," *Birmingham News*, January 22, 2001, News.
29. Condoleezza Rice, interview by Robin Wright and Glenn Kesler, *Washington Post*, July 26, 2005, http://www.state.gov/secretary/rm/2005/50414.htm (accessed October 26, 2007).
30. Christopher Parkes, "Leaders for a New Millennium: Package Still Under Wraps—Condoleezza Rice," *Financial Times* (London), December 28, 1995, 8.
31. Bill Workman, "Stanford Cuts Budget Third Straight Year," *San Francisco Chronicle*, November 11, 1993, C3; Bill Workman, "Stanford Chief Tries to Soothe Faculty on Cuts," San Francisco Chronicle, November 12, 1993, D3.
32. James Robinson, "Velvet-Glove Forcefulness: Six years of provostial challenges and achievements," *Stanford Report*, June 9, 1999, http://news-service.stanford.edu/news/1999/june9/rice-69.html (accessed October 25, 2007).
33. Bill Workman, "Stanford Goes Off Campus For Legal Aid," *San Francisco Chronicle*, May 4, 1994, D5.
34. Bill Workman, "Stanford Students Rally, Begin Hunger Strike," *San Francisco Chronicle*, May 6, 1994, A20.

35. Evan Thomas, John Barry, Richard Wolffe, Martha Brant, Daniel Klaidman, Nadine Joseph, "The Quiet Power of Condi Rice," *Newsweek*, December 16, 2002, 24.
36. Linda Wade, *Condoleezza Rice* (Hockessin, DE: Mitchell Lane Publishers, 2005), 27.
37. Condoleezza Rice, interview by Oprah Winfrey, "Oprah Talks to Condoleezza Rice," *O: The Oprah Magazine*, February 2002.
38. Stanford University News Service, "Provost Rice at Founder's Day Calls for Strength in Adversity," news release, March 8, 1994, http://news-service.stanford.edu/pr/94/940308Arc4392.html (accessed October 26, 2007).
39. Mark Simon, "Stanford May Cut Tuition Perk," *San Francisco Chronicle*, October 21, 1996, A13.
40. James Robinson, "Changes Proposed in Tuition Benefits for Employees," *Stanford Report*, December 9, 1998, http://news-service.stanford.edu/news/1998/december9/emptuition129.html (accessed October 26, 2007).
41. Bill Workman, "Stanford Chief Hits *Wall Street Journal* Piece," *San Francisco Chronicle*, October 11, 1995, A13.
42. "Not College Material," *New York Times*.
43. Robinson, "Velvet-Glove Forcefulness."
44. Bill Workman, "Women Acting to Advance Their Cause at Stanford," *San Francisco Chronicle*, May 14, 1998, A19.
45. Bill Workman, "Female Faculty Say Stanford Has Promotion Bias," *San Francisco Chronicle*, May 14, 1999, A19.
46. Workman, "Women Acting to Advance."
47. Bill Workman, "Stanford Chief Defends Hiring, Tenure Policy," *San Francisco Chronicle*, February 5, 1999, A19.
48. Thomas, Barry, Wolffe, Brant, Klaidman, and Joseph, "Quiet Power of Condi Rice," 24.
49. Parkes, "Leaders for a New Millennium," 8.
50. Bill Workman, "Housing Shortage Protested at Stanford," *San Francisco Chronicle*, May 28, 1998, A16.
51. Stanford University News Service, "Provost Rice at Founders' Day Calls for Strength in Adversity," news release, March 8, 1994, http://news-service.stanford.edu/pr/94/940308Arc4392.html (accessed October 26, 2007).
52. Parkes, "Leaders for a New Millennium," 8.
53. James Bennet, "Chelsea and 1,649 Other Freshmen Arrive at Stanford," *New York Times*, 20 Sept. 1997, A9.
54. Jonathan Curiel, "Rice Still Stretching Her Horizons," *San Francisco Chronicle*, February 9, 1993, B3.
55. James H. Kennedy, "City Native and Bayou La Batre Doctor Among 'Time' Promising Young Leaders," *Birmingham News*, December 1, 1994, 501.

56. Ibid.
57. Parkes, "Leaders for a New Millennium," 8.
58. Ibid.
59. "Stanford Scholar Held Prisoner in China for Past 10 Months," *San Francisco Chronicle*, October 29, 1998, A23.
60. Helen Cheng, "Hua Di convicted by Chinese a second time," *Stanford Daily*, February 6, 2001, http://daily.stanford.edu/article/2001/2/6/huaDi ConvictedByChineseASecondTime (accessed October 26, 2007).
61. Philip Zelikow and Condoleezza Rice, *Germany Unified and Europe Transformed: A Study in Statecraft* (Cambridge, MA: Harvard University Press, 2002).
62. Jim Hoagland, "This Year's Cinderella," *Washington Post*, December 24, 1995, C09.
63. Pamela Burdman, "Search for Chancellor Winding Up," *San Francisco Chronicle*, January 31, 1997, A19.
64. Joanne Davidson, "DU Friends and Alums Rise to the Occasion," *Denver Post*, March 18, 1999, E-02.
65. Ale Beam, "Playing, and Losing, at Agemanship," *Boston Globe*, February 3, 1999, D1.
66. Kathleen O'Toole, "Rice Implores Graduates to Reap Benefits of Crossing Cultural Boundaries," *Stanford Report*, June 16, 1999, http://news-service.stanford.edu/news/1999/june16/classday2-616.html (accessed October 26, 2007).
67. Ibid.
68. "Rice on Students, Tough Decisions and Her Oil Tanker," Farm Report, *Stanford Magazine*, May/June 1999.
69. Jay Nordlinger, "Star in Waiting," *National Review*, August 30, 1999, http://www.nationalreview.com/flashback/nordlinger200411170605.asp (October 25, 2007).

Chapter 11

1. "Fantastic Four," *Texas Monthly*, August 1999, 111.
2. "Bush's Foreign Policy Tutor," *New York Times*, June 16, 2000.
3. "Pumping Iron, Digging Gold, Pressing Flesh," *Newsweek*, November 20, 2000, 50.
4. Ibid.
5. Antonia Felix, *Condi: The Condoleezza Rice Story* (New York: Newmarket Press, 2005), 9.
6. "Fantastic Four," *Texas Monthly*, August 1999, 111.
7. Michael Kranish, "Bush Cramming Before Campaigning," *Boston Globe*, June 6, 1999, A1.

8. Brooke Lea Foster, "Being Condi," *Washingtonian*, March 2007, 54–59, 153–155.
9. Geneva Overholser, "Profile of a Heavy Hitter," *Washington Post*, September 7, 1999, A19.
10. Christin Ditchfield, *Condoleezza Rice: National Security Advisor* (New York: Franklin Watts, 2003), 67.
11. "Fantastic Four," 111.
12. Ibid.
13. Overholser, "Profile of a Heavy Hitter."
14. Jim Yardley, "Eyes of Texas are on a Ranch Bush Wants," *New York Times*, August 8, 1999, 1.
15. Julia Reed, "The President's Prodigy," *Vogue*, October 2001, 403.
16. Yardley, "Eyes of Texas."
17. Reed, "The President's Prodigy," 403, 448.
18. Yardley, "Eyes of Texas."
19. Reed, "The President's Prodigy," 448.
20. George W. Bush, "A New Strategic Relationship" (speech, Reagan Library, Simi, CA, November 19, 1999).
21. Romesh Ratnesar, "Condi Rice Can't Lose," *Time*, September 20, 1999, http://www.time.com/time/magazine/article/0,9171,1101990927-31242, 00.html (accessed October 26, 2007).
22. Elaine Sciolino, "Compulsion to Achieve," *New York Times*, December 18, 2000.
23. Jay Nordlinger, "Star in Waiting," *National Review*, August 30, 1999, http://www.nationalreview.com/flashback/nordlinger200411170605.asp (October 25, 2007).
24. Mark Dennis, "Bush Channels Reagan on Foreign Policy," *Salon.com*, November 20, 1999, http://www.salon.com/news/feature/1999/11/20/foreign/index.html (accessed October 26, 2007).
25. Overholser, "Profile of a Heavy Hitter."
26. Nicholas Lemann, "Without a Doubt: Has Condoleezza Rice Changed George W. Bush, or Has He Changed Her?" *The New Yorker*, October 14, 2002, 164.
27. Condoleezza Rice, "Campaign 2000: Promoting the National Interest," *Foreign Affairs* 71, no. 1 (January/February 2000) http://www.foreignaffairs.org/20000101faessay5/condoleezza-rice/campaign-2000-promoting-the-national-interest.html (accessed October 26, 2007).
28. Rice, "Promoting the National Interest."
29. Ibid.
30. Patrick Smyth and Joe Carroll, "U.S. Presence in Balkans Becomes Election Issue," *Irish Times* (Dublin), October 23, 2000, 13.

31. Jay Nordlinger, "The GOP's Burden: The Color of the Convention," *National Review* 52, no. 16 (August 28, 2000): 19–20.
32. "Philadelphia II: Winners & Losers," *National Review* 52, no. 16 (August 28, 2000).
33. Condoleezza Rice, "America's Unique Opportunity," *PBS Online NewsHour*, 1 August 2000, http://www.pbs.org/newshour/election2000/gopconvention/condoleezza_rice.html (accessed October 25, 2007).
34. George Will, "Why Condoleezza Rice Is a Republican, and Why More African Americans Will Be," *Pittsburgh Post-Gazette*, August 7, 2000, A-11.
35. Ben Stein, "Prime Stein," *The American Spectator*, October 2000.
36. Ann Reilly Dowd, "What Makes Condi Run," *AARP Magazine*, September/October 2005, http://www.aarpmagazine.org/people/condoleeza.html (accessed October 26, 2007).
37. Leslie Montgomery, *The Faith of Condoleezza Rice* (Wheaton, IL: Crossway Books, 2007), 157.
38. Foster, "Being Condi," 54–59, 153–55.
39. Wil Haywood, "'Honored to Have the Chance,' To Her Parents, Failure in Life was Never an Option for 'Condi' Rice," *Boston Globe*, December 21, 2000.
40. "The Birth of an Arab-American Lobby," *The Economist*, October 14, 2000.
41. Judy Keen, "Barbara Bush to Captain 'Women Tour,'" *USA Today*, October 16, 2000, 16A.
42. T. Trent Gegax, Evan Thomas, Peter Goldman, et. al., "What a Long, Strange Trip," *Newsweek*, November 20, 2000, 30.
43. "Bush's World," *The Economist*, January 6, 2001.
44. Reed, "The President's Prodigy," 398.
45. Ibid., 399.
46. Haywood, "Honored to Have the Chance."
47. Foster, "Being Condi," 54–59, 153–55.
48. George W. Bush, "Remarks at the Announcement of Appointments," *New York Times*, December 18, 2000, 23.
49. Haywood, "Honored to Have the Chance," A1.
50. Bush, "Remarks at the Announcement," 23.
51. Haywood, "'Honored to Have the Chance," A1.
52. Foster, "Being Condi," 54–59, 153–55.
53. Ibid.
54. Marcus Mabry, *Twice as Good: Condoleezza Rice and Her Path to Power* (New York: Rodale Books, 2007), 165.
55. Dale Russakoff, "Lessons of Might and Right," *Washington Post*, September 9, 2001, W23.
56. Ibid.

CHAPTER 12

1. Condoleeza Rice, Remarks at Paul H. Nitze School of Advanced International Studies at Johns Hopkins, April 29, 2002. http://www.whitehouse.gov/news/release/2002/04/20020429-9 (accessed June 5, 2007).
2. National Commission on Terrorist Attacks Upon the United States, *9/11 Commission Report*, (New York: W.W. Norton and Company, 2004), 200–201.
3. Condoleezza Rice, "Dr. Condoleezza Rice's Opening Remarks to Commission on Terrorist Attacks" (Hart Senate Office Building, Washington, DC, April 8, 2004) http://www.whitehouse.gov/news/releases/2004/04/20040408.html (accessed October 26, 2007).
4. Julia Reed, "The President's Prodigy," *Vogue*, October 2001, 403.
5. Brooke Lea Foster, "Being Condi," *Washingtonian*, March 2007, 54–59, 153–55.
6. Rice, "Rice's Opening Remarks."
7. National Commission on Terrorist Attacks Upon the United States, *9/11 Commission Report*, 200.
8. Rice, "Rice's Opening Remarks."
9. Foster, "Being Condi," 54–59, 153–55.
10. Condoleezza Rice, "Campaign 2000: Promoting the National Interest," *Foreign Affairs* 71, no. i (January/February 2000) http://www.foreignaffairs.org/20000101faessay5/condoleezza-rice/campaign-2000-promoting-the-national-interest.html (accessed October 26, 2007).
11. James Mann, *Rise of the Vulcans: The History of Bush's War Cabinet* (New York: Viking, 2004), 282.
12. Reed, "The President's Prodigy," 448.
13. Jamie McIntyre, "U.S. Reconnaissance Planes Take Flight Again Near China," *CNNfyi.com*, May 7, 2001, http://cnnstudentnews.cnn.com/2001/fyi/news/05/07/us.china/index.html (accessed October 26, 2007).
14. Toby Harnden and Simon Davis, "Americans Welcome 'Valiant' Spy Crew," *The Daily Telegraph*, April 13, 2001, 4.
15. Reed, "The President's Prodigy," 448.
16. Nicholas Lemann, "Without a Doubt: Has Condoleezza Rice Changed George W. Bush, or Has He Changed Her?" *The New Yorker*, October 14, 2002, 164.
17. Nicholas Kralev, "Political Punch in a Package of Charm," *Financial Times* (London), 26 Feb. 2000, 3.
18. Sheryl Henderson Blunt, "The Unflappable Condi Rice: Why the world's most powerful woman asks God for help," *Christianity Today*, August 22, 2003, http://www.ctlibrary.com/ct/2003/september/1.42.html (accessed October 25, 2007).

19. Jennifer Wells, "World Awaits Rice's Definition of Danger," *Toronto Star*, April 4, 2004, A02.
20. Foster, "Being Condi," 54–59, 153–55.
21. George W. Bush, "Remarks by the President in an Address to Faculty and Students of Warsaw University" (address, Warsaw, Poland, June 15, 2001), http://www.whitehouse.gov/news/releases/2001/06/20010615-1.html (accessed October 26, 2007).
22. Reed, "The President's Prodigy," 449.
23. Ibid.
24. Condoleezza Rice, "Press Briefing by National Security Advisor Condoleezza Rice" (address, Warsaw Marriott Hotel, Warsaw, Poland, June 15, 2001), http://www.whitehouse.gov/news/releases/2001/06/20010615-2.html (accessed October 26, 2007).
25. Rice, "Rice's Opening Remarks."
26. Rice, "Press Briefing."
27. Robin Wright, "Top Focus on 9/11 Wasn't on Terrorism," *Washington Post*, April 1, 2004, A01.
28. Karen Hughes, *Ten Minutes from Normal* (New York: Viking Penguin, 2004), 246.
29. Ibid.
30. George W. Bush, "Address to a Joint Session of Congress and the American People" (United States Capitol, Washington, DC, September 20, 2001), http://www.whitehouse.gov/news/releases/2001/09/20010920-8.html (accessed October 26, 2007).
31. George Bush, Presidential Address to the Nation, (location, city, October 7, 2001), http://www.whitehouse.gov/news/release/2001/10/20011007.8html (site now discontinued).
32. Mann, *Rise of the Vulcans*, 308.
33. Bernard Ryan, *Condoleezza Rice: Secretary of State* (New York: Ferguson/Facts on File, 2004), 73.
34. Condoleezza Rice, "Remarks on Terrorism and Foreign Policy" (keynote address, Paul H. Nitze School of Advanced International Studies at Johns Hopkins, Washington, DC, April 29, 2002), http://www.whitehouse.gov/news/releases/2002/04/20020429-9.html (accessed October 26, 2007).
35. George Washington to Henry Knox, 8 March 1787, in *George Washington: A Collection*, ed. William B. Allen (Indianapolis: Liberty Fund, 1988), 356.
36. Rice, "Terrorism and Foreign Policy."
37. Ibid.
38. Condoleezza Rice, "A Balance of Power that Favors Freedom," *U.S. National Security Strategy: A New Era* (Washington, DC: U.S. Department of State, Dec. 2002), 6.

39. Ibid., 8
40. Condoleeza Rice, "Remarks by National Security Advisor Dr. Condoleeza Rice at the National Prayer Breakfast," Feb. 6, 2003. http://www.luthersem.edu/mysse/OT2116-Prophets/Rice-NationalPrayerbreakfast.htm (accessed Aug. 3, 2007).
41. Mann, *Rise of the Vulcans*, 331.
42. Condoleezza Rice, "National Security Advisor Condoleezza Rice Remarks to Veterans of Foreign Wars" (address, 104th Annual Convention of Veterans of Foreign Wars, San Antonio, TX, August 25, 2003) http://www.whitehouse.gov/news/releases/2003/08/20030825-1.html (accessed June 6, 2007).
43. Mann, *Rise of the Vulcans*, 337.
44. Ibid., 349.
45. "Saddam Statue Toppled in Central Baghdad," *CNN.com*, April 9, 2003, http://www.cnn.com/2003/WORLD/meast/04/09/sprj.irq.statue/ (accessed October 26, 2007).
46. George W. Bush, "Bush Makes Historic Speech Aboard Warship," *CNN.com*, May 1, 2003, http://www.cnn.com/2003/US/05/01/bush.transcript/ (accessed October 26, 2007).
47. Mike Allen, "Inside Bush's Top-Secret Trip," *Washington Post*, November 28, 2003, A47.
48. Ibid.
49. L. Paul Bremer, *My Year in Iraq: The Struggle to Build a Future of Hope* (New York: Simon and Schuster, 2006), 237-39.
50. George W. Bush, "President Bush Meets With Troops in Iraq on Thanksgiving" (address, Baghdad, November 27, 2003), http://www.whitehouse.gov/news/releases/2003/11/20031127.html (accessed October 26, 2007).
51. Laura J. Winter and Tracy Connor, "'I Was Just Looking for a Warm Meal Somewhere," *New York Daily News*, November 28, 2003, 6.
52. Raja Mishra and Bryan Bender, "Hussein Captured," *Boston Globe*, December 15, 2003, A1.
53. Condoleezza Rice, "National Security Advisor Dr. Condoleezza Rice Discusses War on Terror at Reagan Library and Museum" (speech, Reagan Library, Simi, CA, February 28, 2004) http://www.whitehouse.gov/news/releases/2004/02/20040228-1.html (accessed October 26, 2007).
54. "White House U-Turn on 9/11 Inquiry," BBC News, 31 March 2004, http://newsvote.bbc.co.uk/mpapps/pagetools/print/news.bbc.co.uk/2/hi/americas/3583639.stm (accessed October 26, 2007).
55. Tom Shales, "Cool, Calm Condoleezza Rice," *Washington Post*, April 9, 2004, C01.
56. Rice, "Commission on Terrorist Attacks."
57. Ibid.

58. Ibid.
59. Shales, "Cool, Calm Condoleezza Rice."
60. Ibid.
61. Ibid.
62. Ibid.
63. Ibid.
64. Glenn Kessler, "Rice Hitting the Road to Speak," *Washington Post*, October 20, 2004, A02.
65. J. Patrick Coolican, "Despite Violence, Iraqi Elections Will Occur as Scheduled, Rice Says," *Seattle Times*, September 8, 2004, A9.
66. Ann Reilly Dowd, "What Makes Condi Run," *AARP Magazine*, September/October 2005, http://www.aarpmagazine.org/people/condoleeza.html (accessed October 26, 2007).
67. Ibid.; Foster, "Being Condi," 54–59, 153–55.
68. Foster, "Being Condi," 54–59, 153–55.
69. Ibid.; see Bob Woodward, *State of Denial: Bush at War, Part III* (New York: Simon and Schuster, 2006), 358–359.

Chapter 13

1. Condoleeza Rice, "Walking in Faith: Rice Finds Strength in Religion," *Washington Times*, August 27, 2002, A02.
2. Tatiana Serafin, "#1 Condoleezza Rice," *Forbes*, November 2005, http://www.forbes.com/lists/2005/11/MTNG.html (accessed October 26, 2007).
3. Condoleezza Rice, "Opening Remarks by Secretary of State-Designate Condoleezza Rice" (Senate Foreign Relations Committee, Washington, DC, January 18, 2005), http://www.state.gov/secretary/rm/2005/40991.htm (accessed October 26, 2007).
4. Ed Henry, "Rice Confirmed as Secretary of State," *CNN.com*, January 26, 2005, http://www.cnn.com/2005/ALLPOLITICS/01/26/rice.confirmation (accessed October 26, 2007).
5. Brooke Lea Foster, "Being Condi," *Washingtonian*, March 2007, 54–59, 153–55.
6. U.S. Department of State, "Condoleezza Rice Sworn in as 66th U.S. Secretary of State," news release, January 28, 2005, http://usinfo.state.gov/special/Archive/2005/Jan/28-638748.html (accessed October 26, 2007).
7. U.S. Department of State, "President Thanks Secretary of State Rice at Swearing-in Ceremony," news release, January 28, 2005, http://www.whitehouse.gov/news/releases/2005/01/20050128-2.html (accessed October 26, 2007).

8. U.S. Department of State, "President Thanks Rice."
9. Foster, "Being Condi," 54–59, 153–55.
10. Condoleezza Rice, "The Promise of Democratic Peace," *Washington Post*, December 11, 2005, B07.
11. Condoleezza Rice, interview by Robin Wright and Glenn Kesler, *Washington Post*, July 26, 2005, http://www.state.gov/secretary/rm/2005/50414.htm (accessed October 26, 2007).
12. Patrick Goodenough, "Rice Attends Church in Country Where Religious Freedom is Relentlessly Restricted," *CNS News*, March 21,2005. http://www.cnsnews.com/ViewForeignBureaus.asp?Page=%5CForeignBureaus%5Carchive%5C200503%5CFOR20050321b.html (accessed June 5, 2007).
13. Hamish McDonald, "Rice Talks Democracy, Religion in China," *The Age*, March 22, 2005, http://www.theage.com.au/news/World/Rice-talks-democracy-religion-in-China/2005/03/21/1111253953601.html (accessed June 5, 2007).
14. Patrick Goodenough, "Rice Attends Church in Country Where Religious Freedom is Relentlessly Restricted," CNS News, March 21, 2005. http://www.CNSnews.com/ViewForeignBureaus.asp?Page=%5CForeignBureaus%5Carchive%5C200503%5CFOR20050321b.html (accessed June 5, 2007).
15. Joel Brinkley, "Rice Sounds a Theme in Visit to Beijing Protestant Church," *New York Times*, March 21, 2005, 7.
16. Kevin Flower, Enes Dulami, and Kianne Sadeq, "Rice Makes Surprise Visit to Iraq," *CNN.com*, May 15, 2005, http://www.cnn.com/2005/WORLD/meast/05/15/iraq.main/ (accessed October 26, 2007).
17. Glenn Kessler, "Rice Drops Plans for Visit to Egypt," *Washington Post*, February 26, 2005, A14.
18. Daniel Williams, "Egypt Frees an Aspiring Candidate," *Washington Post*, March 13, 2005, A16.
19. Condoleezza Rice, "Remarks at the American University in Cairo," (keynote address, Cairo, Egypt, June 20, 2005), http://www.state.gov/secretary/rm/2005/48328.htm (accessed October 26, 2007).
20. "America's Best Leaders: Condoleezza Rice," *U.S. News and World Report*, October 31, 2005, http://www.usnews.com/usnews/news/articles/051031/31rice.htm (accessed October 26, 2007).
21. "Rice Calls for Mid-East democracy," *BBC News*, June 20, 2005, http://news.bbc.co.uk/1/hi/world/middle_east/4109902.stm (accessed October 26, 2007).
22. "Rosa Parks Lies in State in Washington," *CBC News*, October 30, 2005, http://www.cbc.ca/world/story/2005/10/30/parks-remembered051030.html, (accessed October 26, 2007).

23. Condoleezza Rice, "Transformational Diplomacy" (keynote address, Georgetown University, Washington, DC, January 18, 2006) http://www.state.gov/secretary/rm/2006/59306.htm (accessed October 26, 2007).
24. Ibid.
25. Rice, interview by Robin Wright and Glenn Kesler.
26. Robert Booth, "Jack Becomes Embedded While Condi Loses Sleep," *The Guardian*, April 3, 2006, http://politics.guardian.co.uk/print/0,,329448821-110481,00.html (accessed October 26, 2007).
27. Foster, "Being Condi," 54–59, 153–55.
28. "Travels with the Secretary," U.S. Department of State, http://www.state.gov/secretary/trvl/ (accessed October 26, 2007).
29. "Beckham: The Air Miles, the Health Risks," *Times Online*, August 24, 2007, url (accessed date).
30. Condoleezza Rice, "Remarks at the Independent Women's Forum Upon Receiving Woman of Valor Award" (keynote address, Andrew W. Mellon Auditorium, Washington, DC, May 10, 2006) http://www.state.gov/secretary/rm/2006/66139.htm (accessed October 26, 2007).
31. Condoleezza Rice, "Iraq: A New Way Forward," January 11, 2007, accessed 20 June 2007.
32. Associated Press and Reuters, "Senate Opposition to Bush Plan Grows," MSNBC, January 11, 2007, http://www.msnbc.msn.com/id/16579285/ (accessed October 26, 2007).
33. "Woman of the World," *Reader's Digest*, September 2006, #.
34. Author, "Article," *The News Tribune* (Tacoma), September 5, 2007.
35. "Poll: We Like Condi, but Who's Karl?" *CNN.com*, April 26, 2006, http://www.cnn.com/politics/04/26/poll.administration (accessed June 4, 2007; site now discontinued).
36. U.S. Department of State, "Secretary Rice Plays Brahms at ASEAN Gala Dinner," news release, July 27, 2006, http://www.state.gov/r/pa/ei/pix/2006/69691.htm (accessed October 26, 2007).
37. Jacqueline Trescott, "High-Powered Duet for Arts Medalists: Yo-Yo Ma Teams With Condoleezza Rice," *Washington Post*, April 23, 2002, C01.
38. Condoleezza Rice, interview by Gilbert Kaplan, *Mad About Music: Condoleezza Rice*, WNYC, January 2, 2005, http://www.wnyc.org/shows/mam/episodes/2005/01/02 (accessed October 25, 2007).
39. Anthony Tommasini, "Condoleezza Rice on Piano," *New York Times*, April 9, 2006, http://www.nytimes.com/2006/04/09/arts/music/09tomm.html?ex=1302235200&en=9b7986206bf57c24&ei=5088&partner=rssnyt&emc=rss (accessed October 25, 2007).
40. Foster, "Being Condi," 54–59, 153–55.
41. Ibid.

42. Ibid.
43. Evan Thomas, John Barry, Richard Wolffe, Martha Brant, Daniel Klaidman, Nadine Joseph, "The Quiet Power of Condi Rice," *Newsweek*, December 16, 2002, 24.
44. Amy Fine Collins, "Vanity Fair Presents the 67th Annual Best-Dressed List 2006," *Vanity Fair*, September 2006, 323.
45. Robin Givhan, "Condoleezza Rice's Commanding Clothes," *Washington Post*, February 25, 2005, C01.
46. Ann Reilly Dowd, "What Makes Condi Run," *AARP Magazine*, September/October 2005, http://www.aarpmagazine.org/people/condoleeza.html (accessed October 26, 2007).
47. George J. Tanber, "Rice Sees Wide World of Sports," *ESPN.com*, February 27, 2007 http://sports.espn.go.com/espn/blackhistory2007/news/story?id=2780487, (accessed October 26, 2007).
48. Dale Russakoff, "How Football Helped Shape Condoleezza the Strategist," *The Standard*, February 7, 2005 http://www.eastandard.net/archives/cl/hm_news/news.php?articleid=12571&date=7/2/2005 (accessed October 25, 2007).
49. Condoleezza Rice, interview by Oprah Winfrey, "Secrets of Women Who Rule," *The Oprah Winfrey Show*, NBC, October 2003.
50. Condoleezza Rice, "Walking in Faith: Rice Finds Strength in Religion," *Washington Times*, August 27, 2002, A02.
51. Dowd, "What Makes Condi Run."
52. Rice, "Walking in Faith."
53. Condoleezza Rice, "Title" (address, National Presbyterian Church, Washington, DC, August 2002).
54. Condoleezza Rice, "Rice Says Faith in God is an Important Part of Her Personal and Public Life," *Christian Examiner*, October 2002.
55. Jay Nordlinger, "Star in Waiting," *National Review*, August 30, 1999, http://www.nationalreview.com/flashback/nordlinger200411170605.asp (October 25, 2007).

Epilogue

1. "Transcript for March 13," *NBC News' Meet the Press*, NBC, May 13, 2005, http://www.msnbc.msn.com/id/7173024/ (accessed October 26, 2007).
2. Condoleezza Rice, "Remarks at Espacio USA Conference" (address, Inter-American Development Bank, Washington, DC, May 5, 2006), http://www.state.gov/secretary/rm/2006/65936.htm (accessed October 26, 2007).
3. Condoleezza Rice, interview by Brian Mullahy, KUTV-TV, August 29, 2006,

http://www.state.gov/secretary/rm/2006/71637.htm (accessed October 26, 2007).

4. Scott Lindlaw, "Rice Lays Groundwork for Calif. Return," *San Jose Mercury News*, May 25, 2007, http://www.mercurynews.com/search/ci_5984022?nclick_check=1 (accessed June 5, 2007).
5. Foster, "Being Condi," 54–59, 153–55.
6. Tannette Johnson-Elie, "A Lesson from Rice in Individuality," *Milwaukee Journal Sentinel*, November 20, 2002.
7. Condoleezza Rice, "The Promise of Democratic Peace," *Washington Post*, December 11, 2005, B07.

Index

Acknowledgments

Many people were helpful in making this book possible. Some directly and others indirectly. First and foremost, I thank my husband Floyd for his encouragement, support, valuable ideas, and editing of the first draft. In addition to Floyd, I also thank my children for being so understanding when I was busy writing and working on the book. Life around our house was out of the ordinary and things like nice home-cooked meals were few and far between. My son Patrick gave me helpful suggestions to polish the manuscript and was a source of encouragement, while my daughter Olivia was always so sweet and understanding through it all. Olivia was my own personal cheerleader. Although my son Peter was living away at college through most of the writing, he often called to inquire about my progress and he gave me a word of encouragement.

Of course the book would have never come into being without the wonderful and talented staff at Thomas Nelson Publishing. David Dunham, Joel Miller, Kristen Parrish, Alice Sullivan, and Heather

Skelton were all of tremendous help with editorial comments, encouragement, and keen insights. Thank you for being so understanding and patient when I was confronted with unavoidable delays.

A special thank you goes to my researcher and assistant, Hans Zeiger. I would have never been able to make my deadline without your help. You were especially helpful in the area of foreign policy. I appreciate your diligence and insight.

This book would not have been possible without the help of many friends and family members. Some of those include my friends at Calvary Chapel Santa Barbara and especially the ladies from my book club. You were there when I first thought of writing the book and were so supportive with your prayers and encouragement: Julie, Eliot, Lori, Connie, Tina, Carol, Betty, Martha, Jen, Karen, and Cheryl.

Since my move back to Washington, old and new friends and family have been equally helpful with prayer and support, including my wonderful parents, John and Eleanora Adams, my sisters, Nancy Smith, Linda Charcas, and Susan Healow, and my dear friend Gail Potts. In addition, my in-laws, Floyd and Nadine Brown, helped me by spending time and giving attention to Olivia. Also friends from Life Center Church and those in my home group and women's Bible study group were always ready with support and prayer. I have seen God working throughout the course of writing this book. I give God praise; He has given me strength, insight, perseverance, and hope throughout this endeavor.

About the Author

Mary Beth Brown is a bestselling author and speaker.

Her most recent book, *Hand of Providence: the Strong and Quiet Faith of Ronald Reagan* was published by Thomas Nelson in March of 2004. It appeared on both the *New York Times* and *USA Today* best-seller lists. She blogs at www.2minuteview.com.

In 1988, working from her kitchen table with her husband Floyd Brown, they founded Citizens United. Today Citizens United is one of America's most effective and recognized citizen advocacy organizations.

A graduate of the University of Washington, she was a founder of the Mothers Campaign for Family in that state. She has been a delegate to several Republican conventions and has testified before the Washington State Senate on education, child and family issues.

She currently resides in University Place, Washington, with her husband and children.